Public Camp Orders and the Power of Microstructures in the Thai-Burmese Borderland

Public Camp Orders and the Power of Microstructures in the Thai-Burmese Borderland

Annett Bochmann

LEXINGTON BOOKS
Lanham • Boulder • New York • London

Published by Lexington Books
An imprint of The Rowman & Littlefield Publishing Group, Inc.
4501 Forbes Boulevard, Suite 200, Lanham, Maryland 20706
www.rowman.com

86-90 Paul Street, London EC2A 4NE, United Kingdom

British Library Cataloguing in Publication Information Available

Library of Congress Cataloging-in-Publication Data

Names: Bochmann, Annett, author.
Title: Public camp orders and the power of microstructures in the
    Thai-Burmese borderland / Annett Bochmann.
Description: Lanham : Lexington Books, 2021. | Includes bibliographical
    references and index. | Summary: "Based on ethnographic field research
    between 2011 and 2014, Public Camp Orders and the Power of
    Microstructures in the Thai-Burmese Borderland makes a unique
    contribution to empirical and theoretical discourses on camp
    institutions, (forced) migration, and border regimes. Focusing on public
    camp life, everyday interactions, and the concept of microstructures,
    this ethnography explores local practices of mobility, governance, and
    economy in the context of plural and temporary environments"—Provided
    by publisher.
Identifiers: LCCN 2021014707 (print) | LCCN 2021014708 (ebook) | ISBN
    9781793608956 (cloth) | ISBN 9781793608963 (epub)
    9781793608970 (pbk)
Subjects: LCSH: Refugees—Burma—Social conditions. |
    Refugees—Thailand—Social conditions. | Refugee camps—Sociological
    aspects. | Burma—Emigration and immigration—Social aspects. |
    Thailand—Emigration and immigration—Social aspects.
Classification: LCC HV640.5.B93 B63 2021 (print) | LCC HV640.5.B93
    (ebook) | DDC 305.9/0691409591—dc23
LC record available at https://lccn.loc.gov/2021014707
LC ebook record available at https://lccn.loc.gov/2021014708

This study is dedicated to people displaced
and forced to be (im)mobile in this world,
and to their strength and power
in dealing with their situations.

Contents

Acknowledgments

This study is the result of research conducted between 2011 and 2017 while I was a member of a research training group at Hildesheim University and Johannes Gutenberg University in Mainz, and later a research assistant and lecturer at Siegen University. I would like to thank the German Research Foundation for financing the extensive field research. I am indebted to a multitude of people who contributed to the progression of my thesis, all of whom I cannot name.

First, I would like to thank my supervisors, Stephan Wolff and Katharina Inhetveen, who pioneered this work with their different ways of approaching social phenomena. I am very grateful for the fruitful analytical discussions with all my colleagues and friends in Berlin, Frankfurt, Hildesheim and Siegen. I would especially like to thank Lucia Artner, Tom Güte and Thomas Scheffer and all the members of the research group 'political ethnography' in Berlin. I also have to thank Jörg Bergmann and Joanna Pfaff-Czarnecka who contributed a great deal to this work, especially at the beginning in conceptualising this study. Georg Hubmann invested a lot of time and great effort in finalising this book project. Thank you so much.

But most important to mention are all the people I met during my field research in Myanmar/Burma and Thailand. I would like to express my deep gratitude to the people I met during my stays in the camps and in the borderlands, who kindly shared their lifeworlds with me. I am immeasurably grateful to the staff members and students of the college in which I was allowed to work. But, in particular, I wish to thank Naw Bway Wah and Khu Khu Sher and their warm-hearted and caring families, not least because I could count on them in difficult situations. Juliana Chris, thank you very much for your great effort!

Finally, I have to express my deep gratitude to Paw Moo, Doh Doh Moo, Katerina Jane, Jan Glourieux, Marlon Schröter, Tina Friede, and Annekatrin and Jürgen Bochmann. They all grounded this monograph, perhaps without knowing it.

Introduction

PLURALISMS AND TEMPORARINESS

Since the 1950s, armed conflicts between the Burmese army and various communities in the borderlands of Myanmar,[1] who have sought autonomy and self-determination, led to forced labour, village destructions, torture, massacres and other forms of violence. This eventually led to large scale displacements in the region. People living southeast of Myanmar have systematically crossed the border and fled to Thailand, especially since the 1970s. They have established themselves in agreement with local Thai authorities in over thirty small village-like and fairly self-reliant settlements along the borderland. Tolerated by the host state, the settlements were controlled by refugee representatives who were strongly connected to authorities of the political resistance groups of the home region. The government of Thailand expected the situation to be temporary. Even today, the settlements that turned into camps are perceived as temporary shelter areas where long-term housing remains forbidden. The host state also does not allow the United Nations High Commissioner for Refugees (UNHCR) to take care of the day-to-day management or the overall monitoring of the camps and strongly restricts expatriates from working in these areas. Among other issues, these state restrictions support a level of self-governance, for which Burmese refugee camps in Thailand are renowned. They are characterised by a high degree of community autonomy with powerful refugee representative organisations, which were formed out of the former resistance groups in Myanmar, holding a great deal of control.[2] But, while in 1995 governance and jurisdiction structures were in the hands of camp residents'[3] representative organisations, in 2013 camp residents needed to be 'trained, encouraged and supported' by humanitarian aid agencies 'to take responsibility for their own lives' (TBC

2013 Jan–Jun, 67). The international aid programmes conducted in Burmese refugee camps became similar to those in other refugee camp contexts and remind us of the 'biopolitics of care' (Turner 2006, 46) and the 'regime of humanitarian government' (Agier 2011, 145).

Refugee camps are not simply a product of armed conflicts in a region but remain an international answer to forced migration flows, despite the fact that for decades scholars have shared a very critical perception of camps (e.g. Harrell-Bond 1986). Not only can this be seen in the recent political debate in the European Union that proclaims the establishment of refugee camp institutions along the African-European border. According to UNHCR, 65.3 million people have been forcibly displaced worldwide and 8.59 million people of concern are living in refugee camps (UNHCR 2015).[4] Displacement is primarily an ongoing challenge in regions in the Global South (UNHCR 2015). Hence, the geographical picture is clear: the majority of refugee camps or refugee settlements are located in Africa, Asia and the Middle East. Although most refugee camps are still located in the Global South, they are financed primarily by Western donors and organised by humanitarian agencies from the United States and the European Union but also from Japan.

The political rationality behind building camps is easy to understand. Camps seem to give a somewhat plausible organisational and political answer to the question of how to deal with mass influxes of people who are fleeing violence and persecution but are expected to return to their home countries. It has been assumed that centralised accommodations are less expensive and make it easier to support, regulate and control people. In this way, camps enable, for example, an administratively efficient model for aid delivery and bureaucratic acts. In addition, it is anticipated that the problem of a high number of populations seeking temporary protection is thereby contained in a camp bubble, in order that these populations do not cause trouble or initiate transformative changes in the host countries. Moreover, it is presumed that as soon as the situation changes in the camp residents' home regions, it will be simpler to organise and enforce the return of these populations and to close the camps again. Camps are established not only to ensure ease of control and to simplify logistics in dealing with large numbers of people, but are also based on the maintenance of temporariness, or the interim nature of people's stays. Camps are established in emergency situations intended to immediately and temporarily provide protection, safety and control. In this sense, refugee camps are the logical consequence of the global norm of the nation-state system where every person must belong to a territory and a people. It demonstrates the logic of the refugee status: the refugee camps are supposed to be a temporary solution. Camps materialise and institutionalise the temporary stay of displaced people. However, refugee camps usually continue to exist beyond any semblance of the word 'temporary' and the duration of the initial emergency: the average duration of refugee encampment is close to twenty years (Milner and Loescher 2011, 3). There are refugee situations that even endure for much longer. The most prominent cases of long-term encampment are the Palestinian refugee camps in Lebanon, Gaza and West Bank that have been housing people for more than six decades. Burmese refugee camps in Thailand which are addressed in this research have been in existence for more than thirty years. That is why the considerations made in this book refer to long-term encampment and stays of displaced people. This needs to be distinguished from situations of short-term crisis relief and newly established refugee settlements or camps.

The short introduction of the case of Burmese refugee camps in Thailand and the global relevance of the topic highlight two intermingled social complexities accompanied with refugee camps: pluralism and temporariness. The pluralism of refugee camps relates to contested sovereignties of the diverse actors involved in accomplishing camp orders. The camp order is characterised by different modes and structures of the host state, international humanitarian agencies and refugee representative organisations but also, as the case of Burmese refugee camps demonstrate, of pre-camp authorities. At the same time, the legal and political pluralistic setting is based on the fact that these shelters are supposed to be temporary establishments. This situation leads to the question of how social order is locally established in interim spaces where different actors are supposed to hold authority and sovereignty. Four central concerns drove the research process of this study: (1) How do locally involved people, such as camp residents and local state authorities, make sense of this pluralistic situation and achieve order and reliability? (2) How are these plural governance structures built up locally? (3) How is public camp life organised in these temporary states? (4) How is normality and stability achieved in everyday practices?

From a social theory and historical perspective, camps are perceived as anomalies, exceptions to the ordinary social order. Human collectives are forced to stay in a temporary space where rules and norms exist that differ from the environment. Camps appear as institutions exemplifying immobility and exceptionality where collectives are not able to escape from designated territories, and thus are easily controlled and regulated. The political philosopher Giorgio Agamben contributes, in particular, to this perception of camps, describing them as spaces of absolute power over populations that are stripped off political identity and agency, and existing outside the protection of law (1998, 166). He perceives camps as a state of exception created by sovereign states where the camp collective can be subject to various forms of violence without legal consequences. Agamben stands at the end of a long line of theories on camps, which creates the impression that, primarily, it is the political and legal order that has power over camp life and larger structures are shaping camp social orders. These theoretical perspectives are in contrast to research findings of current studies conducted in refugee camps in the Global South. The supposedly enclosed character of camps is often not achieved in practice (Jansen 2018; Jacobsen 2005). But, the enclosed character of the camp as an institution is necessary for the theoretical assumptions because the pursuit of power depends on the accessibility of the group being controlled. Additionally, more and more refugee camp scholars highlight the plurality of sovereignties, multiplicity of governing actors and hybrid power relations (Hanafi and Long 2010; McConnachie 2012; Ramadan and Fregonese 2017; Maestri 2017).

Having identified this theory-empiricism gap, the starting point of this research was to look at camps beyond drawing analogies and parallels to existing camp theories and top-down approaches but rather investigate people's methods and practices in everyday life to make the camp environment reasonable and understandable. Based on an extensive ethnography, this book offers a novel explanation on how we can theoretically and methodologically grasp camp orders as an association of powerful, local and quite stable *sui generis* microstructures. Throughout my field research, I identified that camp governance, temporality, mobility and economy are social domains that particularly challenge theoretical camp conceptions. These domains became the main focus of the research introduced here.

The key argument of this book is that social orders of camps emerge from micro-interactions in which, for example, residents and local authorities collectively engage in establishing structures to organise public camp life. The findings of this study show that camp orders are a product of the creativity and power of local actors and are deeply rooted in situational dynamics. Within unreliable, indeterminate and temporary environments, locally and situationally produced microstructures order public camp life and provide a high level of normality and stability. Public camp secrets, local governance structures and performances enabling mobility and economic practices are examples of such microstructures. The power of these microstructures illustrates how local actors deal with political and legal provisions; how they are an answer to ambivalent humanitarian aid and state regulations, pre-camp structures or even non-regulations; and how and when they deal with controversies or conflict. In other words, what can be observed through these microstructures is a deeply established, permanent and simultaneously interim space, in which people constantly work to overcome and normalise temporariness and instability. These findings are surprising because, as pointed out before, social theory tends to describe camp life as liminal, closed and insecure states of exception. Faced with these powerful microstructures, this monograph makes a unique contribution not only to empirical but also to theoretical discourses on camps and immobility, migration and refuge.

Furthermore, this book points to the relevance of social interactions, situations and practices among local participants and their role in structuring life in exceptional spaces. It introduces an alternative theoretical approach to camp studies emphasising the local social construction that does not neglect larger structures of power but rather highlights the necessary incorporation of them into local practices. The findings of this study illuminate the significance of microstructures that deserve much more theoretical and empirical attention than they hitherto received in camp theory and studies.

PUBLIC CAMP ORDERS, EVERYDAY LIFE AND MICROSTRUCTURES

The terms *public order* in the title of this monograph are borrowed and inspired by two books: *Relations in Public: Microstudies of the Public Order* (1971) and *Behaviour in Public Places: Notes on the Organisation of Gatherings* (1963). In these studies, Goffman analyses everyday behaviours that are generally below the level of immediate awareness. He focusses on embodied unspoken codes of social understandings and claims the necessity of these perspectives for the orderly conduct of collectives or society. He studies the everyday human traffic and 'the patterning of ordinary social contacts' (1963, 4) and thus provides a grammar of the unspoken language used in public spaces. Referring to these studies, public camp life is linked to practices in any part of the camp to which camp members and, in particular, camp residents have free access to, such as street corners, shops, the *store*, or gatherings such as, for example, ration distributions and cultural events or meetings of all kinds in public. Public life can, roughly, be contrasted to behaviour in more isolated areas (such as private homes or offices) where only family members, friends or invitees are able to gather. This study shows that public camp life happens also outside the territory of the camps. That means life outside the camp includes public camp orders. With the term 'camp member(s)', this study refers to actors who are involved in establishing camp orders. This does not only include camp residents, local state authorities and NGO staff members but also camp visitors or villagers living nearby. As a result of the main research finding, this study also avoids speaking of (one) 'camp order' because this implies the existence of one omnipresent camp order controlling and perpetuating people's everyday lives. There is not one camp order that determines everyday life, interactions or events in public camp life. Rather, the terms 'camp orders' or 'camp orderings' are preferred to highlight that camp orders are something people work on locally, that people do, and need to make relevant including camp residents, state authorities, aid agency workers and other participants. That means that, for example, analysing the various regulations and programmes that exist in camp contexts does not offer much insight into how public camp life is organised. Powerful regulations from 'outside' are not simply realised but need to be made relevant, and are locally adapted and modified to particular situations. That is why orders of public camp life also include political and legal orders.

This, in turn, is not something people work on continuously and constantly; rather, camp orders are situationally achieved and are made relevant in particular (and not all) situations, events, and activities. The camp frame or context goes unnoticed and becomes irrelevant in many aspects of everyday life. Thus, local camp orders are a possible object of investigation and research focus to be taken up in this book. Throughout my extensive field work, several public camp orders were identified—for instance when taking a closer look at the daily loudspeaker announcements, local governance systems, and people's working and mobility practices. When looking at these practices, I also gained insights into how political and legal camp structures, such as formal regulations, become socially relevant and alive. Governance[5] and jurisdictional[6] structures refer to formal regulations, policies and rules introduced by different actors involved in establishing camp institutions. In the case of refugee camps, these are regulations produced by state and humanitarian agencies as well as refugee representative organisations and pre-camp actors such as local authorities of the camp residents' home region. This study shows how and when camp residents (as well as visitors, local state authorities and other members of the camp) who are part of public camp life, interactively make camp orders relevant, including political and legal orders. Further, this research explores how people react towards regulations and rules and how people mediate these in concrete situations of public camp life. Residents do this by establishing very powerful local microstructures, which regulate and order public camp life. The concept of social microstructures as it is defined here derives from my empirical observations and my methodological background that is strongly informed by Harold Garfinkel, Erving Goffman and Georg Simmel.

Social microstructures[7] are established in face-to-face communication and interactions among participants in situations and events and are characterised by the following features:

Rooting and maintaining in situational and local dynamics
Non-documentation

Stability and durability
Reliability
Resistance
Autonomy and sovereignty

Social microstructures are deeply rooted in situational and local dynamics but also need to be maintained in situations based on interactions among participants. Interactions among participants produce structures that have the potential to be established as microstructures, which need to be maintained or modified among participants over time. Their starting point remains undocumented and usually remain undocumented. Nevertheless, they have the potential to become documented in the near future. Microstructures obtain stability and durability and are not temporary. That is why they provide a certain degree of reliability to participants. Still, microstructures have the potential to conflict with other structures they resist and, therefore, the structure's stability needs to be maintained and worked on continuously. Microstructures are neither a simple appendix, collaboration or implementation, nor a modification of broader structures, rules or regulations. They are able to establish autonomous rules. In this sense, microstructures are protected against rapid changes and temporary conditions, not only because of their need of face-to-face interactions, but also because of an extensive procedure to change them. Even though microstructures incorporate, deal with, interact and are interlinked with legal or political structures, they reserve some degree of autonomy and sovereignty as they are characterised by a high degree of momentum, reality of *sui generis* and strength. Microstructures might be established as a reaction to existing structures but could also be established because of the non-existence of broader structures concerned members are in need of. This book shows how social microstructures regulate public camp life and that they have the power to establish stability in states of plurality, exception and interim, but at the same time are also in need of these states to become powerful. Various examples of powerful microstructures and their interlinkages with other structures in the domains of governance (public camp secrets and public bureaucracy), economy (ordinary exceptionality) and mobility (local and situational border regimes) are introduced. With this, I demonstrate how the 'objective' reality of the camp is not solely a system created by a legal and political order or the external environment; rather, the camp is also a situational accomplishment (or social construction) of concerted activities on the part of people pursuing their daily lives. In this sense, the concept of powerful microstructures makes a contribution to theories on encampment that tend to be dominated by structural deterministic perspectives.

SITUATIONALISM AND ETHNOMETHODOLOGY

This work is based on an ethnomethodologically informed ethnography conducted in the borderlands of Thailand and particularly in Burmese refugee camps between 2011 and 2015. The theoretical background of this ethnography and its findings rests on Simmel's perspectives on the social and society. He argues that neither individuals nor their subjective understandings of the world make up society or social institutions, and nor does society simply determine people's understanding or actions. Instead, Simmel argues that people's forms of interaction, their reciprocal exchanges (*Wechselwirkungen*) make up society and consequently have to be acknowledged as an object of sociological study (Simmel 1917/1970, 12–15). He emphasises that social order and society need to be understood as a process that is created when individuals recognise and influence each other mutually (24). Society begins when individuals find themselves in reciprocal relationships. Reciprocal exchanges between people constitute and establish social institutions and, thus, create social reality. From this perspective, society starts with small, fleeting and almost invisible exchanges among people, such as the gaze and non-verbal interactions (Simmel 1908/1992, 723–24). Consequently, society is understood as an accumulation of different interactions. Bigger social units such as states, organisations, or camps are a product of these ephemeral procedures or microscopic molecular processes (Simmel 1917/1970, 12). However, these small forms of interactions not only constitute social units but, in addition, are continuously part of social units (12–13). As such, Simmel does not perceive society and interaction as two separate entities, instead reciprocal exchanges always have to be interpreted in their social context (Bergmann 2011, 134). These considerations are strongly interlinked with ethnomethodological perspectives (125).

Ethnomethodologists agree with Simmel and assume the pre-existence of interaction in organisations, society or larger social units. That is why people's interactions, practices in particular and 'here and now' situations become the main point of investigation. This so-called methodological situationalism makes the 'reciprocity and the situated character of social actions' (Knorr-Cetina 1981, 15) or 'the episode of situated interaction (including routine)' (19) the ultimate unit of social conduct. Following a methodological situationalism means that the social situation where humans interact is taken to be the main unit of analysis. This perspective contrasts to the dominant methodological collectivism/holism as well as methodological individualism. The former understands collectives, internalised norms and moral obligations or common values as the main motor for social orderings. The latter tends to understand individual's knowledge or attributed meanings as the main motor creating social order. Following, for example, a symbolic interactionism informed research approach, scholars take the meaning, knowledge or interpretations of the world by people as the main point of research investigation (Roberts 2006, 87; Knorr-Cetina 1981).

But this research project follows a methodological situationalism and focusses on situational events and their procedural contexts. This does not exclude the socio-cultural, political and ecological contexts they are embedded in. It is suggested that situational events give reference to the wider context in which they occur. Only through this reference, the wider context becomes relevant for participants and their joint actions: 'macro-social phenomena are unknown and unknowable, unless they can be based upon knowledge derived from the analysis of micro-social situations' (Knorr-Cetina 1981, 8). This assumption is controversial, has led to theoretical debates in sociology (Alexander 1987; Goffman 1983, 8–9; Cicourel 1981), and is linked to epistemological difficulties Simmel already pointed out (1917/1970; 1916/2003). Nevertheless, this study takes the ethnomethodological perspective seriously, particularly when analysing data. Only when references to the context are given in a social situation, it is accessible and relevant to the participants and the ethnographer of the situation. This approach contrasts with Gluckman and the Manchester School that also see the potential of meticulous, extremely detailed analysis of social events (1968, 2). But for them the detailed analysis seems to work solely as an illustration of macro processes (Mitchell 2006; Kapferer 2010, 12). In contrast, ethnomethodologists approach the wider context or macro phenomena only if they are an integral part of the social situation and if they are observable within people's practices (Garfinkel 1996). From this perspective, macro structures are not something researchers acquire access to through a detailed analysis; rather, participants of the situations have to demonstrate and make these macro structures relevant and relate to them in public. The context of the situation or event is only relevant for the analysis and for researchers when participants of the situation refer to it (Sacks 1995; Schegloff 1997). This context-sensitive approach is limiting and methodically very strict. But there are good ethnomethodological reasons for this. The epistemological interest aims to capture the mechanisms that constitute structures or (macro) phenomena, and not the results and the consequences themselves (Rawls 2002; Hirschauer 2014). To gain better access to knowledge regarding how structures and social orders are produced, as explained in the following, we have to accept this methodological limitation. This approach enables us to demystify fixed camp structures or broader structural conditions. It aims to reconstruct how camp structures are produced: in people's practices that create micro structures that are part of creating camp orders.

While a Durkheimian perspective seems to contrast an ethnomethodological way of perceiving social phenomena, Garfinkel explicitly agrees with Durkheim's statements 'that the objective reality of social facts is sociology's fundamental principle' (Rawls 2002, 9). The difference between these two theoretical lines is that ethnomethodology does not agree that the objective reality of social facts is the result of people's conformity and of institutionalised forms of constrains. Hence, the camp or displacement is not treated as a social fact. Instead, social facts such as the camp and displacement are perceived as the ongoing social construction (or local accomplishment, to use ethnomethodological vocabulary) of people's daily activities, which can be experienced by participants as an objectively determined reality. Nevertheless, social facts or objectivity are understood as the product of orderly and endogenous local orders and are an achievement (or social construction) of the immortal ordinary society (Rawls 2002, 9). Every social fact, every objectivity or communality is treated as a 'contingent accomplishment of socially organised common practice' (Garfinkel 1967, 33).

> Thereby, in contrast to certain versions of Durkheim that teach that the objective reality of social facts is sociology's fundamental principle, the lesson is taken instead, and used as a study policy, that the objective reality of social facts as an ongoing accomplishment of the concerted activities of daily life, with the ordinary, artful ways of that accomplishment being by members known, used, and taken for granted, is, for members doing sociology, a fundamental phenomenon. . . . Ethnomethodological studies analyse everyday activities as members' methods for making those same activities visibly-rational-and-reportable-for-all-practical-purposes, i.e. accountable, as organisations of commonplace activities. (Garfinkel 1967, vii)

In this way, the production of social order does not simply result from existing social rules, which are perceived as a simplified conception of characteristics that are relevant for social practices. As the game is not determined by rules, social order is not the result of rules; instead, (the game and) social order is the result of the usage and application of these rules. Hence, the central point of investigation is how rules, structures or norms are implemented in situations, how they are used, and how they are made relevant to each other—or not. How do people show each other what kinds of rules are applied in particular situations? How do people establish social facts? This is what is meant by the assumption that ethnomethodology's programme is 'working out Durkheim's aphorism' (Garfinkel and Rawls 2002; Garfinkel 1967, vii).

Members of any situation possess practical methods, ethnomethods, that accomplish recognisable meanings in social actions and a mutual common-sense understanding. Hence, ethnomethodology 'is interested in methods used by people to make sense of their activities and the ways in which actors. . . maintain order—both to themselves and others because only in the everyday activities social reality is realised' (Garfinkel 1967, vii). Thus, the aim of ethnomethodology is to reconstruct these methods; the ways people in their everyday activities describe, interpret, experience, and at the same time produce social reality and social order. It is important to notice that these practical methods are inherent to activities themselves: 'The activities whereby members produce and manage settings of organised everyday affairs are identical with members' procedures for making those settings accountable' (1). The accounts Garfinkel refers to possess reflexivity: this is a central feature of accounts that refer to the embedded and constitutive character of actions, talk and understanding that always depend on and refer to actual situations and their related context. That is why accounts are understandable only in their related context and possess an indexical character. Participants in a situation refer to the context of their actions to make the meaning of an action understandable, for example, by stating the location, time, external terms and conditions, or by addressing a person or a group. These indexical expressions produce indications or an idea about the meaning of an action. Such an account is characterised by 'indefinite reference to its "object"' (Lynch 2007, 497). Despite having this indexical and highly particular character, ethnomethodology suggests an orderliness of social life, which is practically achieved. Social order is possible because of the rational and ordered characteristic of indexical expressions and utterances that are nevertheless vague and tentative (Garfinkel 1967, 11). The vague and tentative character of indexical expressions and the uncertainty of meanings are the preconditions for undertaking joint activities and mutual understanding. Uncertainty of meaning and the vague nature of communication enables an ongoing process of making sense of actions and, therefore, making the ongoing construction of social order possible. The procedures of an ongoing accomplishment of social order, which members of society take for granted, are the explicit research interest of ethnomethodology. In Garfinkel's words, '[e]thnomethodology reveals social order as a dynamic, an indexical, practical, contingent "ongoing accomplishment" resting upon the organised artful ways what ordinary people engaged in the practices of everyday life, and reflexivity rendered them accountable and meaningful' (vii). That is why the medium of audiovisual recordings are privileged over field notes, observation protocols or interviews.

This methodical approach contrasts with more conventional ethnographies, which tend to look more holistically at culture, beliefs and symbolic meanings rather than looking for ordering properties (Rawls 2008, 709). The micro study of camp life presented here utilises an ethnomethodologically informed perspective and takes this way of approaching social phenomena seriously at all research stages. This interactionist, situational and ethnomethodological approach, which is part of the praxeological family (Schmidt 2012), makes it possible to gain a more nuanced understanding of social orders within camp constellations and human (im)mobility, providing insights into the complex creation of microstructures and their relevance in everyday life. It also helps us to understand the normalising processes in an exceptional or made-to-be exceptional space, in which camp residents or (im)mobile people are meant to live.

Ethnomethodology provides heuristics to stimulate the researcher's perspective on social phenomena but does not establish a toolbox for empirical methods. Rather, empirical methods depend on and have to match the object of investigation, and hence necessitate a 'strong use of the unique adequacy requirement of methods' (Garfinkel and Wieder 1992, 182). Still, ethnomethodology pursues a research agenda that has more of an ethnographic style with long-term field research (Rawls 2008, 709; Lynch 2007, 499; Pollner and Emerson 2001), prioritising 'natural' occurring data, referring to data that has not been set up for research purposes (Hammersley and Atkinson 2007). Naturally occurring data is material that tries to capture social phenomena happening in 'real' life events that are not elicited by the ethnographer, such as experiments, interviews or focus groups. 'Natural' occurring data enables the following of ethnomethodological research agenda and allows a fine-grained analysis of situational dynamics. The epistemological difficulties that go along with such data are known and discussed among ethnomethodologists (Speer 2002, 511ff.; ten Have 1999, 48; Bergmann 1985; 1990). In light of these discussions, the terms 'natural' and 'real' are put in quotation marks.

Gaining field access to Burmese refugee camps was challenging. Other researchers have reflected on these difficulties, emphasising for example, the bureaucratic obstacles and the production of blind spots in research because of the constant accompaniment of NGO staff preventing researchers from moving freely around the camp (Vogler 2007, 59). In other regional camp contexts, scholars were confronted with the requirement of constant guidance while conducting field research (Inhetveen 2010, 105; Agier 2010, 65–66; 2002, 324ff.; Malkki 1989, 100). I also faced the 'bureaucratic jungle' (Vogler 2007) but finally, gained access to the camps through a local CBO (community-based organisation) who asked me to work as a lecturer at a camp college. Based on negotiations between the CBO, local camp and state authorities, I was able to live and move freely in two camps. The challenging field access taught me a lot about camp orders. I faced a camp pluralism; various actors and multiple officials control and regulate the camps. Additionally, I learned that formal regulations (like the rule that expatriates are not allowed to stay in the camp) entail margins of discretion that are again part of local negotiations between the multiple actors involved in producing camp orders (Birkholz, Bochmann and Schank 2019). Field access, however, cannot be understood as something undertaken at the beginning of a research project; rather it represents work that is undertaken throughout the whole research process and differs from ethnographic site to ethnographic site.

To get a general understanding of the camps and the borderlands, ethnographic talks and interviews (Hammersley and Atkinson 2007, 117; Spradley 1979, 59) were conducted with local authorities, camp representatives, aid agency staff members as well as ordinary camp residents, and people living in the borderland area. Some of these talks and interviews were recorded; some are documented in the form of field notes and protocols. The analysis of observation protocols, field notes, ethnographic talks and interviews were additionally necessary to identify the events and practices where camp orders were produced that are relevant to camp members. When zooming in on public camp life and the particular ethnographic sites, the application of other methods (such as collecting audiovisual data) was necessary in order to understand the situational dynamics. The best places to observe and to participate were mostly public spaces where lots of people were involved, such as street corners and shops, and during distribution, cultural events and general meetings of all kinds. The findings in the chapters about the loudspeaker announcements, section meetings, ration distribution events and economic behaviours, as well as camp mobility, are primarily based on a detailed, sequential analysis of different kinds of audiovisual recordings and observation protocols. In order to interpret and analyse the audiovisual data, not only the long-term and extensive field research periods were essential but also the study of camp residents' native languages, such as Burmese and S'gaw Karen. The data was translated together with local camp residents and documented in the form of transcripts.

Additionally, various documents were analysed, for example, the published reports by the Karen Refugee Committee (KRC) from 1984 to date that served as a data basis to understand the historical and political development of the camps. Moreover, legal documents published by camp committees and CBOs as well as the reports by the Consortium[8] and evaluations by international aid agencies and human rights organisations were considered. The analysis of these documents was a great introduction into the complexity and the plural perspectives on refugee camps and their different actors. All in all, my data corpus consists of more than thirty hours of recordings of naturally occurring situations (plus respective transcripts), countless observation protocols and field notes, informal and formal interviews, as well as a huge collection of documents.

When conducting ethnographies, the process of analysing data is not a distinct stage of research but begins already in the pre-fieldwork period, during the process of producing the research design and of course during the data collection (Hammersley and Atkinson 2007, 158; Atkinson and Hammersley 1994; Glaser and Strauss 1967). After the practical field research, the ethnomethodological considerations made above continuously drove the analysis of the data corpus produced in the field; analysing orders of ordinary action (Hester and Francis 2004). The data was analysed according to the following main rules: explore ethno-methods (Garfinkel 1967, vii) as well as the local and practical accomplishments (Zimmerman 1974, 128; Garfinkel 1967), 'there is order at all points' (Sacks 1984, 22), be context sensitive (Bergmann 1988, 43) and follow a sequence and membership categorisation analysis (Moerman 1974, 61; Lepper 2000, 7; Hester and Eglin 1997). The type of data presented in this book, particularly the video data, must be treated with high caution and sensitivity. For this reason, the name of the camps, borderland areas, towns and villages where the main research was conducted are not mentioned throughout this book. The same accounts for the names of gatekeepers, interview partners and interactants. All data was made anonymous.

LAYOUT OF THE BOOK

Chapter 1 is a contribution to more theory-oriented approaches in the context of forced migration studies that lack theoretical grounding (Bakewell 2007, 13). It shows how social theory illuminates aspects of refugee camps and forced migration and how researching in the context of forced migration can contribute to a broader theoretical debate on camps in social science. This chapter elucidates the necessity for social theory on camps to consider the concept of microstructures, which my research particularly highlights. Camp theory tends to overemphasise the power of camp structures imposed by dominant sovereigns. In contrast, many scholars studying refugee camps in the Global South highlight the plurality of sovereignty and governing actors as well as contested power relations. The plural character has to be negotiated and adopted to camp life. I argue and show how this theory-empiricism gap indicates the necessity of integrating bottom-up and praxeological approaches to theories on encampment that tend to be structurally deterministic. Camp governance, temporality, mobility and economy are the social domains particularly challenging theoretical camp conceptions. They also became the main focus of this research.

Chapter 2 outlines the triad of conflict-border-camp and answers the interrelated questions of why, how and by whom are Burmese refugee camps established. The first part provides the reader with the political and historical background to (forced) migration, displacement and the establishment of refugee camps in the Burmese/Myanmar-Thai borderland area. The main argument here is that the violence eventually leading to forced mobilities in Myanmar are not only rooted in power struggles over sovereignties but also in the history of missionary work, colonisation and the processes of forced nationalism and homogenisation. With this argument, Chapter 2 also introduces the reasons for the autonomous movements and civil wars at the state frontier areas of Myanmar and the strong linkages between people living in borderlands extending state borders. The second part of this chapter explains the establishment of the political and legal camp pluralism and introduces the different actors who are part of creating social orders of Burmese refugee camps in Thailand. There are three main arguments that are detailed in this part. First, the camp pluralism is characterised not only by contrary regulations and policies introduced by different political actors but also by the non-regulations of important social domains. Moreover, the camp pluralism is not static but changing over time and set up on a temporary basis even though lasting on a long-term basis. Second, even though Burmese refugee camps are renowned for a high degree of self-governance when looking at aid agency programmes, they strongly resemble other refugee camp contexts. Third, the introduced changing, political and legal pluralism has consequences for everyday life and becomes part of local microstructures.

Chapters 3 through 8 rely heavily on the fine-tuned analysis of audiovisual data conducted during the long-term ethnographic fieldwork in the Thai-Burmese borderlands and show how people deal with the changing political and legal camp pluralism and the long-term temporariness. Chapter 3 introduces loudspeaker announcements that are broadcasted throughout the camps. Neither aid organisations nor host state authorities directly use this system to address the camp public but both ordinary camp residents and camp representatives do. Based on audio recordings of more than eighty announcements, this chapter explains how the loudspeakers are used for information flows in public camp life. This system is established as a local instrument of public ordering, intending to establish discipline, control and urgency among local camp authorities and residents alike. Additionally, this chapter illustrates how self-governance, management and power-knowledge nexus structures are produced and reproduced. Moreover, it demonstrates to what extent loudspeaker announcements create camp communality and maintain the character of the long-term established and permanent-temporariness of public camp life. Loudspeaker announcements do create not only a camp public but also social orders and knowledge of public camp life, including humanitarian aid demands and central state provisions.

Chapter 4 illustrates how local governance structures perform camp orders and highlights the powerful role of communication processes in establishing microstructures. Based on audiovisual recordings of more than six hours of five section meetings, this chapter shows how camp representatives do not simply pass on commands by state and humanitarian regime authorities or simply function as intermediaries but instead have the authority to communicate rules in specific ways in order to modify and establish new rules. For example, the process of creating a public camp secret is introduced as a prevailing microstructure that simultaneously incorporates and deals with humanitarian aid rules while conflicting with them. Various examples are given that make clear that state authority as well as the humanitarian regimes are not absent, although members gain local autonomy to a great extent against the demands of these crucial hierarchies. In light of this finding, the chapter makes clear how representatives in collaboration with residents are successful in using their local authority to maintain and change humanitarian and state structures for the good of camp order and stability. This chapter highlights the power of communicating external rules, the local making of camp orders as well as public camp knowledge and the concept of public secrets.

Chapter 5 starts by introducing the distribution chain and how residents become entitled to receive rations and relevant documentation acts during the distribution processes. Next, the relevance of the distribution event for public camp orders is elaborated in detail: the distribution event structures time and space and creates specific camp membership categories. This chapter explains how camp residents create an elaborate, bureaucratic and public system of distributing food items. This includes section staff members who organise the event but also the food recipients themselves take part in establishing reliable and transparent structures. This chapter explains how this collaborative work accomplishes a form of public bureaucracy and the public examination of camp members. A local disciplinary institution is established and maintained by the camp community itself, rather than being forced on them by humanitarian aid agencies. The case clarifies how powerful locally—and collaboratively—established microstructures are established and re-established. The video recordings and interaction analysis introduced here underline to what extent the camp is not limited to a microcosm of intensive modes of governance and restrictions on the part of humanitarian aid agencies.

Chapter 6 demonstrates how economic activities are deeply embedded in the camp's environment. Additionally, this chapter looks at social networks and human mobility beyond camp and state borders. Many of these activities take place in a legal grey zone, hence, residents are forced to make their work activities occasionally invisible during public camp life. Sometimes, they have to perform a total institution but quickly return to normality. However, in general they do not perform their work activities as something "illegal" but as something ordinary and normal. In the light of various observations in a grocery store, this chapter vividly points out how camp residents deal with ambivalent jurisdictional structures and embed troublesome situations in normal state of affairs. The chapter presents the ways interactants perform the exceptional character of the camp, how 'illegal' practices become visible and how they become normalised. Additionally, pre-camp structures and historical linkages play an extraordinarily important role for these camp orders. This chapter shows how normality is produced locally in precarious, exceptional and unreliable environments and how work activities play an essential role for the normalisation of camp orders.

Chapter 7 elaborates on the findings of detailed analyses of border checkpoint architecture and practices, the public transportation system established by camp residents and human mobility in the Myanmar/Thai border area. The observations introduced here underline the extent to which the camp is not limited to a microcosm of intensive modes of governance and restrictions on the part of a central state authority or NGOs. Instead, camp orderings such as mobility rules are set locally in collaboration with the local home as well as host states and camp authorities. These local systems of mobility change occasionally, for example, when the central state authority is present, but are usually stable and quite reliable for those involved. Moreover, locally established bureaucratic systems dominate and are an answer to central state prohibitions. This chapter also shows, how former camp residents holding Western or Thai citizenship support this system. Additionally, it makes clear the extent to which the long-term temporary nature, together with the peripheral locality of the camp and historical linkages, as well as pre-camp structures, are part of establishing local camp ordering practices.

Chapter 8 outlines the strength and limits of highlighting *sui generis* microstructures established by local camp members in the context of encampment and human (im)mobility. In a first part, I illuminate how the research results of this ethnography contribute to other empirical studies and scientific discourses on refugee camps and a novel understanding of social order of refugee camps. Social camp orders do not only incorporate governance and jurisdictional structures but also microstructures and situationally achieved ethno-methods. The second part of this chapter outlines how the conception of microstructures contributes to a broader theoretical debate in social science on camps and its potential for other research contexts. Moreover, Foucault's heterotopia is revised and it is examined why this concept contributes to an adequate understanding for the refugee camp context. Finally, the key characteristics of different forms of encampment are listed and it is explored how we can research these camp phenomena in order to grasp camp complexities adequately. At the end, a new differentiation of camp models is introduced, ranking from totalised camp systems to situational camp settlements.

NOTES

1. There has been a lot of controversy about the name of the country. In 1989, the military regime changed the country's name from the Union of Burma to the Union of Myanmar, and later to the Republic of the Union of Myanmar, underlining the 'nation building' process of one religion, one language and one ethnicity. Sakhong argues that while the name Burma refers to the plurality of the multi-ethnic, religious and cultural nation-state of the Union of Burma, the term 'Myanmar' refers to the ethnic Burmans and the Buddhists of the country (2013, 19). The background of this argument lies in the word 'Myanmar' itself. Burma is an anglicised name of the country used during colonial times; in Burmese, Burma was called Myanmar Naingantaw— which literally means the royal country of Myanmar, again referring to an old term from classical inscriptions (Steinberg 2015, 3). In the following, the term 'Myanmar' should be used for events occurring after 1989 and the name 'Burma' should be used for events occurring before 1989. Some inconsistencies might occur when processes of longer timeframes during the renaming of the country are described. However, this does not correspond with the country name that camp residents commonly used. They still use the term 'Burma' as the country name.

2. Currently, there are various IDP (internally displaced persons) camps in Myanmar receiving assistance from aid agencies (TBC 2016) and there are nine refugee camps on the Thai side of the Thai-Burmese border; seven are said to be in the hands of the KRC (Karen Refugee Committee, the refugee representative organisation representing Karen refugees) and two in the north of Thailand are in the hands of the KnRC (Karenni Refugee Committee, the refugee organisation representing Karenni refugees).

3. In the following, the term 'camp resident' is used rather than 'refugee' because not everyone who is entitled to get rations and lives in the camp has a UN-registration and is a politically recognised refugee of the national government and the UNHCR. The Royal Thai Government (RTG) does not use the term 'refugee', rather 'displaced person' and also did not sign the UN Refugee Convention. Becoming a refugee in Thailand is a political decision made by the RTG, it is not a legal category. The distinction between (irregular) migrants and refugees in Thailand is difficult to draw.

4. Statistics in the context of migration and displacement have to be treated with caution (Crisp 1999). The figure of 8.59 million, for example, is based on the 'UNHCR Statistical Yearbook' (2014) and does not include camps or settlements for internally displaced persons or people living in camps in Gaza and the West Bank.

5. By governance structures, this research abstractly refers to the political order of the camp, rule processes, and interactions regarding governing. In contrast to government, the term 'governance' refers to all kinds of processes of governing, involving

different actors and not solely referring to a state government or political institution (Bevir 2012, 3).

6. By jurisdictional structures, this research refers to a basic legal system, such as formalised ways of resolving disputes, including legal institutions.

7. The concept also evolved from the works of Karin Knorr-Cetina (1981) and Aaron V. Cicourel (1981).

8. 'The Consortium' is a term used to refer to a number of international aid agencies involved in Burmese refugee camps.

Chapter One

Camp Theory and Research

This chapter makes a contribution to a more theoretically oriented approach in refugee studies that are 'under theorised' (Bakewell 2007, 13). It shows how social theory can be used to illuminate aspects of camps and forced migration and how forced migration research contributes to a broader theoretical debate in social science. In this chapter, I argue that camp theory tends to overemphasise the power of camp structures imposed by a dominant sovereign. In contrast, many scholars studying refugee camps in the Global South highlight the plurality of sovereignty and governing actors as well as contested power relations. This plural character has to be negotiated and adapted to camp life. The identified theory-empiricism gap indicates the necessity of integrating bottom-up and praxeological approaches to theories on encampment (Bochmann 2017a). Based on empirical research, this study on refugee camps elucidates the necessity of social theory on camps in considering the concept of microstructures as being part of encampment and human immobility in general.

In the first part, this chapter discusses characteristics, structural elements and different forms of encampment. Moreover, it critically discusses theories on encampment—their relations and intersections—as well as how they contribute to our understanding of camps. These include the concept of liminality developed by Victor Turner, total and disciplinary institutions explicated by Erving Goffman and Michel Foucault, the idea on heterotopia, biopolitics and governmentality also introduced by Foucault, Hannah Arendt's considerations of totalitarian regimes, Georgio Agamben's thoughts on the state of exception and theories on world culture. The second part outlines research results, applying and contrasting to the earlier discussed theories. Research in African and Asian refugee camp contexts are introduced in specific relation to topics such as camp governance, temporality, mobility and economy. I argue that these social domains particularly challenge theoretical camp conceptions. They also became the main focus of the empirical research outlined in the following chapters.

THEORISING CAMP INSTITUTIONS

Social theory perceives camps as anomalies, where things happen that stand outside the law and ordinary social norms. This is the starting point of the majority of historians and philosophers who state that the first camp opening took place during Cuba's independence wars and the British Boer camps (Kotek and Rigoulot 2001, 45ff., 57ff.). With these camps perceived as institutions of forced settlements at the imperial periphery, the starting point of camp narratives are identified (Stucki 2013, 62). The peak of camp institutions are the Nazi concentration and extermination camps as well as the camps in the Gulag system of the Soviet Union. Currently, refugee camps are the most widespread form of camp across the globe (Schnell 2013). Thus, a wide range of camp institutions exist in history up to the present ranging from machineries of terror (Armanski 1993; Sofsky 1993) to loose settlements (Schnell 2013, 145; Kibreab 1996). Camps are global historical institutions established in different kinds of political systems including democracies as well as dictatorships.

In order to understand different forms of camps, scholars have developed camp cartographies. Kotek and Rigoulot derive three different camp types in the twentieth century based on six functions: detention camps, concentration camps and examination camps (2001, 20–22). These different functions are (1) preventive isolation, (2) punishment and re-education, (3) terrorising civilian populations, (4) exploitation, (5) the transformation of society and (6) extermination (19–20). This distinction is quite similar to Arendt's considerations about different types of camps (1962, 445). Möller differentiates four different types of camps according to their functionalist and dialectic principles: prison camps and other penal institutions, concentration camps, camp for/in war and camps for people in flight (2014). Another way of perceiving camps is explored by Diken and Laustsen, who follow Agamben. They discuss camps and their characteristics as spaces that exemplify modern society: 'All society today is organised according to the logic of the camp' (2005, 7). But before following this overstretched concept of camp institutions, we need to know more about the characteristics and structures that establish camp institutions.

Foucault points to characteristic camp structures in another context by describing the strict implementation of quarantine rules in lazarettos during plagues in the pre-modern world. He identifies that there was a collective forced to stay in temporary spaces in which rules differed from the environment and the 'ordinary order' (1979, 197ff.). Just as these lazarettos, camps are described as social institutions that have solid hierarchies and power relations, occupy confined territories where inmates are not allowed to leave at all or are not able to leave without being controlled (Kotek and Rigoulot 2001; Greiner and Kramer 2014; Möller 2014). In comparison to prisons, psychiatric hospitals or monasteries, these kinds of institutions are not accepted as a long-term socially and legally integrated part of society or of state structures. Camps always carry a kind of provisional, temporary arrangement (Bochmann and Inhetveen 2017). As described by Foucault, lazarettos and camps are provisory institutions established for a large collective with different structures, rules and orders that count in the camp environment. The temporary character and the treatment of a collective, is characteristic of camp institutions. People usually enter prisons, psychiatric clinics or monasteries because of individual reasons related to their biography or illegitimate and deviant behaviours; but the purpose for confinement in camps is mostly attached to a collective carrying particular characteristics such as belonging to ethnic, national, religious or hostile groups. Still, the boundaries between these institutions remain blurred. This has been discussed, for example, in relation to camps in the Gulag system (Schnell 2013, 134) and the Nazi regime (Arendt 1962, 447). Additionally, studies on camps, including Nazi concentration camps as well the camps of the Gulag system, mention the role of prisoner functionaries that supervised other inmates and carried out administrative tasks. This strongly contrasts to prisoners and hospitals as well. In the Gulag system, prisoner functionaries were able to establish very powerful structures that could not be overseen and controlled by the camp management, rather they became (an involuntary) part of the camp management (Schnell 2013, 155–56). Internal camp structures were beyond the control of the camp commanders that, despite of their power, could neither theoretically nor practically wield real power over the camps. This went as far as guard safety being endangered during their patrols and overnight stays becoming too dangerous for them (Applebaum 2003, 2017). Scholars argue that these powerful prisoner functionary structures, established by minority groups within the inmate collective, are one of the main reasons why the Gulag system finally came to an end (Schnell 2013, 162). These observations are certainly not comparable to Nazi concentration camps. Still, the role of the *kapos* (such as camp, barrack or room leader), supplementing the daily management of the camp and forming a secondary hierarchy, should not be underestimated (Gilbert 2005, 101; Kogon 1980; Ludewig-Kedmi 2002; Sofsky 1993). These systems were called 'prisoner self-government' and played an important role in maintaining the Nazi domination and terror of control (Orth 2007, 110ff.). In sum, camps are temporary institutions that necessitate a spatially demarcated territory in which forms of total control and rule over a collective is exercised. Additionally, rules were set up by the camp management that are outside the ordinary jurisdiction order. Self-governance structures are established that supplement the maintenance of order.

Foucault recognises in the concept of the *heterotopia* the potential of an ambivalent position of particular spaces or institutions existing outside of all places (1984). Heterotopia is a very general concept describing an enacted and realised utopia, which also points to relevant characteristics of camp institutions. Moreover, the concept refers to the function for ordinary society, which are applicable for camp contexts as well. Heterotopia is perceived as an opposition, a maximal contrast to society, and yet as a space with its own rules, which reflects, represents, contests and inverts the relation between the structures of ordinary society and heterotopias. Foucault gives six premises, the last three of which are particularly relevant for camp structures are explicated.[1] Heterotopias present 'other' temporal orderings and may refer to temporal jumps or transition points, or breaks in ordinary time structures. Heterotopias always refer to systems of opening and closings that isolate the heterotopia from its surroundings. The degree of the opening and closing can vary strongly, which contrasts to the concept of the total and disciplinary institution where systems of closings dominate. Lastly, the most relevant characteristic of the heterotopia: it has a function for its surroundings and at the same time questions its surroundings. Either the heterotopia creates an illusion, which discovers 'reality' as an illusion, or it creates a real space that is well ordered and, in this way, demonstrate the illusion of an ordered society (Foucault 1984, 8). These considerations help us understand the nature of camp in general. The camp can be perceived as heterotopia with different temporal orderings that exist in a specific surrounding, with relevant systems of closings and openings and the function of demonstrating the illusion of a perfectly ordered and normed society. We encounter all these heterotopian premises in the following theoretical conceptions and theories that have the potential to describe and understand camp institutions (see Bochmann 2017a).

Victor Turner's conception of *liminality* (and the related powerful role of the weak for ordinary society) is fruitful for conceptualising camps because he unravels the interim state of the camp and their residents. Drawing on van Gennep (1909)[2] he focusses on the study of the liminal period in rites of passage, based on research into the rituals of two African tribes (Turner 1964). Liminality is described as the period between the detachment and separation of an individual or a group of people from a fixed point in a social structure (*rites de separation*) and the reincorporation into a stable and fixed point in social structures (*rites d'agrégation*). At these points, the liminal phase is to be found where individuals or groups of people find themselves with an ambiguous or uncertain status in which the classification systems of the ordinary social structures are suspended. Individuals possess neither the characteristics or social positions of the pre-liminal or those of the post-liminal period: 'a limbo of statuslessness' (Turner 1969, 97). People who find themselves in this period 'are neither here nor there; they are betwixt and between the positions assigned and arrayed by law, custom, convention, and ceremonial. . . . Thus, liminality is frequently likened to death, to being in the womb, to invisibility, to darkness, to bisexuality, to the wilderness, and to an eclipse of the sun or moon' (95). Turner describes the behaviour of people who find themselves in liminality as

> normally passive or humble; they must obey their instructors implicitly, and accept arbitrary punishment without complaint. It is as though they are being reduced or ground down to a uniform condition to be fashioned anew and endowed with additional powers to enable them to cope with their new station in life. Among themselves, neophytes tend to develop an intense comradeship and egalitarianism. Secular distinctions of rank and status disappear or are homogenized. (95)

Additionally, Turner characterises the liminal period as a time without status, property or ordinary, secular clothes or things that indicate roles, rankings or positions in the kinship relations of ordinary society. Like van Gennep, Turner argues that these characteristics of liminality are comparable to those of minority groups and groups that live at the borders of social structures. That is why characteristics described in liminality also describe characteristics of marginality and inferiority. Groups that live in such states capture a central function of ordinary society, namely to maintain the identity of a society and 'ordinary' norms of society. In this way, Turner points to the power of the weak in maintaining the social order of ordinary society (108ff.). There are similarities to camp populations and the perspective of society, who view camp populations (similar to van Gennep's and Turner's arguments) as collectives with the same positions, equalising the social diversity they come from or go to. These equalising aspects are captured in the concept of *communitas*, where people exit from the status-bound social order (131). Looking at these ideas of liminality together with the concept of heterotopia is illuminating for camp contexts. Camp spaces are illusions because with their characteristic of liminality—hence, their appearance of lacking social structures—structures and regulations have to be implemented. The camp as a heterotopia, however, is simply not ordered in the way ordinary society or the surroundings are ordered. Moreover, the role of the weak is implemented through camp structures, and the role of ordinary society in producing these homogeneously perceived, weak camp collectives is relevant as well. From the external perspective these collectives lose their position in ordinary social structures. The camp is regulated through a spatial regime where a collective of liminality and marginality is produced through enforcing the perspective of the environment and outsiders. At the same time, the camp is an anomaly functioning as a maintainer of the social order and the norms of society.

Turner himself identifies parallels with Goffman's total institutions (Turner 1969, 108), where liminality may also become permanent and in-stitutionalised (107) and in terms of the loss of personality and individuality (Goffman 1961, 30, 33ff.). A similarity exists also between Turner's descrip-tions on homogenisation and the egalitarianism and the concept of the 'civil death' (16) and the admission procedures that Goffman explicitly calls 'rite[s] of passage' (18). The conceptions of Goffman's total institutions again share characteristics with disciplinary institutions described by Foucault (1979). Total and disciplinary institutions can be characterised as liminal stages in which normal status is lost by inmates and where a new status is to be achieved through the institution. It is a status that aims at producing suitable members of the institution that can later on become suitable members of a society who fits into the normal systems of society.

The concepts of the *total* and *disciplinary institution* refer to an all-encompassing drawdown by a closed institution and its structure of members who are not allowed to leave the premises such as mental hospitals, prisons and monasteries. Foucault and Goffman both emphasise that it is not the illness or the crime that characterises the patient or the prisoner; rather, the institution itself produces its inmates. Goffman describes four main features of a total institution:

1. All spheres of life happen in one place (which he contrasts to the ordinary Western separation of work, free time and sleep) and under one single authority (1961, 44ff.).
2. Daily activities are conducted with other members who are similarly treated and are forced to do the same things. This refers to the equalising processes of the inmates mentioned above.
3. All phases of the day and all activities are planned in detail (45ff.) and are imposed from above, based on 'a system of explicit formal rulings and a body of officials' (6).
4. These enforced activities are part of a rational plan that is directed towards achieving the objectives and official aims of the institution (6).

Among many other characteristics, the total institution expresses itself in the restriction, regulation and control of inmate mobility as well as social communication channels outside the institutions. Further relevant characteristics are a high degree of bureaucracy, the involuntary presence of the inmates, control and supervision as well as a strict separation and (an intended) social distance between the body of officials and the inmates (7).

Simultaneously to Goffman, Foucault studies forms of confinement, but the focus is more on the discursive formation-conditions of modern prisons as an expression of new forms of power—namely the microphysics of power (Foucault 1979). This kind of power is no longer directed towards the body (such as torture) but towards people's souls. According to Foucault, the humanist penal system is not a step towards a humanised society but corresponds with the calculation of modern forms of power to minimise the costs of deviant behaviour. He identifies a new quality of social power relations characterised by the minute observation of details and the control of the smallest aspects of life. This, according to Foucault, is what defines modern humanism, which is exemplified by prisons as well as the military, medicine and education. He explores diverse procedures for discipline and control. As noted earlier, he identifies these procedures already in pre-modern times in the way people dealt with the plague, creating a natural disorder. The answer to this exceptional situation is bureaucratisation and regulation implementation: 'not the collective festival, but strict divisions, not law transgressed but the penetration of regulation into even the smallest details of everyday life through the mediation of the complete hierarchy that assured the capillary functioning of power' (198). Further disciplinary procedures and techniques he discusses, based on research in prisons, are the ordered distribution of bodies in spatial arrangements (144ff.); control of activities and their temporal regulation (150ff.); the combination of time, the arrangement of the space, body and object control as well as their exhaustive usage of controlling activities (194ff.); the permanent visibility that assures the proper functioning of power through the panopticon, and the investigative stance (191, 201ff.). The architectural *gestalt* of the panopticon exemplifies disciplinary power (195ff.). The panopticon produces a form of power which is normalised by the bodies that it occupies and fabricates. This form of power aims minimising the resistance potential and improves the sufficiency of the bodies for ordinary society. Disciplinary institutions oppress undesired behaviour and modulate desired behaviour at the same time, paradoxically enough to repair, to produce and to heal simultaneously.

Analogous to Goffman's total institution, the prison is an institution with apparatuses and techniques that reshape and form individuals. Foucault refers to the total drawdown of individuals through the investigative stance, hierarchical control and surveillance through the techniques of the institution. Moreover, he refers to the function of these institutions for society, linking it already to the concepts of biopolitics and governmentality. Foucault emphasises the links between these institutions and the outside world, and even identifies these structures in the outside world. He argues that these modern institutions train people to behave according to the norms and rules of society and in this way make them productive and have an important function for their environment. Similar to Schmitt, for Foucault the investigation of these closed institutions makes him understand the investigation of normality (Foucault 1980, 329). Schmitt states: 'In the exception the power of real life breaks through the crust of a mechanism that has become torpid by repetition. The exception explains the general itself' (1985, 15). In describing disciplinary techniques, Foucault perfects some of the considerations Goffman makes in the first part of his book. But he does not elaborate on what Goffman identifies as the 'underlife' of inmates, the ways patients 'worked the system'.

Goffman details the *underlife* of the inmates in the second half of his book. Immanent to total institution are margins of discretion. He focusses on the many different kinds of secondary adjustments, which in total institutions tend to be composed not of disruptive adjustments but of contained adjustments, where inmates are able to withdraw from the prescribed role of the institution (Goffman 1961, 200). Important parts of the underlife are adjustments in which inmates work the system, such as obtaining workable assignments (219) in order to obtain extra food (220). Moreover, undercover transportation systems are established. Legitimate transportation systems may also become part of the underlife, where artefacts, objects and messages can be conveyed (254ff.). Even though acts of buying and selling are forbidden by the institution (264), social exchange with the outside world, economic exchanges involving sale or trade are part of the underlife and so also part of the total institution. Additionally, there are undertakings that provide individuals with short-term breaks from the institutions such as sports, drawing, gambling, leatherwork and reading, which Goffman calls 'escape worlds' (309–10). The minimal requirements for building up such an underlife 'are stashes, means of transportation, free places, territories, supplies for economic and social exchange' (305). Still, the total institution is involved, and some everyday activities from morning to night provide amorphous power over the inmates imposed by one authority realised by a body of staff (43ff.).

The underlife plays a central role in camp institutions and is observable in diverse camp contexts on which neither Foucault nor Agamben further elaborate. As noted earlier, various studies of the camps in the Gulag system refer to an underlife (Applebaum 2003, 25ff.; Douglas 2003; Sgovio 1979). But 'inmates' of camps in the Gulag system established power structures that the camp management or body of staff could no longer handle (Schnell 2013, 158). Thus, these power structures cannot be described as an underlife of a total institution because inmates become the body of staff and, in doing so, bring down a main characteristic of the camp as a total institution. Goffman contrasts total institutions to what happens in the ordinary society (such as the division of work, sleep and free time) but does not further elaborate on the relevance of the total institution for ordinary society. As noted, while Foucault does not acknowledge the underlife, he elaborates further on the relevance of disciplinary institutions for ordinary society.

With the conception of *biopolitics*, Foucault links the forms of power such as discipline, control and punishment, particularly in institutions, with processes outside these institutions. Foucault's idea of biopolitics refers to developments in the West of new mechanisms and technologies of power (1977/2014, 166). These are the ongoing inclusion of natural life in the regulation and calculation of power (163). These biopolitics developed together with the previously described disciplinary procedures in institutions such as microphysics of power, the investigative stance and the regulation of large populations or collectives (Foucault 1994, 191, 198). The term 'governmentality' combines this disciplinary power and biopower, where collective bodies, even whole societies, are not only disciplined and controlled but at the same time optimised and made productive. The denoted social and political power over life, applies to the collective body, which is accessible and approachable through administration and bureaucracy similar to disciplinary institutions. Biopolitics is a control apparatus exerted over populations. The aim of biopolitics is to administer, secure, develop and manage the life of collectives. Foucault describes the change in power in the following way:

> Since the classical age the West has undergone a very profound transformation of these mechanisms of power. 'Deduction' has tended to be no longer the major form of power but merely one element among others, working to incite, reinforce, control, monitor, optimise, and organise the forced under it: a power bent on generating forces, making them grow, and ordering them, rather than once dedicated to impeding them, making them submit, or destroying them. (1998, 136ff.)

> New too for the fact that it expanded along three axes: that of pedagogy, having as its objective the specific sexuality of children; that of medicine, whose objective was the sexual physiology peculiar to woman; and last, that of demography, whose objective was the spontaneous or concerted regulation of births. (116)

While disciplinary power aims to control individual bodies, biopolitics aims at equally constituting and regulating large collectives. The instruments of biopolitics include, for example, statistics and general regulations. These procedures are of particular significance in camp contexts because regulations and mechanisms aim at collectives more than individuals. Foucault argues that these kinds of power are not binary, identifiable solely with state, institutions or an apparatus, on the one hand, and oppressed, on the other hand (Foucault 1977/2014, 95). For him, power pervasively circulates and emanates. The ongoing inclusion of these biopolitical mechanisms seems to be highly applicable in camp contexts because the access to a small amount of people in a smaller enclosed space is much easier than in bigger territories with larger populations. Foucault highlights both the fragmented character of power and how power becomes identifiable in the microprocesses of social life (94ff.).

Before Agamben's work is introduced, we should briefly reflect on Arendt's consideration of camps and their links to political regimes, because Agamben follows both Foucault and Arendt. Arendt emphasises the function of camps for a political system. In her *Totalitarianism in Power* (1962), Arendt discusses the role of camps in totalitarian regimes, particularly the Nazi regime and the Soviet Union under Stalin. According to Arendt, these totalitarian regimes are interested in dominating every aspect of people's lives and camps serve as laboratory spaces to demonstrate that 'the fundamental belief of totalitarianism that everything is possible is being verified' (437). To demonstrate the regime's power these 'laboratories were used for experiments of every kind' (438). In this way, she assumes that camps are the most severe institutions that play a relevant part in maintaining totalitarian regimes and rules. She distinguishes between three different camp types: Hades, Purgatory and Hell: Hades are mild camp institutions that she identifies even in non-totalitarian regimes which serve to remove human elements—refugees, stateless persons, asocial, survivors of wars (445). Purgatory includes camps represented by the Soviet Union labour camps. Established by the Nazi regime, Hell is extermination camps (445). According to Arendt, these camp institutions have in common that 'the human masses sealed off in them are treated as if they no longer existed, as if what happened to them where no longer of any interest of anybody, as if they were already dead' (445). She also describes the character of the nihilistic generalisation of inmates (which also has been described by Goffman and Turner). Most importantly, Arendt highlights the state production of the non-juridical person in all types of camps, which successfully establishes the destruction of individuals (455). Added to this claim we also learn from Arendt (and also Giddens) that even in absolute total institutions, powerless situations are difficult to imagine, not least because the powerful depend on the cooperation of the controlled and ruled (Arendt 1970, 51; 1943/1986, 312; Giddens 1988, 64ff.).

With Agamben, the focus switches more to the power of state sovereignty which produces the camp as a state of exception. Agamben follows Foucault's and Arendt's thinking[3] and argues that the camp, in general, is the paradigm for biopolitical processes of the modern world (2002, 127).

Referring to Schmitt, Agamben characterises the camp by *the state of exception* which is permanently realised by the nation-states and thus, becomes the rule (2000, 38). Agamben argues that camps are exemplary zones of indiscernibility because within these spaces the difference between norm and exception becomes blurred (2002, 182ff.). The state sovereign makes a decision regarding inclusion in the political community through the exclusion of people or spaces such as camps where legal status is refused. These characteristics mean that in the state of exception it is possible for individuals to become subject to various forms of violence without legal consequence (183). Agamben understands biopower as the governance or the rule of the state sovereign over the naked life—*zoé*. While Foucault's biopower describes the ordinary state of society, Agamben chooses the perspective of the state of exception exemplified in the camp. Agamben nevertheless follows Foucault's thinking, arguing that camp structures are the paradigm of social life (1998, 118). Agamben scholars have argued that the camp 'signifies a hyper modern differentiation (of "society"), which can no longer be held together by Durkheim's "organic solidarity"' (Diken and Laustsen 2005). They argue that what they understand as the logic of the camp is generalisable to ordinary society. In this way, the camp does not remain an anomaly through which one can better understand the normal order of things (see Goffman 1961) but becomes the normal order of things (Diken and Laustsen 2005, 5).

Theories on *world culture* and *society* provide an additional analytical frame to understand camps. Even though camp institutions are not only spread historically, but also globally, world culture theory is underestimated in camp theory. It has a focus on global, worldwide convergence processes (Meyer 2005, 94). Neo-institutionalism, in particular, points to the political and cultural dimension of the global diffusion of norms and values (Meyer 2010; König 2005b, 375; Meyer et. al. 1997). The idea is that worldwide communication links are transcending national boundaries (Greve and Heintz 2005, 110), which make the increasing global convergence of structures, norms and values, with explicit origins in Western societies, possible (Meyer 1987, 41). These structural convergences are based on the existence of a world culture (Greve and Heintz 2005, 110). The most popular example of these worldwide norms and values are human rights, legal and education systems, and women's rights (König 2005a, 103; Greve and Heintz 2005, 110). The organisations of the United Nation (UN) and international nongovernmental organisations (INGOs) are the carriers of these norms and values (König 2005a, 100; Boli and Thomas 1997). World society theory speaks in favour of theories of confinement and the biopolitical mechanisms attached to camps, where centralised forms of world governance determine organisations and people's norms and values. World society approaches are criticised for being macro-deterministic, focussing only on nation-states, organisations and their legal frameworks and programmes. But they also identify with the concept of structural isomorphism, the gap existing between declaration and realisation (Meyer et al. 1987, 32). Heintz, Müller and Schiener, for example, show in a comparative study on women's rights that even though all states agreed and ratified the same conventions, these conventions were interpreted and realised in radically different ways (2006, 424). Additionally, their empirical results demonstrate that there is an expectation that governments will follow a global or a world culture, but this is realised only in terms of an external façade. The external façade and the rights ratified may be the same (world culture), but the local realisation differs strongly (426). There is dissociation between formal adjustments and the realised implementation, which Hafner-Burton and Tsutsui identify as epiphenomena in the context of human rights: 'international law is epiphenomenal to state power' (2005, 1379). The importance of these theoretical aspects should be recognised also for camp environments.

THE REFUGEE CAMP: MATERIALIZING ANOMALY, AMBIVALENCE AND LIMINALITY

Currently the most widespread camp institutions in the world are camps where refugees are accommodated. There are diverse definitions of the refugee category within various jurisdictions, but many states follow the 1951 Convention Relating to the Status of Refugees and its 1967 Protocol[4] (Shacknove 1985, 274). Many Asian countries such as Thailand do not follow this definition as they are not signatories to these conventions (Davies 2007). Apart from this legal definition, the term 'refugee' is also a social type of generalisation and universalisation of a human collective described as 'others' and 'strangers'. These conceptualisations have been the subject of various sociological studies and theoretical considerations, for example, Simmel's 'Excursus and the Stranger', in which he points to the ambivalent role of the stranger, with its advantages and disadvantages, as being inside and outside (Simmel 1908/1992, 143). Further, Schütz's essay about the stranger (1964), Park's study of the 'Marginalised Man' (1928) and Elias and Scotson's work on the established and the outsiders (1965) point to various phenomena that either deal with aspects of becoming part of a social group, or the role of newcomers and their relation to the 'established'. All these aspects obviously apply to the situation of refugees. The question is then: What is particularly characteristic of the figure of the refugee? and, Why are camps established for people entitled to this status?

A first answer to these questions is given in Arendt's popular essay 'We Refugees' (1943/1986), as well as her considerations in *The Origins of Totalitarism* (1962). Refugees are perceived as a threat to the normal order of the nation-state system but, at the same time, are the necessary 'other' and support for the 'normal' nation-state order. The ambiguous relationship of exclusion and inclusion of the figure of the refugee in the nation-state (system) is dealt with by Malkki (1995b) and Soguk (1999). Both agree that the figure of the refugee undermines and supports the nation-state system simultaneously. Malkki argues that refugees expose the problematic character of the trinity of people-state-territory, which needs to be hidden in order to maintain the 'national order of things' (1992, 25). Like Arendt, she supposes that the refugee is an exception and an anomaly (Arendt 1962, 420; Agamben 1998), and disturbs the symbolic national order where it is assumed that every person belongs to a territory and a people (Malkki 1992, 9). At the same time, refugees are seen as a constitutive element of the national state system (Soguk 1999, 33ff.). The refugee is the 'necessary other' that creates the normalcy of citizens and stabilises the images of citizens and refugees alike (12). State borders and the attempt by states to order people with political status guarantees the constant creation of refugees (Hadad 2008, 56). As long as nation-states try to manage the ordering of people with politically defined legal statuses, such as citizenship, they will simultaneously create a category of the 'other', including refugees. The ambivalent position in the nation-state system has social consequences for these collectives. It leads to the establishment of a collective being perceived as passive victims and apolitical actors existing outside the realm of citizen and social membership (Elford 2008, 65ff.; Agamben 1998; Arendt 1943/1986). They are categorised as marginalised subjects, lacking agency, voice, a face and protection (Soguk 1999, 18; Harrell-Bond 1986, 11; Arendt 1943/1986). Having left behind his origin and been stripped of his former identities, the refugee is socially a 'zombie' whose spectral past survives in a world in which his symbolic capital does not count, and whose presence takes place in a condition of 'social nakedness' (Diken 2004, 88).

The figure of the refugee suits the conception of camps insofar as both are intended to be temporary because refugees are waiting to rejoin the normal nation-state system where everyone belongs to a territory and a nation. An international refugee regime has been developed to respond to the problematic status of the 'others' that the nation-state system produces. The term 'international refugee regime' is used to refer to 'an institutionalised system comprising, first, rules and norms referring to refugee-related actions of organisational, individual and state actors, second, organisations, specifically engaged in these refugee-related actions, and third, operational practices of dealing with refugees' (Inhetveen 2006, 1). Refugee camps or accommodation spaces for refugees materialise the common answer of the refugee regime to this structural problem and institutionalise the ambivalent and temporary position of the refugee figure. In this way, refugee camps also become a threat to nation-states, housing unwanted residents who need to be alternatively regulated. Simultaneously, camps demonstrate, maintain and strengthen the normal state order of things, namely, that every person should belong to a territory and a people.

These considerations echo what Foucault describes as his last premises of heterotopia, and with what Turner describes as characteristic of marginalised, liminalised and interiorised groups of people and their powerful role in ordinary society when it comes to maintaining and stabilising ordinary social orders and norm-systems (Turner 1969, 108ff.). The liminal state has validity in the context of refugees and refugee camps because neither the host nor the origin countries want these people to stay in their territories (Dudley 2010, 61). From a political point of view, refugees are marginal in the global system of nation-states. Further, it has been argued that '[i]n anthropological terms, refugees are people who have undergone a violent "rite" of separation and unless or until they are "incorporated" as citizens into their host state . . . find themselves in "transition" or in a state of "liminality"'. This 'betwixt and between' (Turner 1969) may not only be legal and psychological but social and economic as well (Harrell-Bond and Voutira 1992, 7).[5] While Harrell-Bond and Voutira argue that the liminality refers not only to the legal realm but also to people's lifeworlds, Dudley argues that the critique of the dominance of the nation-state system by academics is an ideological statement itself and may have little relevance for refugees' everyday lives (2010, 61ff.). The process of producing the refugee and refugee camps through the international community (Wright 2014, 460; Turner 2004) and humanitarian agencies (Agier 2011, 19ff., 33–34; Harrell-Bond 1986, 89ff.) are linked to these debates. In particular, the role of the international humanitarian regime or industry is emphasised (Turner 2010; Lischer 2005; Hyndman 2000). In addition, some scholars argue that the 'consciousness' of being a refugee is the product of dominant external others that impose this form of awareness, which is observable particularly in camp contexts (Malkki 1995a, 234; Long 1993, 7ff.; Harrell-Bond 1986, 90). In a comparative study between camp refugees and refugees living in urban areas, Malkki found that '[t]he camp, then, produced "refugees" in a way that the township never seemed to do' (1995a, 235). As mentioned earlier, this was observed also by Goffman (1961) and Foucault (1979) in contexts of clinics and prisons. In contrast to these assumptions emphasising the powerful role of the external environment, scholars also acknowledge refugees' agency (Holzer 2012; Horst 2006;

Essed, Frerks and Schrijvers 2005; Kibreab 1993)—for instance, based on their establishment of self-management and governance structures in camps (McConnachie 2014b; Fiddian-Quasmiyeh 2011; Dzeamesi 2008; Frechette 2002). At the top of refugee-agency debates stands the discussion about 'refugee warriors', refugee camp militarisation and civil-war supporting structures for armed rebels in the home region (Möller 2014, 92ff.; Lischer 2005; Adelman 1998). But all these considerations should not lead one to the conclusion that (camp) refugees are a homogenous group of people. It has been argued that the term 'refugee' is a political and juridical category that does not take into account the social structural characteristics that vary enormously (Horst 2006, 210). Nevertheless, the most prominent theoretical approaches also applied by scholars studying refugee camps do not provide much support for these differences but tend to maintain the picture of a collective of refugees, in general, and particularly of camp refugees.

PLURAL CAMP GOVERNANCE AND LEGAL SYSTEMS

The conception of the total institution has been utilised to identify authoritarian structures, regulations and control inside refugee camps (Schmidt 2003, 6; Baumann 2002, 347; Long 1993, 8). Baumann (2002) compares refugee camps to 'hyper ghettos' and even prisons, as analysed by Wacquant (2001), where people 'learn to live, or rather survive in the here-and-now, bathed in the concentrate of violence and hopelessness brewing within its walls' (Baumann 2002, 345). Baumann argues that the refugee camp is a micro-world that comes close to Goffman's 'total institution' (1961, 347). Hitchcox describes depersonalisation and equalising processes that are similar to techniques applied in total institutions (1990, 150, 153). In this way, refugee camps are compared to controlling institutions like prisons, psychiatric clinics or hospitals in Western societies. Refugee camps are validated as institutions with clear distinctions between inmates and staff, where staff members permanently regulate and observe their inmates and have total access and control over the inmates' behaviour (Goffman 1961, 17). Inhetveen makes use of this ideal type in a heuristic way (2010, 71) but emphasises that this comparison is inappropriate for various reasons (360). To mention but a few: everyday life in a refugee camp is not planned in detail and barely affected by administrative guidelines (382), aid agency staff have weak access to camp refugees and there is permeability of the structural as well as spatial camp borders (384). Moreover, perceiving a refugee camp as a total institution does not take account of the complex structural and institutionalised power relations in refugee camp contexts. Some structures of the total institution may be comparable to particular organisational structures present in refugee camps. But it does not follow that refugee camps are a kind of total institution that Goffman describes (1961, 17). I argue that any underlife similar to that Goffman has in mind would be exhausted in refugee camp contexts. But, surprisingly, studies conceptualising refugee camps as total institutions do not even draw much attention to the underlife Goffman describes. A similar critique can be made regarding the comparison of refugee camps and the 'disciplinary institution' described by Foucault (1979). Harrell-Bond, for example, argues that the dependency of refugee camp residents is not immanent but becomes a reality over time due to the authoritarian structures in camps, which create refugees who no longer make decisions about their own lifeworlds (1999, 138). As Foucault states, delinquents become products of prison life (Foucault 1994, 256), so refugee camps too turn refugees into helpless victims and passive recipients dependent on relief agencies (Harrell-Bond 1986, 283): 'It should be no surprise that once refugees move under the aid umbrella their perceptions and behaviour change. Numerous signals remind them that they are now being cared for by others' (90). Hyndman also writes that camps are institutions 'where refugees are counted, their movement monitored and mapped, their daily routines disciplined and routinized by the institutional machinery of refugee relief agencies' (1997, 17). Analogies between the characteristics dominating prisons, such as control and regulation structures, are drawn out or imposed (Hitchcox 1990, 159). All these considerations point to important phenomena. But along with the critique from Goffman's total institution, these conceptions of the camp as a total and disciplinary institution leads to overlooking the social phenomena relevant in camp life (Malkki 1995a, 237ff.). The following study, as well as research results of studies concerned with mobility, economic behaviour and governance structures in the hands of camp residents, demonstrates that major characteristics described by Foucault and Goffman do not fit these conceptions. Main arguments against a comparison are, for example, that the difference between staff and inmate is blurred and camps are not governed under one authority.

Many scholars are in substantial agreement that there are diverse actors involved in the governing processes in refugee camps and study the relationship between the different governance levels and actors involved in refugee camps such as the international community, donors, aid agencies, state governments and the refugees themselves (Inhetveen 2010; Turner 2004;[6] Fellesson 2003; Hyndman 2000; Malkki 1995a[7]). Many studies highlight the multiplicity and heterogeneity of power relations and describe camp sovereignty as multiple, plural, hybrid and contentious (Hanafi and Long 2010; Maestri 2017; Ramadan and Fregonese 2017). Based on research in refugee camps in Zambia, Inhetveen argues that the political order of a refugee camp is marked by poly-hierarchical structures, and that claims to power—in formal but also informal ways—remain unclear and are disputed (2010, 383). Janmyr argues that refugee camps are characterised by their non-centralised, overlapping systems of governance and dynamic organisation processes generated, transformed and accomplished within the camp and its regional context (2013, 86). There are diverse domains that are not under the control or productive regulations of either the aid agency or the host state. Pluralistic governance structures are emphasised in Burmese refugee camp contexts in Thailand as well (McConnachie 2014b).

Nevertheless, what dominates refugee camp discourses is the argument of the power of the humanitarian aid industry in camp governance structures (Turner 2010; Agier 2010; Hyndman 2000; Harrell-Bond 1986). It has been argued that camp refugees suffer from a dependency syndrome produced by aid agency structures that dominate in refugee camps (Harrell-Bond 1986) and become victims of the modern techniques of relief agencies (Turner 2006, 47; Hyndman 2000, 144). Scholars suppose that aid agencies aim to introduce and impart the values and norms of the international refugee regime that are equal to universal Western values (Inhetveen 2010, 329ff.). Aid agencies enforce a dominant Western bureaucratic system on camp residents (Long 1993, 9).[8] Hyndman states that refugee camps are 'sites of neo-colonial power relations' (1997, 17). Similar to studies about refugee camps, world theory scholars emphasise the strength and the power of an international regime where international organisations, also present in refugee camps, constitute and disseminate world culture. As noted, the humanitarian industry, including Western donors, the UN and NGOs, teach values like human rights, gender and diversity awareness, how to be clean and how to take care of the environment (Jansen 2011, 48). Kibreab, who emphasises refugee agency and speaks against the dependency syndrome (1993), explores how customs and power relations practiced by refugees in their home regions changes (321ff.). Traditional leaders and elders lose their authority of law enforcement because democratic elections are imposed by aid agencies and the elected representatives of the settlement replace these traditional leaders. The election programmes have requirements for elected candidates that traditional leaders cannot fulfil, for example, literacy and English skills (Kibreab 1996, 207–8). Inhetveen also views the international refugee regime as a paradigm for the domain of world culture theory (2010, 29). But the critique applied by world society scholars needs to be applied to refugee camps as well (Heintz, Müller and Schiener 2006, 424). The programmes and policies that aid agencies aim to implement in refugee camp context have to be differentiated from what is implemented and realised in a local context. In reference to Foucault's biopolitics it has been argued that camp refugees are easily accessible in terms of implementing technical and bureaucratic interventions, social control and regulations (Malkki 1995a, 234–35, 236ff.). Thus, refugees become victims, produced through these modern (biopolitical) techniques of relief agencies (Turner 2006, 47; Hyndman 2000, 124, 144; Malkki 2002; 1995a, 236ff.). To give an example that makes these considerations comprehensible and convincing: although refugees make themselves heard, for example, in participation or self-management projects, Turner perceives these kinds of humanitarian projects 'as a specific art of governing that links to . . . biopolitics' (2001, 7). With this he refers to Foucault's understanding of biopolitics, namely that rules from above are replaced by norms within the population (Foucault 1998, 144) and frames the self-governance approaches and empowerment projects that aid agencies initiate as an integral (perfidious) part of biopolitical governance (Turner 2006, 51). Existing political rivalries among camp residents or politically active camp residents disturb the *humanitarian camp project*, where refugees are cared for as apolitical victims and not as political actors (54). Following the humanitarian logic, politically active camp refugees are viewed as those who could potentially cheat and misuse the (humanitarian) camp. Hence, aid-agency initiated self-governance structures to control troublemakers, to teach and train them to follow the logic of the humanitarian industry. These findings correspond to the findings of the current study focusing on the programmes that aid agencies aim to implement, and are illuminating and productive.

However, power relations emerging in local arenas of action, and that are unstable and contested as products of micro-processes of social life, which Foucault also had in mind (1998, 115), do not get enough attention in studies about refugee camps (Bochmann 2019). In particular, Foucault suggests that power is not binary, identifiable solely with the state, institutions or an apparatus, on the one hand, and the oppressed on the other hand (1977/2014, 95). Rather, for Foucault, power is not a property that institutions (or states or organisations) possess; rather, it pervasively circulates and emanates. Notably, Foucault underscores not only the complexity and fragmented character of power, which has been discussed by scholars in refugee studies, but also how power emerges from local arenas of concrete actions and practices (94). This research looks precisely at these local arenas of action and practices where a form of control and discipline is produced and reproduced. Foucault takes power as being intertwined with micro-processes of social life and thus as a phenomenon that emerges within concrete local transactions (93–102). Based on this framework, Foucault's programme can be linked to research that highlights microscopic analysis of social interactions (Knorr-Cetina 1981, 22). For power, as such, is perceived not as an omnipresent feature determining social life but, rather, as a result of very concrete interactions.

Even though Agamben does not refer to (long-term) refugee encampments in the African or Asian contexts, he is referred to in studies about refugee camps. His considerations have been used to argue that refugee camps materialise the state of exception and are spaces of abandonment where the origin of state sovereignty becomes particularly visible (Diken 2004, 96). It has been argued that refugee camps are spaces of 'included exclusions' and vice versa, and that they represent exemplary zones of indistinction because within these spaces the difference between norm and exception becomes blurred (Turner 2010, 6ff.; 2004, 230; Odgen 2008, 48ff.; Turner 2004, 230). Due to these characteristics, the state of exception makes it possible for individuals to be reduced to bare life and perhaps to become subject to various forms of violence without legal consequence. Turner uses Agamben's (together with Foucault's) theoretical framework to explain his empirical research and describes the biopolitical processes in refugee camps in terms of a 'biopolitics of care' produced by aid agency machinery (Turner 2006, 47). He views refugee camps as the result of a decision made by the sovereign (the nation-state's government) but also as a model for biopolitics and biopower not only produced by the sovereign but also by the aid agency industry, which produced the refugee as an apolitical bare life (48). In this way, the conception of Foucault's biopolitics (of care) and Schmitt's understanding of the state of exception, introduced earlier, are interlinked (57). Within these debates, where Agamben and Foucault are mentioned, refugee camps are also framed as non-places (Augé 1995) characterised, for example, by their extraterritoriality, the disposability of meanings and the permanency of transience (Diken 2004, 96). Many scholars study Agamben's considerations critically and demonstrate that his theoretical considerations do not reflect the characteristics of refugees and refugee camp contexts (Schiocchet 2014; Inhetveen 2010, 384ff.; Owens 2009). The power relations described by Agamben are not practices performed by aid agencies or the state government (Inhetveen 2010, 384). Moreover, various studies demonstrate that norms, values, rules and laws in refugee camp contexts are not independent from the outside world, as suggested by Agamben (2002, 178), and, further, that camps are not lawless sites where anything is possible (Holzer 2012). Agamben's camp structures depend on the jurisdiction and political systems producing the camps. When he describes the camp as the laboratory of the experiment of total power and the pure, absolute and unsurpassed space of biopolitics, he pictures a Nazi concentration camp and other forms of prison-like institutions established in the jurisdiction order of (European) nation-states (Agamben 2000, 128). Agamben's conception of the camp is developed based on Western societies and their bureaucratic and jurisdiction systems, which cannot simply be transferred to countries in the Global South. Agamben's theoretical work highlights empirically grounded findings regarding how refugee camps are a product of states and the nation-state order (Malkki 1992). His considerations lose sight of the multiple and complex sovereignties and governing actors of refugee camps as well as neglects the agency and creativity of camp residents. His perspective is state-centred and not focussed on how the state of exception is put into action through actors beyond the state (Maestri 2017, 214). As noted earlier, empirical studies show that refugee camps are not spaces where one sovereign is able to suspend or establish the rule of law. Rather, multiple actors contribute to the state of exception (Hanafi and Long 2010) and camps contain complex power relations and sovereignties (Ramadan 2013; Maestri 2017). Camps are not governed by a single camp logic; instead, poly-hierarchical bureaucratic structures exist (Inhetveen 2010). These findings chime with how other researchers argue that rules, values and norms practised in refugee camps are not independent from the outside world (Lang 2002; Dudley 2010). Agamben's considerations regarding camp contexts are both enriching and necessary for understanding the characteristic political aspects of refugee camps. In particular, they help to elucidate the power of the 'humanitarian industry' (Agier 2011) and the world order of nation-states where every person must belong to a nation (Malkki 1992). Still, with Agamben's conception, power somehow remains a large-scale macro phenomenon and thus risks overlooking power created within interpersonal relations or interaction. That is, power seems to be viewed as repressive and binary: on the one hand, there is a dominating state or institution power; on the other hand, there are those who are dominated. Whilst this makes sense from a macro perspective, from a micro and local perspective empirical research has persuasively demonstrated that sovereignty and power relations in refugee camps are in fact much more complex. The complexity becomes even more evident when considering the power of refugee representative governance structures.

The participation of refugees, or their elected representatives, in the camp administration of the Global South is formalised (IOM/NRC/UNHCR 2015). Refugee camps are partitioned into administrative units that are called sections, sectors, blocks or zones, and elected representatives and a respective committee of section staff members represent these units. This administrative unit structure is a global phenomenon and can be found in camps worldwide. It has been argued that even though these institutionalised structures exist, camp refugees have little governance space because relief agencies set up management structures that dominate political structures in the camp (Inhetveen 2010, 181ff.; Hyndman 1997; Cha and Small 1994) or even camp life (Turner 2010, 7). Scholars even perceive these refugee representative structures as part of the humanitarian biopolitical project (Turner 2006, 51). In-hetveen also concludes that these representatives have the power to intervene in local conflicts, and to collect and administer information about residents, but do not have the power to make decisions about the administrative system in the camp (2010, 181). Moreover, she describes the role of these refugee representatives as intermediaries (165). They inform the humanitarian-led administration about refugees' perspectives (170) and become a mouthpiece for aid agencies to convey information to refugees and to give orders (171). She also mentions corrupt practices by refugee representatives. This points to the role of the humanitarian aid industry perception of camp refugees as apolitical actors or at least places a high importance on keeping refugee camp life civil, independent, and humanitarian (Hilhorst and Jansen 2013, 187; McGuiness 2003, 135ff.). In case refugees become too active, they are either perceived as subverting the camp community in politics or as cheating or misusing the 'good' system that aid agencies aim to implement (Turner 2006, 54–55).

Other studies again have identified strong camp representative structures, extending beyond the aid agency refugee-representative policy. Tibetan refugees in Nepal (Frechette 2002), Liberian refugees in Ghana (Sagy 2009; Dzeamesi 2008) and Sahrawi refugees in Algeria (Fiddian-Qasmiyeh 2011) inhabit camps where humanitarian aid agency structures do not dominate the political system. Powerful (pre-)camp structures established by refugees are identified in these camps. This is also the case for Burmese refugee camps in Thailand where the political, cultural and religious imported (power) structures from the home region have been studied (McConnachie 2014b; Dudley 2010; Lang 2002). Unsurprisingly, camp residents make structures of pre-camp time relevant in these supposedly temporary humanitarian spaces.

The overlapping of these two kinds of refugee representative structures— (1) imposed by the aid agency and (2) imported from pre-camp time—are discussed in this study, as elsewhere (Inhetveen 2013; Kibreab 1993, 321). Scholars studying these relations have concluded that structures imposed by the aid agencies and the imported pre-camp power structures of home regions are productive for camp stability and management (Inhetveen 2013; McConnachie 2012). While in Zambian refugee camps it has been argued that through these pre-camp structures refugees have 'at least some influence on camp politics' (Inhetveen 2013, 59), in Burmese refugee camps the power of pre-camp structures for camp stability has been emphasised (McConnachie 2012). Other scholars draw different conclusions. Strong residents' structures are criticised and problematised. Politically active refugees or strong refugee leaders, whether part of the formal camp structure or not, appear to threaten camp order. Scholars refer to the militarisation and radicalisation of refugee camps and 'refugee warriors' (Salehyan and Gleditsch 2006; Lischer 2005; Robinson 2000; Malkki 1995a). Both strong leaders and structures from the home region can indirectly or even directly support the civil war, which refugees are fleeing from (South 2011, 33ff.; Callahan 2007, 37; Lischer 2005, 6ff.; Adelman 1998, 3). The abuse of humanitarian aid by political and militarised refugee groups has been referred to in diverse contexts (Möller 2014, 92ff.; Hilhorst and Jansen 2013, 187; Lischer 2005, 17; Adelman 1998). Burmese refugee camps are among the examples that are critically discussed (Möller 2014, 94; McConnachie 2012). The most popular and problematic example of powerful camp refugees known as 'refugee warriors' can be found in the Rwandan refugee crises that occurred between 1994 and 1996, where Eastern Congo (former Zaire) became a war zone. One cause was the international support of these refugee groups that conceptualised them as victims and not as active political agents (Lischer 2005, 73ff.). These events show that it is reasonable to maintain camps as humanitarian and apolitical spaces.[9] On the other hand, they also show that total humanitarian regulations, the production of an apolitical life and the biopolitical humanitarian project are difficult to achieve.

Another interesting domain is that of camp jurisdiction structures. Next to security and the physical protection of refugees, the implementation of legal systems and jurisdictions in the camp is the formal responsibility of the host state (Janmyr 2013, 17). Often, states are unwilling or unable to provide effective protection, legal instruments or jurisdiction (Holzer 2015, 165ff.; Janmyr 2013, 345ff.). This is why it has been argued that camp refugees live in a 'legal limbo' with no rights (Knudsen 2009; Diken 2004), which corresponds to Agamben's analysis. The jurisdiction structures demonstrate the realised extraterritoriality of the camp space; while the relevant legal domains, at root and in a practical sense, are established by refugees themselves (Veroff 2010, 72; Sagy 2009, 191; da Costa 2006). Particularly in long-term refugee situations, residents are engaged extensively in different legal practices, discourses and institutions (Holzer 2012, 838). They establish judicial institutions and structures, which often do not comply with the laws of the humanitarian aid industry or the host state (Veroff 2010, 5; da Costa 2006; Griek 2006).[10] While in the Meheba refugee settlement, the courts of the host state may be of greater relevance (Veroff 2010, 72) than in Burmese or in Liberian refugee camps (Sagy 2009, 121); in all cases it is clear that camp refugees tend to keep even 'serious' cases within their family (Veroff 2010, 89) and make use of camp institutions established by refugees (Sagy 2009, 121) rather than referring cases to the 'ordinary' legal institutions of the host region. This may even be in the interest of the host state (49). These findings demonstrate that camp residents may not only have an interest in establishing legal institutions themselves but are also forced to do so. This is also observable in the case of Burmese refugee camps, as explicated in the following chapter.

TEMPORALITY, MOBILITY AND ECONOMY

Refugee camps' time structures differ from the time structures of the total and disciplinary institutions explicated previously. The provisory is one of the main characteristics of camp constellations. As indicated earlier, refugee camps seem to institutionalise a professorial, provisional, interim space. The intentionally impermanent character also corresponds with (inter)national refugee policies (Haddad 2008, 56; Fellesson 2003; Soguk 1999, 18). It has been argued that refugee camps are exceptional spaces where life is caught in a 'temporary limbo' (Abdi 2005; Turner 2004, 236; Bousquet 1987, 43ff.) outside of the time of the common world (Agier 2002a, 323). Refugee camps are (temporary) established institutions or, as stated by Agier, 'extra terri-tory temporary residences' (181). It has been argued that the temporary time perspective dominates camp life (Inhetveen 2010, 23; Loescher and Milner 2005, 36; Baumann 2002, 345; Malkki 1995a, 228; Long 1993, 10), which restricts the possibility for people to make long-term plans (Inhetveen 2010, 255). It has been argued that the refugees' perspectives hold an unfaltering, subjective belief that their situation is temporary, though their exile lasts for many years (Malkki 1989, 400). The argument that refugee camp life is tem-porary has been reiterated for decades: 'life in the camp was uncertain and impermanent, and the future was not in their own hands . . . new relationships formed in the camp therefore were seen as transitory, no matter how impor-tant they were in replacing kin and friends left behind in Vietnam' (Bousquet 1987, 46). According to Bousquet, 'For the refugees, life in camp meant wait-ing for a departure date whose timing could not be predicted, while they could only regard the ties formed with camp-mates as ephemeral' (47). Studying the environmental impact of refugee settlements, Kibreab also concludes that the perception that it is temporary causes a lack of long-term commitment to the environment (1996, 315–20): 'The effect of the existing institutional arrangement, i.e. the conceptualisation of the refugee problem as a transient phenomenon, on the environment is manifold' (315). Further:

[T]he camp ceases to be a provisional place, a space of transit that is inhabited while awaiting a hypothetical return home. (Mbembe 2000, 270)

Refugee camps boast a new quality: a 'frozen transience' and on-going, lasting state of temporariness, a duration patched together of moments none of which is lived through as an element of, and a contribution to, perpetuity. For the inmates of a refugee camp, the prospect of long-term sequels and consequences is not part of the experience. The inmates of refugee camps live, literally, from day to day—and the content of life are unaffected by the knowledge, that days combine into months and years. (Baumann 2002, 114)

[Camp refugees] learn to live or rather survive from day to day in the immediacy of the moment anything in the despair brewing inside the walls. (115)

[T]he life of refugees and the situation of the camps are models of uncertainty. They are spaces and population administered in the mode of emergency and exception, where time seems to have been stopped for an undetermined period. A camp is an emergency intervention that has been on 'stand-by' for months or years. . . . The common term for all these spaces could well be that of 'waiting room'. (Agier 2011, 72)

Other scholars again argue differently, for example, that refugee camps become urban or village-like. Jansen conceptualises the camp as an accidental city, stressing the diversification and organisation of livelihoods, division of labour (Jansen 2011, 123), people's choices to come and go (225) and processes of place-making (227): 'The camp as an accidental city became a place where a diversity of social arrangements or options emerge' (232). The camp is 'a temporary place that slowly shakes its features of temporality through processes of place-making that are similar to forms of urbanisation, with no end in sight as of yet' (Jansen 2009, 12). Others also point to the urbanisation processes of camp environments (Herz 2013; Dorai 2010; Montclos and Kagwanja 2000). Moreover, there are many studies focussing on mobility and economic behaviour in refugee camp contexts that clearly show that important areas of people's everyday lives do not come to a standstill. These studies demonstrate the creativity and agency of people living in such restricted life conditions. These findings additionally show a more differentiated picture on the temporary character of camp contexts.

The picture of refugee camps is determined by the idea of camp residents forced into immobility. Refugee camps have been perceived as isolated and excluded areas with few connections to a wider network, outside of the time of a common, ordinary and predictable outside world (Agier 2002a, 323). The camp population seems to be forced to stay inside the camps. This is often solely the legal framework given by the host states (Bakewell 2014, 129ff.; Jacobsen 2014, 105; Bochmann 2010; 2017b) and may even be in the interest of the aid agency industry because it makes it easier to access, regulate and control the camp collective (Bakewell 2014, 128; Turner 2006). However, this forced immobility or controlled mobility is not comparable to that experienced by the inmates of total or disciplinary institutions that Foucault and Goffman had in mind. Refugees or displaced persons often do not have opportunities for legal mobility but still they are (forced to be "illegally") mobile outside the camps. There are different scales and perspectives on mobility in the camp context such as daily, temporary, permanent, long-term, voluntary or involuntary as well as outside or inside mobility. Hyndman emphasises that aid agencies, which decide on where houses/homes, offices or fields are allowed to be established, regulate and plan the long-term settlement of camp residents (2000, 87ff.). Inhetveen distinguishes between the more regulated long-term settlement and non-regulated short-term mobility in camps (2010, 360). She points out that the enforcement of long-term settlement regulations is systematically lacking, to the woe of aid agencies (362ff.). Scholars have more consensuses about the crossing of camp borders, namely that mobility restrictions related to crossing camp borders are not strongly enforced (Bochmann 2017b; Inhetveen 2010, 360ff.; Turner 2010, 16ff.; Dorai 2010, 5). Moreover, camp residents establish ties to their environment and cross the camp borders daily. Although sanctions are occasionally imposed on those who venture outside of the designated camp areas, cross-border mobility is characteristic for most refugee camp situations (Jacobsen 2005, 5) and is one of the most important livelihood strategies for refugees (Horst 2006; Jacobsen 2005, 10).

Similar to the 'forced immobility picture' is the picture of the (economic) inactivity of camp residents, which is obviously interlinked with the dimension of (im)mobility. These working inactivities are often the legal framework given by host states (Jansen 2009, 1). Unsurprisingly, social exclusion and marginalisation mechanisms for camp residents are identified (Jacobsen 2014, 109). However, there are also host states that allow camp residents the right to work and a significant degree of freedom of movement, such as Uganda (Betts et al. 2014, 4) and Ghana for Liberian refugees (Holzer 2015). Although host states restrict forced migrants from working, the strength of economic activities are highlighted especially in the African context (Jansen 2011, 124ff.; Werker 2007; Horst 2006, 83ff.; Riak Akuei 2005; Agier 2002a, 329ff.; Montclos and Kagwanja 2000; Wilson 1992, 116ff.). Even within restrictive frameworks, 'refugee livelihood strategies' within the camp and even beyond camp borders are carried out with positive effects for the camp surroundings (Brees 2009, 27; Jacobsen 2005, 34). As camps are often established in more remote, underdeveloped regions, the establishment of refugee camps economically revitalises the regional areas surrounding the camps (van Hoyweghen 2001). Moreover, there are 'camps' that are simply huge agricultural settlements where people are able to make a living from agricultural work (Inhetveen 2010; Pottier 1996, 331; Kibreab 1987; 1996).

These results, as well as identifying transnational phenomena in camp contexts (Lindley 2010; Horst 2006, 123ff.), open up the understanding of refugee camps as human forms of confinement. The establishment of transnational networks and the respective flows of remittances, goods and information, and the significant role of people's livelihoods are studied in the camp context and elsewhere (Fiddian-Qasmiyeh 2011; Lindley 2010; Horst 2006, 128; van Hear 2003; Shami 1996; Bochmann and Daroussis 2011). The relevance of transnational activities and networks are stressed in Burmese refugee camps too, where strong economic, social and political ties and linkages to the country of origin, as well as abroad, are identified (Brees 2009, 25, 30). Brees states that, due to sanctions in Myanmar, refugees' transfer remittances were conducted through informal 'bundi' systems where a trusted person acts as an intermediary who delivers the money to the recipient (27). But, at the same time, the government of Myanmar encourages people to work abroad in order to remit. It is an attractive source of income for the junta, as migrants are asked to register legally and pay taxes, in short: 'remittance capturing' (Brees 2009, 29; Turnell, Vicary and Bradford 2008, 12). Brees analyses the impact and the effect of this transnational process for Myanmar by focussing on financial remittances and social-political engagement. She furthermore argues that money has been used for household needs in particular. The drawback of transnational cash transfers is also discussed. While the structural problems in the camp do not change, financial inequality among the camp population increases (Levitt and Nyberg-Sörensen 2004, 7). It has been argued that the dependency syndrome established by aid agencies (Harrell-Bond 1986) is replaced by these social networks (Horst 2006, 5). Moreover, remittances are used to support armed conflicts, again referring to powerful structures established by refugees themselves (van Hear 2006). The phenomena of camp-resident mobility, economic behaviour and activities beyond the camp borders are discussed as a fourth solution, next to resettlement, repatriation and reintegration (2006). However, like the established "illegal" mobilities, these economic activities are also mostly established semi-(il)legally; they include 'transnational smuggling businesses . . . through a myriad of actors such as local junta and rebel leaders, Thai or Burmese businessmen and police and immigration officers' (Brees 2009, 30).

In sum, camp theories are useful heuristic instruments for understanding the governance structures and power relations of refugee camps. World culture theory is also illuminating when it comes to understanding refugee camp orders, particularly when studying the biopolitical regulations that aid agencies intend to implement. The ideal type of a camp may be described as having the characteristics of a total and disciplinary institution but is better described using the idea of biopolitics, because camp regulations and mechanisms are oriented towards collectives; the notion of confinement, in particular, is oriented towards a collective and not towards individuals, as is the case for prisons and mental hospitals. The biopolitics and governmentality described by Foucault is fruitful in this context because, in comparison to its environment, a small collective is accessible within a fairly restrictive space in which mechanisms of control, discipline and regulation are easier to implement. What is problematic about these theories is that the provisory character and the political and legal pluralism of such institutions are not given much attention. All these theories are, basically, structurally deterministic and emphasise the role of sovereigns and the power of the regulations, institutions and rules implemented in camps. Camp theory tends to overemphasise the top-down logic of camp regime structures and power over camp life. Indeed, the role of the sovereigns in producing refugees and refugee camps cannot be overlooked. From these perspectives, a camp *dispositif* is created that has the capacity to control and model people's behaviours, while any ability to act outside of these regulating mechanisms are rarely taken into consideration. Moreover, Foucault's considerations on power relations emerging in local areas of action has been neglected, which has the potential to be linked to the microscopic analysis of social interactions. In particular, the camp as a plural and provisory space enables the establishment of local structures that make it possible to break the Goffmanian underlife (Goffman 1961), as this and many other studies of refugee camps demonstrate. These theoretical gaps serve as starting points for this research: to look at refugee camps beyond drawing analogies and conceptual parallels to correctional and deterministic camp institutions, but to investigate people's methods and practices in establishing and maintaining camp structures, as well as their relevance in camp life. Moreover, the contradiction between theory and empirical studies on refugee camps particularly allow a critical reflection on theoretical camp approaches. These inconsistencies also serve as a starting point to understand camps as contradictory spaces where institutions constrain, human creativity intersects and micro-processes intersect. The need for more micro analytical research is not only empirically but also theoretically based.

NOTES

1. (1) In the first premise he distinguishes between two existing heterotopias: crises heterotopias describe places that are sacred and reserved for people who are in a state of crisis such as menstruating women and adolescents (Foucault 1984, 5). Deviation heterotopias are spaces for individuals who show deviant behaviour, such as psychiatric hospitals or prisons. (2) Society can modify, disturb and produce new heterotopias. And the function or purpose of a heterotopia is changeable. (3) The third principle describes how they are able to encompass several spaces that are incompatible in themselves, such as the theatres, cinemas or gardens (6).

2. Van Gennep introduces the idea of liminality in the context of rituals in small-scale societies, which mark the transition from childhood to becoming a full member of a tribe or social group (1909). He describes three rites of passage that mark the move from childhood to adulthood: the pre-liminal, the liminal and the post-liminal. He claims that this three-fold sequential structure of rites demarcates transitions and is a universal phenomenon, applicable to all kinds of societies.

3. Agamben's considerations in 'Homo Sacer' are based on, and combine, Foucault's, Arendt's and Schmitt's thinking (2002, 127–98).

4. The 1951 Refugee Convention Art 1A(2).

5. Nevertheless, it has been argued that camp refugee 'communities' (or their elites) are busy trying to be identified in terms of nationality (Dudley 2010, 61; see also Malkki 1995a).

6. Turner, for example, argues that refugees do not seek recognition from nation-states but from the international community in terms of media coverage and relief supplies (Turner 2004, 228).

7. Malkki studies refugees in Tanzania. Her central interest is in showing how displacement and deterritorialisation shapes the construction of nationality, identity and history (1995a, 1). Moreover, she emphasises the connection between historical memory and the national consciousness of refugees, assuming that refugees are liminal and positioned in the order of the nation-state system. She argues, moreover, that in contrast to camp refugees, urban refugees do not develop a construction of one identity as a nation. The camp 'community' constructs a national identity and at the same time still pollutes the 'national order of things' (1995b).

8. Long (1993) studies Laotian refugees in Thailand, focussing on the relation between relief workers and refugees and the differences between camp generations and their ways of dealing with the situation.

9. A more differentiated discussion on refugee warriors and the dilemma of humanitarian aid is given by Lischer (2005).

10. Further anthropological or sociological literature focussing on jurisdiction structures in refugee camps (rather than legal rules and procedures) in the Global South is rare.

Chapter Two

Conflict—Border—Camp

The Union of Myanmar is the largest country of mainland Southeast Asia, with a total population of around 51.5 million people (Spoorenberg 2015). Burma was, and Myanmar still is, confronted with conflicts occurring in the process of state formation and the difficulties that go along with nation-building processes. The nation-state system is so familiar to us that it is hard to imagine the world in a different way. However, it is only in the last century that the notion of a unique group connected to a specific territory became reality in most parts of the world. This globally diffused idea became extraordinarily problematic in today's territory of Myanmar, which is among the most ethnically diverse and complex countries in the world.[1] That is one of the reasons on why armed conflicts between the central government and ethnic minority groups aspiring to regional autonomy have continued since its independence in 1947. In the following, more background information and reasons are provided that answer the interrelated questions, Why and by whom have camps been established and what do they look like?

This chapter outlines the triad of conflict–border–camp and is divided into two main parts. The first part provides the political and historical background of the establishment of Burmese refugee camps in Thailand. The main argument here is that the violence eventually leading to forced mobilities in Myanmar are rooted not only in power struggles over sovereignties, but also in the history of missionary work, colonialisation and processes of (forced) nationalism and homogenisation. This chapter introduces the reasons for the autonomous movements and civil wars at the state's frontier areas and the strong social linkages between people living in the borderlands of Myanmar and its neighbouring countries. The second part of this chapter explains the temporary establishment of the political and legal camp pluralism and introduces its different actors. There are three main arguments that are worked out in this

part. First, the camp pluralism is characterised not only by contrary regulations and policies introduced by different political actors but also by the non-
regulations of important social domains. Moreover, the camp pluralism is set
up temporarily and is not static but changes over time. Second, even though
Burmese refugee camps are renowned for a high degree of self-governance,
aid agency programmes strongly bring to mind 'biopolitics of care' (Turner
2006, 46). Third, the introduced changing, political and legal pluralism has
consequences for everyday life and becomes part of local microstructures.

BRITISH COLONISATION AND CHRISTIAN MISSIONARY

In pre-colonial times, different kingdoms existed in today's territory of
Myanmar. The Konbaung Dynasty, formerly known as the Alompra Dynasty,
was the last to rule the lands of the Burmans (Topich and Leitich 2013, 37).
Burmans were ruled by their kings; the frontier areas, inhabited by other
ethnic groups, were largely unaffected by this government system. The Shan,
for instance, had their own monarchy, while the Chin and Kachin had a kind
of chieftaincy system. Three Anglo-Burmese wars resulted in the identification of what we today call the Union of Myanmar and ended a millennium of
Burmese monarchy in 1885. A province called Burma in British India was established (Harvey 1967). The formerly independent mini-states of the different ethnic groups, covering more than 40 per cent of the total land area, were
incorporated into one new union (Smith 1999, 27). The British colonisers
had done little to reduce existing historic tensions between the Burmans and
the people living at the state frontiers. The colonisers perceived themselves
as 'protector[s] of the minorities against the allegedly inevitable exploitation
of the majority population group, the Bamar' (Taylor 2007, 76). The British
divided Burma into two areas of control (Smith 1999, 27): One area where
mostly ethnic Burmans lived, 'Ministerial Burma', was under direct British
control. This area today marks the seven regions of Myanmar. The more
peripheral areas, where other ethnic groups dominated, are today the seven
states of Myanmar and were only indirectly under British control. Local elites
of the ethnic groups were enabled to control these areas. In this way the seven
states and the major ethnic groups became more cohesive and yet retained
their own political structures. Additionally, the British also predominantly
recruited people from ethnic minorities for the Burmese army. These two
colonial practices contributed to the ethnic conflicts the country has faced
since independence (Steinberg 2013, 30). South argues that ethnic identity
was diffuse in pre-colonial times and was reinforced during colonial times
(2015, 161). Taylor also states that imperialism undermined pre-modern

conceptualisations of social solidarities and reinforced ethnicity, which generated new social and political processes, institutions and actions (2007, 76). Moreover, the Japanese occupation in the Second World War intensified conflicts. While ethnic Burmans deserted and joined the Japanese army, people of ethnic minorities mainly remained loyal to the British colonisers.

Parallel to these developments the idea of nation-building also spread. The leadership organisations of ethnic groups such as the (mainly Christian) Karen National Union (KNU), founded in 1947, attempted to create a Karen nation-state out of a linguistically plural group of people (77). Christian missionaries greatly contributed to the processes of ethnic homogenisation and in the building of a common pan-Karen identity (Leigh 2011; Gravers 2007; Marshall 1922/1997). American Christians missionised some Karen hill tribes around 1830, which provided a way of distinguishing converts to other Karen groups, such as Buddhism, before that time (296). The religious division amongst the Karen became problematic during the civil war, a topic that will be discussed later. In this regard, Gravers explicates the complex historical relationships between religion, language, nationalism and ethnicity:

> The missionaries later understated the differences in favour of a selected, common tradition in order to promote a Christian Karen culture and secure a proper translation of the Bible. By inventing new words, metaphors and concepts, mainly from Sgaw Karen, the missionaries worked to create a single presentation of Karen custom, knowledge and identity despite the considerable local differences. (2007, 231–32)

Inspired and supported by the British colonisers, who promoted the idea of independent states for different ethnic groups, the Karen were not the only ethnic group that wanted to establish an independent nation-state. Various ethnic and nationalistic inspired elites mobilised ethnic communities to gain access to, and control of, resources. They wanted to gain power in order to demand fair treatment for the groups they sought to represent (South 2015, 161).

CENTRAL STATE STRUGGLES

In 1947–1948, Burma gained independence from its British colonisers and a constitution was passed under Aung San, the last premier of British Crown Colony of Burma and deputy chairman of the executive Council of Burma, with federalist principles and with the philosophy of 'Unity in Diversity' (Smith 1994, 26). In principle, a multi-ethnic parliamentary democracy was established, including Shan and Karen personnel in important governance positions. For various reasons, however, communist and democratic movements, the military and parties representing ethnic groups all boycotted the political progress and stabilisation of the central state. These problematic beginnings indicate the power struggles that this state faced in the upcoming decades. Further, the country had to deal with economic difficulties and questions relating to seeking regional independence and autonomy of the ethnic groups in the frontier areas (Steinberg 2013, 58).

Due to these persistent struggles and conflicts, the military were able to seise power through a military coup in 1962. They formed a military junta to rule the country together with one political party, the Burma Socialist Programme Party (BSPP). The Tatmadaw, the armed force of Burma that was founded by Aung San, became instrumental in establishing the military regime. They enforced the regime's edicts, maintained order and suppressed 'civil unrest' (Selth 2015, 15). Not much information is given about the Tatmadaw, for example, regarding how large the armed forces actually were. But it is stated that there are also deep divisions and conflicts within the institution itself (16). The Tatmadaw became strongly engaged in the armed conflict on the frontiers trying to combat insurgents. In 1974, a new constitution was approved, wherein Burma was defined as a unity state with a one-party socialist system and a socialist economy under the control of the military (Steinberg 2013, 70). Added to this, the Burmese territory was divided into seven divisions/regions dominated by ethnic Burmans—Sagaing, Mandalay, Magwe, Pegu/Bago, Rangoon/Yangon, Irrawaddy/Ayeyarwardy and Tenasserim/Tanintharyi)—and seven states dominated by other ethnic groups—Kachin state, Shan state, Karenni state, Karen state, Mon state, Arakan state and Chin state (Smith 1999, 30). The distinction between region/division and state, however, did not have much practical significance in terms of a more or less political and administrative autonomy. The government wanted to primarily eliminate the counter insurgency movements and did not grant secession rights to ethnic groups living in the borderlands (Smith 1994, 26). In 1988, widespread student protests against the military junta led to a second military coup, after which the 1974 constitution was suspended (Steinberg 2013, 76ff.). This made democratic elections possible. In 1990, elections were held and won by the newly formed party, the National League for Democracy (NLD), led by Aung San Suu Kyi. The NLD was not able to form a government because military leaders did not accept the election results due to alleged irregularities in the election process. Aung San Suu Kyi was placed under house arrest. Many democratic activists and NLD members fled to the border areas after the election, which were controlled by armed ethnic groups such as the KNU. Many of these pro-democratic activists were also trained and armed by the ethnic groups and subsequently formed armed resistance groups. Again, the central state established a new military junta, the State Law and Order Restoration Council (SLORC), later renamed the State Peace and Development Council (SPDC) from 1997. The regime worked on a new constitution, but opposition leaders were imprisoned or forced into exile. While many did not expect much from these constitution-drafting processes, some saw the potential (South 2004; Butenschön, Stiansen and Vollan 2015, 216ff.).

Only eight years later, a new constitution was finalised and approved in a referendum in 2008. The new constitution enshrined the political power of the military but also allowed for new elections. However, the opposition refused to recognise the new constitution and the NLD, under Aung San Suu Kyi, boycotted the elections held in 2010. After the 2010 elections, a civilian government was installed, strongly assisted by the military. A former general, Thein Sein, became president and engaged in democratisation processes. Aung San Suu Kyi was also released from house arrest and met Thein Sein several times. Since the reform-oriented government was inaugurated, the Tatmadaw has still had privileges; however, its role is better described as a 'veto player' rather than as the hegemonic player it was previously (MacDonald 2013). Nevertheless, leadership is closely linked to the military, which still exerts much control and there are legal ways to return the country to military control (Selth 2015, 17). Since these reform processes, the country slowly opened its economic system. Until 2010, the country was economically quite isolated from the West, but Myanmar has always enjoyed strong ties with China (Steinberg and Hongwei 2012), India, Thailand, Korea and the ASEAN—Association of Southeast Asian Nations (Steinberg 2015, 5). Thailand, for example, regarded as a traditional enemy, is currently the second largest investor in the country and Myanmar now supplies Thailand with its electricity (7). In 2012, moves towards democratic development under Thein Sein led the NLD to participate in by-elections to fill vacant seats, which they won and subsequently engaged with the government. The change from an authoritarian military regime to a functional constitutional republic was a surprise to most scholars (Taylor 2015, 5). Even though the military continues to have significant political power, the government seems to have accepted the change from military rule to a multi-party democratic system. After the 2015 election, the NLD won the majority of seats in the national parliament. A more detailed overview of the power-sharing arrangements, their pre-conditions and existing systems in present Myanmar is given by Butenschön, Stiansen and Vollan (2015, 231). Many questions remain about the future of Myanmar, but one is of particular importance: ending the ongoing armed conflicts between ethnic groups and the central government and finding solutions for balanced power between the central state and the authorities of the border regions (Pritchard 2016, 9).

ARMED INSURGENCY IN THE BORDERLANDS

The largest ethnic group in Myanmar is Burmans, but there are various other socially constructed ethnic groups: Shan, Karen (Kayin), Karenni (Kayah), Arakan (Rakhin), Chinese, Indian, Mon, Khmer, Wa (whose main territory is part of the Shan state), Kachin, Naga, Lahu (whose main territory is also part of the Shan state), Kokang (whose main territory is also part of the Shan state), Akhu and Rohinga. The majority of these populations live in the borderlands. However, these ethnic categories are better understood as conglomerates of diverse groups or as umbrella terms for multiple sub-groups. Many of these groups can be subdivided into several categories, signifying differences in language, custom and culture, such as the Chin's forty-plus sub-groups (Smith 1994, 36). No reliable numbers exist of ethnic populations because the government's published figures play down the numbers, and resistance groups tend to exaggerate the numbers (Smith 1999, 30). For example, estimations for the Karen population range from three to seven million (Thawnghmung 2012, xvii). Nevertheless, next to the Burmans, the Karen are probably the second largest group and the Shan are the third (South 2008, map 2). However, there is disagreement regarding whether the Shan or the Karen is the second largest ethnic group in Burma. Scholars, such as Barth (1969) and Moerman (1965; 1974; 1993), have discussed ethnic categories, identities and boundaries extensively. There is a common view among scholars that the concept of ethnicity integrates processes of identification, including self-identification towards a group, but also that it highlights differences in relation to others; and further, that ethnic identities are fluid and contested and have different (political) functions to fulfil. McConnachie, for example, shows, in the case of the Karen, that ethnic identification has a significant political meaning (2014b, 23ff.). Gravers also states that '[i]n the case of the Karen, ethnic boundaries and the model of a nation (and of the Kawthoolei state) had the double function of erasing the internal differences while depicting the external i.e. with the Burmese' (2007, 229). But the aim here is not to elaborate the production of ethnicity, ethnic boundary (un)making and its function, but rather to show how the central government has dealt both with ethnic diversity and with ethnic groups' desire for autonomy, which has led to mass displacement and the establishment of Burmese refugee camps in Thailand.

The constitution of 1947 guaranteed Shan, Kachin and Karenni (Kayah) authorities who participated in the constitution negotiation processes, the autonomy to agree on their own constitution and to develop their own public services ten years after independence (Smith 1999, 24). But authorities of other ethnic groups, such as the Karen, Mon and Arakan, were not invited to these negotiations. In addition, they were not recognised in the constitution or granted autonomy (79). Based on unofficial promises of independence for the ethnic minorities made by the colonisers after the war, these ethnic groups expected something different (Steinberg 2013, 42). That is why, in 1949, Karen and Arakan groups, in collaboration with communist groups, were among the first to rebel against the central government, seeking independence and secession (Smith 1999, 100). During these times the Shan, Kachin and Karenni still remained loyal to the national government based on the understanding of having the right to autonomy after ten years of independence. But these groups also began to protest after the promise was not fulfilled. After the 1962 military coup of the central government, a quasi-federal union that emphasised a unitary state, with a national culture and language, was established in which Burmans controlled the state's governmental systems. Indeed, the government tried to build up a homogeneous unitary state. It has been argued that this forced assimilation, homogenisation and nationalisation was one of the causes of the militarisation of the state and the subsequent insurgencies in ethnic areas (Sakhong 2013, 3). 'Since the 1962 coup, many ethnic minorities believe that there has been an underlying, though unacknowledged, policy of "Burmanisation", which initially appeared to accelerate after the events of 1988' (Smith 1994, 35).

With the help of their armed wings, not only the KNU but also other politically organised groups such as the Kachin Independence Organisation (KIO) gained full control of large territories along the border. The frontier territories of Burma came under control of organisations representing ethnic groups that were able to (re)establish quasi-state capabilities and regional command structures (Smith 1999, 28). In response, the military junta divided the country into white, brown and black areas (Lang 2002, 40). White zones were controlled by the Tatmadaw and brown zones were contested areas. The armed ethnic groups controlled black zones. In 1965, the Four-Cut Policy was initiated, aiming to transfer black areas into brown and later into white areas (South 2011, 12). This was the counter-insurgency strategy for the upcoming decades. Forced displacement was also part of this policy, often in combination with the confiscation of land and other properties, as well as forced labour and physical and sexual violence (Lang 2002, 38ff.). Ethnic insurgents controlled large parts of the country until the 1970s, but with the realisation of the Four-Cut Policy many lost full control of their once-extensive liberated zones.

The civil wars on various border fronts demonstrate that the situation is not reducible to a political conflict between the central government and the ethnic groups. The ethnic groups are highly diverse and reflect the country's heterogeneity. Similar to state actors, various motivations drive these groups, including economic and resource-oriented needs. The border areas are rich in timber, opium and other natural resources. But there are also conflicting ideological perspectives and personal rivalries (South 2015, 169). Two examples are given below displaying the complexity of the situation in regards to strong linkages to the economic interest as well as internal power struggles among ethnic groups.

The United Wa State Army (UWSA) is thought to be responsible for displacing over forty-eight thousand people between 1999 and 2002 from Shan, Lahu and Akha villages in the south of Shan State (Keenan 2013, 73). The UWSA is the military arm of the United Wa State party, representing the Wa ethnic group.

> The move was necessitated by the UWSA's relocation of over 125,000, over a quarter of the entire population of ethnic Wa (as well as other including Lahu and Haw Chinese) from the north east to the more fertile south . . . there is much speculation that the move was likely engineered for the purpose of expanding territory and increasing business opportunities with Thailand. It is also claimed that the military junta may have sought to use the UWSA as a proxy against the Shan State Army—South which has headquarters in the area. (73)

The situation of the Wa is currently described as fairly stable, because the northern UWSA is recognised as an autonomous region under the 2008 constitution (South 2015, 172ff.). Even though Tatmadaw leaders are dissatisfied with the entrenched autonomy of the UWSA (Keenan 2013, 73ff.), they are allied with the UWSA in fighting against Shan nationalists. The Wa state is part of the Shan state. The Chinese community, the Kokang Special Region (KSR), also enjoys a high degree of autonomy, which other ethnic minorities aim to achieve as well. The KSR is also called a state within the Shan state (Kyu 2016, 13). There are not only power struggles between ethnic groups, as is visible in the Shan state between the Chinese and the Shan community, but power struggles also exist within ethnic groups, such as the Karen.

As noted earlier, one important element of the Karen homogenisation processes is religion. At the same time, religion became a subject of conflict—including a Buddhist rebellion against the Christian leadership in the KNU. The military arm of the KNU, the Karen National Liberation Army (KNLA), was known as the strongest and largest resistance group in Burma. The KNLA was weakened in 1994 because a faction of its troops broke away and formed the Democratic Karen Buddhist Army (DKBA). The DKBA signed a cease-fire with the central government of Myanmar and supported the military offensive of the Tatmadaw against the KNU. In 1995, the former headquarters of the KNU in Manerplaw fell. This led to massive displacement, where members of the KNU and KNLA, their families and also villagers from eastern Burma fled to IDP (internally displaced persons) camps or to Thai territory.

Currently, the borderland areas can be described as mixed administration areas. Many are not under the control of any one party. The border territories remain 'areas of disputed authority and influence' that 'blur into each other, with frontiers shifting over time in accordance with the season and the dynamics of armed and state-society conflict' (South 2011, 12). Affected communities have to deal with multiple authorities, such as the state government and the military, one or more ethnic armed groups, local militias and other informal power-holders (South 2015, 177). In some areas the situation became more stable after a time, and local people reported that taxes paid to the Myanmar Army and armed rebel groups have been decreasing since then (165).

It has been argued that democratic developments and the ethnic Burman political elite are not necessarily quelling the ethnic conflicts. Despite the democratic developments in 2011, the conflicts between armed ethnic groups have escalated, particularly in Kachin, Karen and Shan states (Turnell 2012, 160), but there have been serious attempts by the government to solve these conflicts. Between 2011 and 2012, the government and many armed ethnic groups agreed on preliminary or full cease-fire agreements (South 2015, 164). However, the peace agreements and the path to a national cease-fire agreement fall under the shadow of the continuous fighting between the Tatmadaw and armed ethnic groups, especially in the Kachin and Shan states (O'Connor 2016). The reasons for the current stagnation of negotiations for a nationwide cease-fire agreement are diverse (South 2015, 171). To mention just a few problems: (1) The 2008 constitution hardly allows changes towards decentralisation processes. The central government continuously tries to expand its authority in former conflict-affected areas. (2) While the Burmans, and also ethnic minorities living in central parts of the country, accept the dominant concept of a 'Burmese identity', populations in the border areas violently reject it. They feel oppressed by the central government and the Burman political elite. (3) Many of the ethnic groups have para-government structures in their regions and these structures are widely perceived as legitimate among the population. (4) Ethnic group authorities and leaders regard the current political structure as illegitimate (171). They demand negotiations under the conditions of the 1947 constitution or a basic constitutional change that includes a federal state solution. (5) The ethnic political parties always supported the democratisation process, and the NLD, who won the central elections in 2015, promised to support a federal solution. The NLD also stated that peace was the party's top priority; to achieve this goal, they have to closely cooperate with the military, which still has 25 per cent of the parliamentary seats. Additionally, one has to consider the fact that the NLD is dominated by ethnic Burmans. Steinberg summarises this by pointing out that President Thein Sein has repeatedly called for respect for all peoples and cultures, 'but the military's previous attempts at cultural "Myanmarification" have been evident over decades' (7).[2] (6) Additionally, 'conflict actors' motivation for reaching cease-fires are not limited to war weariness [and] political vision . . . but include the desires of military and political elites to benefit from business opportunities, including the exploitation of natural resources' (175). (7) Lastly, not all insurgent groups are involved in the peace negotiations (Myanmar Peace Monitor 2017).

The ethnic conflicts at the frontier areas of Burma/Myanmar count among the most protracted and long-lasting civil wars in the world (Callahan 2013). The communities in the affected regions suffer a great deal from these conflicts and face serious human rights abuses on both sides (South 2015, 161). The forced relocations, always a war strategy of the Tatmadaw, as well as the various forms of military harassment in the frontier areas, resulted in mass internal displacement as well as crossings of Myanmar's border. Internal displacement is widespread in Myanmar, with at least one million people displaced since the armed conflicts started (Lang 2002, 75). People from Burma/ Myanmar, particularly from the Karen, Karenni and Mon ethnic groups mainly living in Southeast Burma, have crossed the border and fled to Thailand. Historically, the regions along the state border of Myanmar, the frontier border areas mainly in the hands of ethnic groups, are characterised by strong political, economic and social ties between the communities of neighbouring states and the armed resistance groups and their communities. Relations exist in the borderland regions that stretch beyond national boundaries (see Lang 2002, 138ff). Ethnic groups control(led) the border crossings and trade routes (Smith 1994, 21). Today, many border communities in Myanmar rely on crossing the border for their livelihoods (see Kyu 2016, 26; Aung 2016, 52; Brees 2009). While central state authorities perceive these activities as "illegal," local or regional authorities and people who are involved in such activities do not categorise them as such. This is also the case for the Myanmar-Thai borderlands, home to different ethnic groups including the Karen, Karenni, Mon, Shan and others. Strong historical, economic, political and social links in the border region exist, dominated by the different ethnic groups on both the Burmese/Myanmar and Thai side of the border (see Lang 2002, 137ff.). Until the end of the 1990s, the borderland area in Myanmar was in the political hands of ethnic groups and so was the flourishing trade and economic market established in collaboration with local Thai authorities (138ff.).

The close relations between the ethnic groups beyond state borders became highly relevant during (forced) migration processes. Local Thai authorities and village leaders, mostly of the same ethnicity, sympathised with forced migrants and allowed them to establish settlements at the Thai side of the border in a relatively welcoming environment. Additionally, the central Thai government's liberal policy towards refugees further ameliorated the process via a non-enforcement of strict border controls. In the past, Thailand has also supported insurgent groups and indirectly allowed them to smuggle weapons and other goods across the border. This policy changed in the 1990s for various reasons. One reason is that the Royal Thai Government (RTG) relations to the central government of Myanmar improved and the states signed a major economic agreement (Steinberg 2015). Still, the RTG tolerates refugee representative organisations, which established and maintain facilities, offices and homes in the border areas near Thai towns. This enables them to oversee the activities of the refugee representative bodies of individual camps, to coordinate the assistance provided by aid agencies and also to communicate with local Thai governance actors. Currently, there are two main working refugee committees in the Thai-Burmese borderland: the Karen Refugee Committee (KRC) and the Karenni Refugee Committee (KnRC). Organised along ethnic lines, other refugee committees also exist such as the Mon National Relief Committee (MnRC), the Shan Refugee Organisation (SRO) and the Chin Refugee Committee (CRC).

However, it is not only ethnic groups but also ethnic Burmans who were involved in pro-democratic and communist activities and fled the regime to regions, where ethnic armed groups ruled, and then crossed the border to Thailand. A town at the Thai-Burmese border became a centre for active pro-democratic organisations and opposition groups. No one can estimate the exact numbers of people who have crossed and continue to cross the border on a daily basis from Burma/Myanmar to Thailand since the conflicts in the region decreased. Even more difficult is identifying the exact reasons for the border crossings, which were and are necessary to distinguish between *de facto* and *de jure* refugees (South 2007).

THE CONVERSION OF POLITICAL
AND LEGAL CAMP PLURALISM

In the 1970s and 1980s, forced migrants of different ethnicities have established themselves across thirty small village-like, fairly self-reliant settlements along the Thai-Burmese borderland areas. Refugee representative organisations such as the KRC managed and organised these settlements in collaboration with smaller aid agencies on a temporary basis. However, when the armed conflict crossed the border and Thai villages were attacked as well, the Thai government decided to consolidate the settlements into larger, more camp-like institutions at the end of 1990s. Among other outcomes, these consolidations led to the stronger relevance of humanitarian aid structures as well as the loss of self-governance and reliability on the part of camp residents. While the United Nations High Commissioner for Refugees (UNHCR) is usually the most powerful actor in refugee camps worldwide (Voutira and Harrell-Bond 1996), it plays a minor role in Burmese refugee camps as the Thai government granted UNHCR only a restrictive mandate to operate in Thailand. While the limited presence of UNHCR and the strength of refugee representative structures in Burmese refugee camps are quite unique, the presence of the international refugee regime is comparable to refugee camps worldwide. Still, the political order of Burmese refugee camps makes clear that there is no central power such as the humanitarian regime or a state sovereign that regulates the camps. Rather, we find a concerted and re-negotiated form of plural governance and jurisdiction structures and multiple political actors that are part of establishing camp orders: (1) home state actors and pre-camp structures; (2) refugee representative bodies and structures subdivided into regional, camp and section levels; (3) the host state authorities, subdivided into national, district and provincial levels; and (4) NGOs and structures of the international refugee regime.

Home State & Pre-Camp Structures	Refugee Representatives Bodies and Structures	Host State Structures	Structures of the International Refugee Regime

The nature of authority as described by Voutira and Harrell-Bond (1996, 210) contrasts to the political order of Burmese refugee camps because camp administration and management are also in the hands of refugee representative bodies and based on pre-camp structures. This camp pluralism confirms existing arguments scholars make relating to power relations in refugee camps and other regional contexts. Camp sovereignty and authority is described as multiple (Hanafi and Long 2010), poly-hierarchical (Inhetveen 2010), hybrid (Ramadan and Fregonese 2017) and contentious (Maestri 2017). This research builds on findings that frame camps as 'multiply inflected, contradictory spaces' (Peteet 2005, 31) where institutional and structural constrains, human creativity and micro processes intersect. In the following, a rough picture is drawn on the multiple actors, their relations and their role in setting up different formal regulations, policies and rules. These actors and structures are important because they become part of public camp life and social microstructures but are also made relevant and brought into situations and interactions described in the upcoming chapters.

Home State Authorities and Camp Representative Bodies

Without the conflicts between the authorities of the ethnic groups and the central government in Burma/Myanmar, the mass displacement would not have occurred. Burmese state authorities are less relevant for the political orders of Burmese refugee camps in Thailand even though they had an influence on Thai policy consolidating the settlements into larger camps in the 1990s. A much stronger relevance to the political order of the camps have the quasi-state actors in Southeast Myanmar such as the KNU, pre-camp village structures in the home region of camp residents as well as the regional entanglements in the borderland. At the beginning, the village-like settlements of forced migrants were regarded as relatively stable, secure and self-reliant. One reason for this is the strong historical, economic, political and social links in the border region dominated by the different ethnic groups on both the Burmese and Thai side of the border (see Lang 2002, 137ff.). Until the end of the 1990s, the borderland area in Myanmar was in the political control of ethnic groups and so were the flourishing trade and economic markets established in collaboration with local Thai authorities (138ff.). But when the KNU were pushed back by the Burmese military, they also lost territory and authority in the border region. Additionally, the established settlements in Thailand and their authorities, but also Thai-Karen villages, were economically affected. As stated above, the KNU can be viewed as having been the de facto state authority in Karen territories of Eastern Burma since the 1950s (McConnachie 2014b, 28–29).

A second reason for these relatively stable self-governance structures are the strong links between KNU-related organisations and the newly established refugee representative bodies such as KRC. The first people who crossed the border to live in Thailand were political elites and their families, who started to organise the settlements. While scholars state that the first refugee settlements were established in 1984 (McConnachie 2014b, 2), it is very likely that the first settlements were established earlier. The KRC, the refugee representative organisation of the Karen, suggests, that the first settlements were established before 1974 (KRC 1984). This is further supported by the fact that the first refugee committee, called the Karen Christian Relief Committee, was created in 1975 by authorities of the home region after the first Karen people crossed the border to Thailand (KRC May 2010, 2). In 1984, the name changed to Karen Refugee Committee (KRC). The KNU authorities established this committee to oversee 'their' Karen populations in Thailand (BBC 1997, 35). While the KNU structures and authorities have a strong relevance in the local governance of Karen villages in Southeast Myanmar (McConnachie 2014b, 60, 71ff.), the KNU structures became more relevant in the context of the refugee settlements (that later on became camps). The nationalist party was able to exercise power over the camp governance system because of a stable and accessible environment in Thailand (see McConnachie 2012, 11). 'KNU leaders took key roles in the KRC' (McConnachie 2014b, 97) not only because of their education and experiences in setting up administration structures, but also because of their pre-camp relations with the local Thai authorities and experiences with Western donors (Thawnghmung 2008, 21). The departments of the KNU in Myanmar, for example, served as a model in the camps and were branches of these departments. The education department of the KNU in Myanmar, Karen state, also administered the education structure in the camps in Thailand (McConnachie 2012, 11). Similar observations were made in reference to the KnRC: first a political elite of Karenni people crossed the border, established settlements and set up governance and political structures. The refugees that followed differed from this political elite: 'Unlike pre-existing members of the refugee population, at least at first, these new arrivals had little or no conception of the KNPP's nationalist ideals or of a Pan-Karenni identity' (Dudley 2010, 33). Dudley describes how the justice system was systematically controlled by Karenni National Progressive Party (KNPP) members, who even designated men as judges in the camp (41). Camp leaders dealt only with minor offences and imposed brief imprisonment and a temporary withholding of rations (41). It was the KNPP that created a camp structure and controlled the justice system. These links between the political elites and the refugee committees were strongly criticised, often with the claim that the armed resistance groups manipulate aid agencies (through refugee committee personnel) that indirectly but also directly maintain(ed) the different ethnic, militarised conflicts in Burma (see South 2011; Thawnghmung 2008). McConnachie gives a more productive argument, namely, that cooperation with armed ethnic groups may 'transform approaches to governance within the refugee community' (2012, 31) and that in the case of Burmese refugee camps they actually 'became a partner for aid agencies and helped in service delivery and also in governance within the refugee community' (30).

Another reason for the stable governance structures of these settlements can be located in the pre-camp structures of village sovereignty and strong village leaders (McConnachie 2014b, 45). A centralised system of governance or a justice system (such as a Burmese national court system or a KNU justice system) did not reach villages in Southeast Myanmar and so did not have much relevance in village governance (60). Studies on villages in Southeast Burma highlight the relevance and importance of village structures that are acknowledged and mainly referred to by ordinary village people. For example, local dispute-resolution practices at a village level exist(ed) (see Andersen 1979, 320). A prison system focussing on containment does not dominate, but sanction options used by village leaders involved fines, punishments focussing on the body of the offender and expulsion from the village (Marshall 1922/1997, 288; Scott 2009, 264). Today, village leaders are the primary arbitrators of justice, offering mechanisms for resolving disputes and managing community affairs (TBC 2013, 26–27). These pre-camp structures were applied and imported to the settlements in Thailand too, and resulted in quite powerful and autonomous structures at the individual camp and section level. The power of camp and section leaders in the political order of Burmese refugee camps were also observable during field research, particularly when it came to the daily affairs of the camp. Historically, camp leaders acted quasi-autonomously also because of the difficult accessibility of the camp territory. Section and camp leaders and their respective staff live in the camps and are, until today, responsible for the day-to-day governance and management of the individual camp or section. As a result, governance systems varied significantly from camp to camp, including the organisation of different working areas and different camp authorities (Thailand Burma Border Consortium (TBBC) 2011 Jan–Jun, 158; 2006 Jan–Jun, 52). Looking at the different camp rules that remain in place reveals this quasi-autonomous standing.[3] Although section structures are the bottommost administrative unit of refugee representative structures, in my observations it is evident that they are quite powerful within the camp itself. The section unit is a social establishment that governs and orders relevant parts of public life in the camp. This study particularly highlights the relevance and significance of these section structures for public life in the camp and for ordinary residents that refugee camp scholars tend to overlook. Section structures are political structures camp residents encounter on a daily basis. Section committee members are the ones who communicate to ordinary residents the regulations and rules given by aid agencies, state actors, or refugee and committee representative bodies. The relevance of these local governance systems is discussed in more detail in chapters 5, 6 and 7.

Currently, Burmese camps in Thailand are governed by civilian structures, but 'lines of communication remain blurred' (McConnachie 2014b, 31). The KRC is viewed as a quasi-legislative and quasi-executive governance body for seven camps where the main research has been conducted. Refugee representative organisations such as refugee committees, individual camp committees and section committees play a major role in the governance system of the camps. Aid agencies and ordinary camp residents, together with state actors, recognise these representative bodies as relevant actors for the political and administrative order of Burmese camp residents in Thailand. The strength of these refugee representative structures is not only the result of the strong linkages in the region, for example, between the political groups of the home

region, local Thai authorities and the established refugee representative organisations. The strength of the refugee committees is also a result of Thai national policies of acknowledging and tolerating these refugee committees in
Thai territory outside the camps; their refusal to become involved in internal
camp affairs; and not allowing permanent expatriate staff in the settlement.

The Host State

After requests by the KRC and aid agencies in 1984, the Ministry of Interior
(MOI) of the RTG officially invited non-governmental organisations that had
worked with Indochinese refugees in the past to provide assistance to Karen
people fleeing the fighting between the Burmese Army and armed ethnic
groups.[4] The government of Thailand expected the situation to be temporary
and restricted assistance from aid agencies to a minimum level. Currently,
the government does not allow UNHCR to take care of the day-to-day
management or the overall monitoring of the camps and restricts expatriates
from working in these areas. Among other issues, these restrictions support
a level of self-governance for which Burmese refugee camps in Thailand are
renowned. The Thai state, moreover, provides a weak legal framework for
asylum seekers or forced migrants.

In Thailand, there is no specific national legislation pertaining to asylum
seekers, refugee protection or refugee status determination. Thailand is neither party to the 1951 Geneva Refugee Convention nor its 1967 Protocol.
The 1951 Convention Relating to the Status of Refugees plus the text of its
Protocol[5] is a legal document defining the term refugee, the rights of refugees
and the legal obligations of the signatories. In comparison to African countries, most Southeast Asian and South Asian countries reject this 'Eurocentric
1951 Convention' (Davies 2007, 23ff.). According to a staff member of the
MOI, the reason for their not being signatories to the convention is because
the standards required by it are too high and unrealisable, considering the
influx of displaced persons over many centuries (Lang 2002, 94ff.). The government fears being restricted by these conventions in terms of their national
sovereignty and prefers to retain a large margin of discretion in dealing with
refugee flows (Loescher and Milner 2005). In addition, there are also no
other national legal documents relating specifically to the status of refugees
or asylum seekers in Thailand. The relevant legal act that impacts asylum
seekers/refugees is the general Thai Immigration Act of 1979. According
to this act, people who enter the country without proper travel documents
are called 'illegal aliens' that, if identified as such, should be detained and
sent back to their home country (Immigration Act, B.E.: 2552, section 29).
However, under special circumstances the MOI can refuse to comply with

these regulations. Although these people are considered to be 'illegal aliens' under the Immigration Act, the Thai government may tolerate certain groups or individuals through cabinet approval (Immigration Act, B.E: 2552, section 17). This was used by the Thai government of 1984 to tolerate people of the Karen ethnic group fleeing Myanmar, and allowed them to temporarily reside in designated areas. Later on, the RTG also tolerated displaced persons of the Karenni and Mon ethnic groups with cabinet approval, and allowed them to establish settlements. Thai authorities name and document these people as 'displaced persons fleeing fighting' who have to reside in 'temporary shelter areas' (Immigration Act, B.E.: 2552). This illuminates an initial contradiction: the terms refugee and refugee camp are not officially used by government officials, but are systematically used by aid agencies, community-based organisations and refugee committees. Moreover, although Thai national law relating to 'displaced persons' requires refugees to reside in these areas, district and provincial authorities allow(ed) the political leaders of these ethnic groups and their families to live outside of these designated areas (Lang 2002, 141ff.). These leaders constituted the refugee committees that represent the aforementioned 'displaced persons'. Even without a comprehensive legal framework, the MOI provides general regulations, policies and guidelines for the government bodies, humanitarian aid agencies and other relevant agencies that are involved in providing services and assistance (Jackson and Associates 2012, 14). But only a few documents relating to these policies and regulations are accessible to the public. The MOI has a subdivision called the Operation Centre for Displaced People and works together with the Committee for Coordination of Services to Displaced Persons in Thailand (CCSDPT). The later institution is a formal body representing international aid agencies in Thailand involved with 'displaced persons fleeing fighting'. The CCSDPT was established by aid agencies in 1975 as a communication network in the context of the Indochina refugee crises. The committee is a platform and a stage for advocacy work where negotiations are undertaken between the MOI, aid agencies and the UNHCR.[6] Through this committee and its subcommittees, the MOI sets its guidelines for the aid industry.

   In the beginning, aid agencies worked with the established CCSDPT Karen subcommittee to coordinate their work. In 1989, the KnRC and the MnRC asked for assistance with their settlements as well (Dudley 2010, 33; Lang 2002, 102). Subsequently, the name of the subcommittee changed from the Karen to the Burman, next to other committees mostly referring to Indochinese refugees.[7] In 1991, seven years after the MOI asked aid agencies to assist 'displaced persons' from Myanmar, the ministry gave these aid agencies their first formal approval and permission to provide assistance under specific guidelines to specific ethnic groups—Mon, Karenni and Karen—throughout four provinces (BBC 1991, 26). These formal guidelines were based on earlier informal arrangements. To give some examples of these formal regulations: To offer assistance, the respective aid organisation must submit a proposal to the MOI (through the CCSDPT) and request permission. Only with the permission of the MOI, aid organisations were allowed to coordinate and work with the provincial authorities (MOI Regulations 1991; BBC 1992, 31). Additionally, organisations must submit records to the MOI as well as to provincial and district authorities detailing the supplies that will be delivered as well as expected delivery rates. Then aid organisations, but also the provincial authorities, have to wait for approval by the MOI for these reports. Provincial offices then give approval to the district authorities (MOI Regulations 1991; BBC 1992, 31). Only after these formal procedures are aid agencies allowed to deliver rations. This already indicates how provincial, as well as district, authorities are strongly involved in these procedures. Another example is that relief agency staff must be kept to a minimum, and permanent expatriates are not allowed in the camps. It was decided that the assistance should be low-profile and limited to food, clothing and medical care. In 1994, the MOI modified some of these formal guidelines, for example, the regulation of the bureaucratic procedure for aid agencies. From then on, aid agencies had to submit records of their work every six months to the MOI and quarterly reports to the provincial offices. Moreover, the ministry officially allowed aid agency to support sanitation and education services in the 'temporary shelter areas' (BBC 1995 Jul–Dec, 21). The MOI also decided that aid agency staff would have to apply for border passes, which allowed them to access the designated areas. Still, expatriates could not stay permanently in the camps and overnight stays remained forbidden. Considering these national restrictions on the aid industry, the aid organisations were forced to work directly with the refugee committees and refugee representative bodies.

In the 1990s, the RTG began to carry out protective, stricter and more controlling policies in the settlements. Thai military personnel started to police the settlements. Before that time, state authorities were not present at all. The background of this policy change lay in security: the Myanmar army had attacked refugee settlements, which also affected Thai villages (Lang 2002, 154ff.). The conflict at the Myanmar border had thus spread to Thai territory. In response, several (forced) camp consolidations were carried out, combining small, village-like settlements into larger camps, fences were erected to mark the camp space, and the Thai military started to control movements in and out of the camps (see BBC 1993 Jan–Jun, 9). The Thai army also burned down camps because they assumed that these settlements were being used by armed ethnic groups (BBC 1992 Jan–Jun, 9). The relocations were conducted in collaboration between the provincial, district and national

Thai authorities. However, the Thai military presence in Burmese refugee camps was and is still low-key in comparison to Indochinese camps, which were systematically surrounded by heavy surveillance (Lang 2002, 91). In 1998, the RTG allowed UNHCR to play a minor role in the Myanmar-Thai border area mainly in an advisory capacity, monitoring and assisting some of these difficult relocations. In 1998, as a result of the relocations there were three Karenni camps (instead of six, as in 1995), ten Karen camps (instead of twenty-four, as in 1995) and three Mon camps (instead of five, as in 1995) with an overall population of 111,900 people. These numbers are based on the camp committee registers published in the reports of aid agencies (BBC 1998, Jul–Dec, 9; 1995 Jul–Dec, 9). Until 1999, no other form of registration, neither by state nor aid agencies, was conducted, which again highlights the autonomy of individual camp structures.

Local state authorities are relevant when it comes to realising national regulations introduced previously in relation to camp governance structures. The national guidelines given by the MOI leave space for discretion on the part of provincial and district authorities, which also take care of non-regulations and take part in establishing contrasting regulations to state regulations.[8] Their power becomes most obvious through the prism of the beginning of the camps when it was not the RTG/MOI but instead mainly provincial and district authorities that negotiated with the political leaders of the ethnic groups to decide where the populations should be located or where exactly established settlements were allowed to stay (BBC 1994 Jan–Jun, 3; 1992 Jul–Dec, 4–5). It is noteworthy in this context that Thailand is a unitary state, but state services are divided into three different governmental levels: the central government (RTG), the provincial government and the district government. There are seventy-six Thai provinces, each led by a governor (*Phu Wa Ratchakan Changwat*), whom the MOI appoints. Each province is again divided into districts (*Amphoe*) and each district has a deputy district chief (*Nai Amphoe*), also appointed by the MOI. In those districts containing 'temporary shelter areas', the MOI usually appoints the respective deputy district chief as the 'camp commander'. Among camp residents he is referred to as the *Palad*. Legally the *Palad* functions under the MOI responsible for his district (where the 'temporary shelters' are also located). He himself is seldom present in the camps but regular meetings take place between him and the camp leader outside the camp. The meetings are not formally scheduled, as one camp leader explained to me.[9] The power of local state authorities, but also the peripheral locality of camps, makes it possible for the district officers to allow foreigners to work as teachers and live in the camps despite the official prohibition of expatriates (see also Dudley 2010, 39). Under the jurisdiction of the camp commander, voluntary corps are present in all the camps on a daily basis. Camp residents call them *Or Sor*.[10] Officially, they are responsible for the security and the maintenance of the formal entry/exit point of the camps. These Thai security personnel are poorly trained, poorly paid, and recruited from local communities. The *Or Sor* units and the camp commander are flexible in their practices and in realising given regulations.[11] The relationships between *Or Sor* members and camp authorities, especially the camp security staff, but also ordinary camp members, are complex and discussed in more detail in chapter 7. Due to their daily presence, they play an important role in public camp life.

The International Refugee Regime

The Thai government's idea was that residents of the 'temporary shelter areas' would stay on a short-term basis and would be provided with minimum assistance by aid agencies. Although the MOI tried to restrict the international aid apparatus, the aid agencies' low-profile programme changed to a larger-scale programme. But Burmese refugee camps in Thailand are renowned for a high degree of community autonomy and for their self-governance, with control in the hands of refugee representatives (McConnachie 2014b, 92ff., 140; Dudley 2010; Banki and Lang 2008; Lang 2002). Not only scholars but also aid agencies and KRC reports emphasise this characteristic of self-governance (TBBC 2004; KRC 2003). By contrast, the programme reports, published twice a year by the aid agencies involved in these camps, show another picture by identifying camp residents as people in need of training, encouragement and support, so 'that they are able to take responsibility for their own lives' (TBBC 2004 Jan–Jun, 24; TBC 2013 Jan–Jun, 67). This perspective is reminiscent of the refugee empowerment approaches that Turner identifies as an integral part of a 'biopolitics of care', where the international norms of aid agencies are replaced by the refugee population in UNHRC-managed camps (Turner 2006, 46) or what Agier describes as the international humanitarian governance apparatus (2011, 199ff.). Currently, more than twenty international aid agencies are actively involved in different areas, such as health, education, shelter, livelihood, food and nutrition, and camp management. The aid agency reports clearly show that the transformation process from a small-scale aid programme to a high-profile aid programme, where self-governance and self-reliability are pushed further into the background, is also a result of the humanitarian apparatus. This finding is mainly based on an analysis of the reports by aid agencies themselves from 1984 until 2016, where it is made transparent that there is a very strong attempt to control and regulate not only the administration of rationed goods but also the governance and jurisdiction system.

As noted, at the beginning, settlements of forced migrants were basically managed by refugee representative bodies constituted by political leaders and authorities of the home region. In the 1980s and the beginning of the 1990s, these aid organisations mainly worked through the refugee committees, organisations that ought to represent refugee populations. In 1984, different aid agencies supported them and started a programme in collaboration called the Consortium of Christian Agencies (CCA). The governance, administration and jurisdiction structures, including registration, food distribution, sanitation and camp security, were solely in the hands of KRC and individual camp leaders (Bowles 1998, 12). The needs of camp residents were counted on the basis of monthly reports on population statistics and records given by refugee and camp committees (BBC 1991, 10). They also conducted the administration process for these goods and performed quality checks on the supplies (BBC 1992 Jan–Jun, 36). The Consortium basically arranged and organised the transportation of the supplies, including the necessary permits from local Thai authorities. The programme was limited to the supply of rice, fish paste, salt, chillies, supplementary feeding, mosquito nets, blanket and some school supplies. Elephants have been used to access the settlements with these goods (BBC 1993, 37).

Due to the many name changes of the aid programme in the camps (CCA, BBC, TBBC, TBC), the terms—Consortium, leading aid agency or TBC—are used to refer to the international aid agencies involved in Burmese refugee camps. The name changes follow stronger formalisations and transformation in the programme's mission. In the beginning, the programme was informally organised and called the Consortium of Christian Agencies (CCA). The name changed to Burma Border Consortium (BBC) in 1991, when the Consortium started to work under the formal mandate of the MOI. In 2004, the name changed to Thailand Burma Border Consortium (TBBC), when it was decided that the Consortium would be registered as a charitable company in London; and stronger regulations and controls were introduced in camp administration and management. In 2013, the name changed again to The Border Consortium (TBC), when another new mission was developed, focussing more on (re)establishing a self-reliance system (TBC 2013 Jun–Dec, 14). The term Consortium also highlights the fact that various agencies are involved that also have to deal with internal conflicts and different points of view towards implementing programmes (see Inhetveen 2010, 119ff.). The following main reasons were identified as to why the aid programme had to be extended, changed and better controlled and why, instead of three people managing the programme as in 1995, by 2012 more than ninety-seven people worked for the Consortium in Thailand (TBBC 2012 Jan-Jun, 91).

(1) Bowles and other researchers ascribe these changes to the political circumstances in 1995, when the Burmese Army, supported by the DKBA attacked the camps (Bowles 1998, 12ff.). As mentioned earlier: the KNLA was weakened in 1994 because a faction of its troops broke away and formed the Democratic Karen Buddhist Army (DKBA). The group split because of the Christian leadership that dominated the KNU and the KNLA. Thompson agrees with Bowles and argues that these attacks threatened the security of the settlements, which resulted in changed guidelines and policies by the RTG/ MOI to which the leading agency needed to react (Thompson 2008, 26ff.). Thompson and Lang also argue that by the time the settlements were attacked, the flourishing informal links at the border were attacked too (see Lang 2002, 137ff.), which strongly threatened the self-reliance as well as the economic stability of the settlements. But these informal links in the border area have never been completely destroyed and continue to exist (Brees 2008).

(2) Another reason for these changes was the strong critique by human rights organisations and academics of the links between the KNU and refugee/ camp committees. South claims that aid funds were used for military purposes, indirectly supporting and maintaining the conflict in Myanmar (2011, 61ff.). Thawnghmung argues that soldiers were recruited by these organisations (2008, 23). This critique and the pressure from donors led agencies to supervise and get more involved in the camp management and governance system (see McConnachie 2012, 10ff.). (3) Moreover, the background of the transformation is visible when reviewing and analysing the Consortium's programmes and their reports from 1984 to today. These reports demonstrate that donors and the Consortium share an interest in implementing specific internationally accepted norms and values in the camps, such as gender sensitivity, democratic values, human rights, transparency, rationalisation and standardisation. Moreover, the reports show that the content of the programmes and their development does not exist in a national vacuum but is strongly tied to international discourses and norms under the 'regime of humanitarian government' (Agier 2011, 145). The term 'humanitarian order' is used by Agier to refer, on the one hand, to a set of norms used and referred to by international humanitarian aid agencies and, on the other hand, to the organisational systems of these agencies (210). This humanitarian government apparatus includes large international NGOs (203), which are also involved in Burmese refugee camps that rely on donations from the European Union, various individual European countries, North America, Australia and Japan (TBC 2013 Jan–Jun, 108). Since 1994, the Consortium has undergone several evaluations that were conducted by international aid evaluation agencies. These evaluations and their recommendations went along with changes in the programme aiming to implement international norms and values. More-

over, international standards changed the programme in working areas of aid agencies, for example, in the context of nutrition and food, camp governance and jurisdiction structures. The published reports clearly show that similar mechanisms and programmes conducted in other refugee camps in the world are observable and strongly remind us about what Turner described as a 'biopolitics of care' (Turner 2006, 46) or what Agier called the 'regime of humanitarian government' (Agier 2011, 145). However, these are only the regulations, policies and programmes the aid agencies aim to implement and do not tell us much about the way these regulations are locally realised. Moreover, aid agencies do not only perceive Burmese camp residents as recipients but also as partners in the refugee representative organisations that should realise the aid agency programmes in the camps themselves (TBBC 2010 Jul–Dec, 114). This leaves refugee representative organisation staff members and camp residents space to manoeuvre in realising aid agency regulation. This is observable also in the context of the MOI guidelines that are implemented and realised by district authorities and the local *Or Sor* that are present in the camp on a daily basis.

Example: Legal Pluralism and Local Justice

The legal system established in the camps serves as another example for the described entanglements between the different actors and pluralism of governing Burmese refugee camps (see McConnachie 2014b; Burma Lawyers' Council 2007). First, jurisdiction structures within the camp make the non-regulation of important areas visible. While the host state is legally responsible for the (legal) order of camps, in the case of Burmese refugee camps this is (or was) an area of state non-regulation. There is no interest on the part of Thai officials in getting involved in internal camp affairs, such as integrating the Thai justice system into these temporary shelter areas. Thus, the legal order and jurisdiction structures became a responsible area for refugee representative organisations or camp residents themselves.

Based on my field observations in camps located in very rural areas, most disputes and crimes are still addressed at a very local or section level. Camp committee members or other actors such as KRC, CBOs, NGOs or local state authorities get involved occasionally (see McConnachie 2014b). People mainly handle conflicts and problems internally before involving external and formal structures. People tend not to involve other parties in problems or conflicts in order to avoid the attention of other residents or the camp public. This also relates to the pre-camp structures discussed earlier. Camp residents structure themselves in ways derived also from pre-camp structures of their home regions where, for example, disputes, conflicts and crimes are solved on a local village level or, in the case of the camp life, on a section level. Section leaders explained to me that they seldom send people to the camp leader.[12] The perception by aid agencies of these legal camp orders became clear when I told an interviewee about a case of detention in a section. My observation made her upset and she told me that this is prohibited.[13] The interviewee's angry reaction shows the aid agency staff members' perception that they have the power and knowledge to deal with such cases and know what kind of punishments are allowed to be applied to cases.

But what rules are applied in case the camp leader or camp committee members get involved? The historically quasi-autonomous camp structures resulted in having and applying different rules from camp to camp.[14] But camp authorities and justice committees (which were later established based on aid agency pressure) refer to not only their individual camp rules but also to KRC rules and the KNU law (McConnachie 2014b, 71ff.). This is stated in the individual camp rules. The KNU law has been or is still used, for example, as a reference and applied in cases of 'marital disputes'.[15] Moreover, it is documented in the camp rules that very serious cases could also be referred to the KNU or the KRC. But according to camp leaders[16] and KRC staff members,[17] very few cases are actually referred to the KRC.

These structures, however, are not supported but rather strongly criticised by aid agency representatives and scientific scholars alike. As an answer to this legal system, aid agencies try to implement their concepts of 'adequate' jurisdiction structures and programmes in collaboration with refugee representatives. In 2006, the UNHCR[18] and International Rescue Commission (IRC) set up a programme to bring the judicial camp system in line with the legal standards of the Thai judicial system, to integrate more serious cases into the Thai justice system and to implement a human rights-based approach (see McConnachie 2014b, 132). The IRC programme started in 2006[19] in the Karenni camps and was extended, in 2008, to Mae La Camp and, in 2010, to Umpien and Nupo Camps. The idea of this programme is to promote the rule of law and access to justice in the camps. The programme, on the one hand, provides advice and counselling, including training in Thai[20] and international law, and on the other, offers material and practical assistance in solving incidents. Moreover, it encourages local stakeholders, defined as local police and prosecutors, juvenile justice and municipal officials and camp leaders to discuss and collaborate. The Legal Assistance Centre (LAC) wants to make sure that serious crimes are referred to the Thai justice system and encourages camp committees not to detain camp residents for breaking rules but to usher them through rehabilitation (Human Rights Watch 2012, 54). Additionally, UNHCR, RTG, the refugee committees and the IRC started to negotiate about formal camp rules and a document formalising a quasi-justice system for the refugee camps. Unsurprisingly, this process was marked by a lot of conflict between the actors but a one-hundred-page document explicating a detailed set of rules and procedures called 'Mediation and Dispute Resolution Guidelines' was finalised.[21] In this document, it is clearly stated that camp committees deal with civil cases only and formal criminal cases should be referred to the Thai justice system. Although the LAC and their programme were not relevant in the camps, where the main field research was conducted for this research, this programme shows how refugee representative organisations lose their power in dealing with disputes and problems. It also minimises the recognition and acknowledgement of camp leaders by ordinary residents. Moreover, the legal system highlights the plurality of legal systems that come into play in camp context.

It has been demonstrated that governance and jurisdiction structures in Burmese refugee camps are not centralised; rather, different organisations are involved in establishing plural existing structures. The case of Burmese refugee camps may be unique because self-governance structures are historically institutionalised and refugee representative organisations are highly relevant in establishing governance structures, which cannot simply be viewed as an extension or self-governance project of the humanitarian regime. Some institutionalised and locally accepted self-governance structures were established before aid agencies became involved. The characteristic self-governance structures are not a result of an aid agency programme or mission but a result of historical linkages in the region beyond state borders, imported pre-camp structures, a strong link to the authorities of the home region and refugee representative organisations, as well as regulations of the host state. For example, aid agencies are restricted by the host government and, as such, are forced to work through refugee representatives who implement the aid agency programmes. Thus, camp and section committees and also the KRC are strongly linked with, dependant on and forced to work with, but also in-between, home state actors, aid agencies and host state actors. That is why Burmese refugee camps cannot be solely characterised by a self-governance system: the governance structures are strongly interlinked to other organisations. The camp consolidations in the 1990s and the resettlement programme that began in 1996 demonstrate how powerful the host state and the humanitarian industry has become.

The regulations and policies that these camp actors on different levels produce and aim at implementing vary and may be contrary or ambivalent. The production of contrary and ambivalent regulations and rules are not limited to different organisations but can be produced by one 'sovereign'. Specific areas such as jurisdiction structures are under-regulated or not regulated at all and changing over time. Additionally, in many areas, there are wide gaps between regulations and rules and the local adaption and realisations of these. The strong discrepancies I have noted during field research between regulations and local realisations do not seem to be limited to Burmese refugee camps in Thailand. We can identify many similarities to other refugee camps and contexts, for example in restrictions on mobility that are not strongly enforced locally (Horst 2006; Jacobsen 2005). In other areas, given regulations are systematically unrealised or frequently change. Local, alternative solutions need to be found to these ambivalent and changing regulations as well as to non-regulated areas. People involved in establishing and maintaining camp structures not only have to interpret and deal with regulations, but also have to deal with changes, non-regulations and ambivalent regulations particular to a local level. Examples are given throughout this research.

It is crucial to notice that these governance and jurisdiction structures described here are a characteristic result of the temporary perspective taken towards camps. The temporary perspective is indeed the very basis for building up such an extraordinary, highly complex and ambiguous governing system, which allows manifold organisations working together. The temporary perspective launched the establishment of such systems and their organisations (for example, the refugee representative organisations). Over the years, these temporary governance and jurisdiction structures have become relatively stable, reliable and more long-term, with huge budgets and large staffs. These extraordinary and territorial governance structures are based on a temporary perspective but at the same time institutionalise, establish and maintain a long-term temporariness. They make up an established, interim space.

Most importantly, this chapter highlights the relevance and significance of the camps' section structures, particularly for public life in the camp and for ordinary residents. These are the jurisdictions and governance structures that camp residents encounter most regularly and where local solutions need to be found to non-regulations, changing systems, ambivalent regulations or unrealised regulations. The following chapters zoom in on public life in the camp, where social orders are introduced through which the governance and jurisdiction structures become relevant and alive for camp residents. All these structures, more based on administrative, organisation, legal or political governance levels, are part of microstructures. Social microstructures regulate public camp life and have the power to establish stability in states of plurality, exception and interim, but are also in need of these states to become powerful. The following chapters discuss examples of these powerful microstructures and their interlinkages with structures described here in the domains of local governance, economy and mobility.

NOTES

1. More than one hundred thirty-five ethnic groups (Pritchard 2016, 9) or 'national races' (Kipgen 2014, 235ff.) have been recognised by the central government.

2. For a more elaborate discussion of the rise of Buddhist nationalism, see Lall (2016, 185ff.).

3. (File copy with author of three different camp rules).

4. There are major differences in Thai policies regarding Indochinese refugees and Burmese refugees (see McConnachie 2014a, 631ff.; Lang 2002, 81ff.).

5. The protocol basically removes temporal and geographic restrictions from the convention.

6. Until 1998 the UNHRC had no mandate to assist Burmese refugee settlements but was involved in CCSDPT committees related to Vietnamese refugees.

7. In 1997–1998 the Burma subcommittee effectively became the CCSDPT because the Indochinese refugee crisis was largely solved. Since then, the main populations of displaced persons in Thailand have come from Myanmar.

8. Apart from these local authorities, there are various national agencies who are responsible for the security of the Thai-Burmese border area and also relevant in implementing these national guidelines relating to refugee camps: the Royal Thai Army and its paramilitary proxy force, the Tahan Phran rangers; Thai police and immigration police; and the paramilitary Border Patrol Police (see Lang 2002, 95ff.).

9. (Interview protocol, camp leader 3).

10. McConnachie uses the term 'para-military group' for this group (2012, 18). In KRC reports the term 'Thai camp security personnel' is used (KRC Nov 2006, 4).

11. Human Rights Watch states that they are corrupt and abuse their power (2012, 138).

12. (Interview protocol, section leader 1).

13. (Interview Protocol, TBC 2).

14. (File copy with author of different camp rules).

15. (Interview protocol, camp leader 2).

16. (Interview protocol, camp leader 1).

17. (Field notes, KRC).

18. Only in 1999 did the RTG allow the UNHCR to become a fully operational actor in the Burmese-Thai borderlands, and the UNHCR opened three offices in the area. The role of the UNHRC was and is still limited to monitoring and protection practices, but it also assisted in the relocation of the camps. Moreover, it played an important role in registering refugees. The UNHCR has been allowed to exercise a protection mandate in the camps since 1998 and during the relocations helped with registration procedures, the LAC project and the Resettlement Programme. While state officials rejected reintegration, and since repatriation was not possible because of the ongoing conflict, resettlement was the only solution. The Thai government agreed to the resettlement option and, since 2005, many camp residents have resettled to third countries, mainly the United States but also Australia, Canada, Norway and other European countries.

19. In 2004, the UNHCR began talks with refugee communities and local Thai authorities about Thai law and how it could relate to jurisdiction structures in the camp (TBBC 2004 Jan–Jun, 27).

20. A staff member from the KRC told me that in these trainings they teach forest law, for example, but not Thai labour law (field notes, KRC).

21. (File copy with author).

Chapter Three

Public Camp Orders,
Temporality and Discipline

The scratchy nasal voice coming from the loudspeakers between five to twenty times a day are a central part of communicating and establishing public camp life. The rough sound sometimes starts early in the morning, around five o'clock, and stops in the evening around seven o'clock. Occasionally it wakes people up, it annoys them but from time to time it also makes them laugh. Primarily, these regular announcements are a necessary form of communication in the camp, fulfilling different functions. Camp representatives and residents use this public system. Hence, the term *public* refers not only to the listening audience but also to the operators who make use of the system. Aid agency or Thai-authority staff members do not operate the system but are potential listeners.

This chapter shows how the loudspeaker system creates a camp public. First, it discusses the limited communication channels used in the camp. Second, the relevance and the function of the public address system and its general features are introduced. The main body of the chapter is concerned with the loudspeaker announcements themselves and answers the questions of how the loudspeaker system is used and how local camp orders are constituted through these announcements. The speeches given by operators of the loudspeaker system are analysed as performances of certain practices. They constitute social pressure, forms of discipline and authority, public knowledge and self-governance structures. Additionally, the announcements establish and maintain the long-term temporary character of organising and managing public camp life. A rough subdivision is made between two different forms of messages that also structure the chapter: public 'private' messaging and public messaging. The former is defined as an announcement related to actions that need to be undertaken immediately by ordinary residents. Addressed are residents who are unavailable and they are asked to go somewhere or to do something immediately. The urgency makes it reasonable that these private messages are made public and are audible for the wider camp public. Public messaging relates primarily to camp or section governance but also to announcements that communicate general, long-term and immediate, short-term behavioural codes in the camp.

The data basis of the findings constitutes eighty-five announcements. One part of the announcements was captured with a recorder. Additionally, a person who lived next to a loudspeaker, regularly made transcripts of the loudspeaker announcements on a piece of paper. The findings are based on analysing these announcements and, additionally, observation protocols of scenes, situations and interactions between people related to loudspeaker announcements.

THE PUBLIC EARSHOT:
COMMUNICATION TECHNOLOGY AND RELEVANCE

The public address system (PAS) is a communication technology not exclusively used in camp environments. This system is a simple technique for transmitting important information to a larger public or for guiding many people. It is used in different settings (libraries, schools, hospitals, sports fields, industrial sites, athletic stadiums and underground railways) as an alert system for emergency cases, or in the context of crowd management and mass communication. In Thailand and Myanmar, political parties and advertising agencies commonly use this system to convey information to the public in villages and towns. The loudspeaker system is also commonly used in temple environments. In Vietnam, daily broadcasts are part of everyday life as well and used to deliver community information. Especially in coastal areas, the PAS is used as an alert system. In these contexts, it is used to address a lot of people at once; individuals are seldom addressed. But in shopping malls, trains or train stations, individuals are occasionally called, for example, when a child is lost. Considering the relevance this system can have in diverse social contexts, it is surprising that no scientific studies have addressed this technique with a focus on its social character. In contrast to the use of PAS in other contexts, ordinary camp residents can use the equipment as well as camp representatives. It is not only legitimate authorities who use the system to communicate to a wider public. It is a PAS used by the public, to address the public and which creates the camp public.

The audio equipment consists of an input source, amplifier, control, equipment and loudspeakers. The first four components are usually located in public camp buildings such as a hospital office where patients are registered and the supply of medication takes place.[1] The microphone is neither located in a locked or enclosed space nor do camp or section authorities control the content of the message that is spread, and no one is responsible for deciding whether a person is eligible to use the equipment or not.[2] The microphone is publicly accessible.[3] The operator speaks into the microphone and the sound of his voice is transmitted through the connected cables to the speakers. Two to four speakers depending on the size of the section are hung on bigger trees, which allow the operator to broadcast over a designated area and, thus, to address a larger public. The catchment area of the camp's PAS, which can include up to five sections, does not correspond with the section administrative system, instead, several sections share one microphone and one section has several speakers. That is why it is not possible to address everyone in the camp at the same time, but only residents that live in certain parts of the camp. Microphone operators can communicate with each other so that different operators may communicate the same kind of message at the same time. Even though it is not often undertaken, it is possible to unplug speakers. This is an important function when information refers to only one specific section. Still, when a person makes an announcement in the catchment area, the information becomes public immediately. Exchange or discussion is limited, but as this chapter will show, immediate responses are usually expected. An announcement can be the first part of a sequence—a request, where the operator expects the addressee to respond—or the second part of a sequence—an answer to a request. Operators do not usually introduce themselves, regardless of whether the message is private or public. The speaker creates herself as an author through the way she speaks into the microphone and, of course, in the first instance as someone who can speak through the loudspeaker. The system has technical limitations because in some areas it is impossible to understand what has been said, or the speakers are broken. Apart from these limitations, everyone in the area hears (and might listen to) the same information at the same time. Operators use the microphone because they expect people in the catchment area to hear, listen and react to the message they convey. In contrast to posters, these loudspeaker messages are 'fleeting'. In case people are not present and thus not able to listen, they do not get the information unless it is repeated at a later point in time or the information is forwarded via face-to-face interaction.

It is important to notice that even though the loudspeaker is omnipresent and audible for most people, they do not necessarily listen to the announcements. When I asked about the content of recent announcements, residents could not always give me adequate answers. Potential listeners usually did not stop their conversations when announcements were made but acted as if they were ignoring them. After loudspeaker announcements had been made, people occasionally commented on them. Once, for example, a very long announcement was made around five o'clock in the morning and repeated twice. People complained about this announcement regarding the time and the length.[4] Other objections about the announcements were that loudspeaker announcements are generally too long, not understandable or disturbing as well as that the loudspeakers are broken and there is no money to repair them. Due to the frequency of the announcements, living next to a speaker can be quite annoying.[5] During announcements some operators even refer to this annoyance.[6] In general, section staff members' attention is more focussed on the announcements than on the residents.[7] These observations show how people are used to the PA and its limitations, but this does not bind its importance and relevance.

In order to understand the relevance and importance of loudspeaker announcements, as well as their characteristics, the limited forms of communication channels that are accessible for camp residents are shortly introduced. So-called mass communication channels such as posters, bulletin boards, newspapers and radios are typically one-sided communication channels for which direct and immediate responses are not expected (Pearce 2009, 624). These public communication channels have no direct and immediate response, they are response-unilateral, and are limited in the camp to posters and bulletin boards. Current newspapers are not available in the camp on a regular basis. This is surprising because people leave and enter the camp on a regular basis. Internet access is officially forbidden according to host state regulations. Still, some camps have access to telecommunication networks—mobile phones, smartphones and internet messaging—such as in Mae La Camp. Residents of these camps profit from the public Thai infrastructure. Others, especially camps located in rural and difficult-to-access areas, do not profit from these network accessibilities but have the advantage of fewer interactions and thus less control by state authorities. As noted, this is not a matter of technical capability; national guidelines by the MOI do not allow access to these technologies. All camps have a phone, which is intended to be used by the camp management to exchange information with other authorities outside the camp. Residents use this phone too, but the room where the phone is located is usually overcrowded, and private communication is impossible. Security staff, section leaders and the camp leader use a local and camp-internal form of telecommunication to communicate with one another: walkie-talkies. In the section where most of my research was conducted, this equipment was introduced only at the end of 2012, financed by tax-like contributions collected by section representatives from ordinary section residents (see page 142 for more details on this issue).

An official public postal service is not available in the camp itself. People must leave the camp and go to the post offices in Thai towns in order to use the post. Few camp residents do leave and go to the Thai towns nearby or to Karen areas in Burma and come back to the camp on a regular basis. Usually, they take packages and letters to the post office in a Thai town on behalf of other camp residents. Thus, an informal postal system has been established. Many camp residents leave the camp area to get access to phones. Around thirty to sixty minutes walking distance away, many so-called phone shops have been set up by local Thai villagers since 2008–2009, when the resettlement programme started. The owners are Thai citizens, but it is usually camp residents that work at the phone shops and take care of the day to day running of business. Camp residents use these phones to communicate with friends and relatives living outside the camp. But the phone conversations remain public in some way, since there are four to six phones per room. Usually, many people are present while a person makes a call. People living outside the camp also call these phones to leave messages for their relatives in the camp. Phone users who pick up the phone or the phone shop managers pass these messages on to the respective person in the camp or to people who may meet the particular person in the camp. When returning to the camp from the phone shops to the the following conversations regularly occur:

Dramu, your friend XY's sister in Canada called, tell her to call her back.[8]

Your husband called, call him back.[9]

I was walking along the street and a woman I've never met before said to me: Are you the German dramu? Your husband called. Your son is sick. Call him back.[10]

These examples indicate already the outstanding importance of social interactions among physically co-present people in camp environments for the purpose of forwarding messages. The forwarding of messages to and from ordinary people in the camp requires social interaction and co-presence, as phone or other telecommunication channels do not exist. It is very common camp practice to visit each other to gossip, exchange, give or receive news or information. People in the camp do this constantly. They visit friends or relatives from other sections or their immediate neighbourhood. The term 'body-to-body messaging' is used to refer to a dominant practice of forwarding messages, as the example above demonstrates. Family members from Canada call the phone shops and whoever is present takes the message to the camp and communicates it to people who may know the intended recipient. Residents pass not only letters, materials, things and packages but also messages on to friends and relatives through (unknown) people who are going to other sections and outside of the camp. Friends and strangers become deliverers of messages. Analog to the informal postal system, a body-to-body messaging system exists. But in case messages are urgent, ordinary residents might use the loudspeaker system instead of the time-consuming body-to-body messaging system. Here, information is conveyed immediately to the camp public as the following announcement will show.

PRESSURE, DISCIPLINE AND URGENCY

All in all, twenty-three (out of eighty-four announcements) of public 'private' messages were recorded, representing around one-third of all documented announcements. As noted, these announcements relate to actions to be undertaken immediately by people who are unavailable at a specific time and in a specific locality. This legitimises the private messages being made public. In addition, the lack of alternative communication channels for communicating messages over distances within the camp leads people to use the PAS to forward messages that are urgent. The system functions in lieu of body-to-body messaging. These three aspects show cause for residents to make loudspeaker announcements; the examples that follow display these aspects clearly:

> Hello! Hello! Naw Gay Paw, who lives in section 2, if you hear this, please go to the phone shop right now. Your mom wants you to come to Naw Pa Klae K'lot phone shop. So, if you hear this please go to the phone shop right now.[11]

> (*One-second pause*)

> Hello! Hello! A lady who is living in the women's organisation dormitory. If you hear this, please go to Naw Pa Klae K'lot's phone shop now because Dai Naw Mu's mum would like to talk to you. Please go there right now. Dai Mu's mum called you, go to Naw Pa Klae K'lot. She would like to talk to you. Please go there right now.[12]

This announcement consists of two different messages. Both messages start with a very clear beginning, the repetition of a form of greeting: 'Hello! Hello!' This form of greeting is not intended to elicit a greeting in response but is first and foremost used to get people's attention. The same greeting in the second part of the announcement has another function. It is used to isolate the first message from the second and again to get the attention of a wider audience. The attention of the listener is requested again in the repetition of this form of greeting.

In the first message the speaker calls a name followed by a broad locality: 'section 2'. The operator assumes that these two categories will provide
enough information for the listeners to identify the addressee. Obviously, the
name is not enough, but identification is possible through the reference to the
person's residence. This is a very common practice in loudspeaker announcements to identify addressees. Although the speaker talks to the addressee
directly—'if you hear this'—she[13] acknowledges the possibility of the person
not hearing the information by the addressee. This if-clause is evidence of the
fact that speakers are aware of the limitations of the PAS when addressing individuals and the possibility of the addressee not hearing the announcement.
After the if-clause the operator makes a request that consists of the following elements: activity ('go to'), locality ('the phone shop'), temporal adverb
('right now'), reason ('your mom wants you') and a personalised locality,
namely, a particular phone shop located outside the camp ('Naw Pa Klae
K'lot's phone shop'). Besides mentioning a locality, the speaker emphasises
the urgent nature of the activity—an immediate reaction is expected. The
speaker distances herself from the message by mentioning the principle of
this request: 'your mom'. At the end a personalised locality is given, with the
phone shop owner's name. The speaker uses again an if-clause—'if you hear
this'—and repeats the activity as well as the temporal adverb. The one who is
calling is the animator and the author, but not the principle of the message.[14]
This is also recognisable in the second part of the announcement.

In the second part of the announcement the speaker expects hearers to
identify the addressee not via name and section but through details regarding
gender and a specific locality—'a lady who is living in the women's organisation dormitory'. The speaker addresses all women living in this dormitory.
Apart from this, the following request is like the sequential order of the first
message, using an if-clause, mentioning the activity, a personalised locality
and the reason as well as initiator of the request. In this notice someone's
mom is the initiator of the request. The speaker does not mention the name
but only a membership category. Like the first message, the speaker repeats
the temporal adverbs ('now') connected to the activity to emphasise the urgent and immediate character of the request. Furthermore, the request, with
the initiator and the reason, is repeated.

These announcements are very typical of public 'private' messages: repetitions are common, but paraphrases are avoided. Operators try to avoid
sharing more information than necessary and to keep the messages short. It is
characteristic of such messages that they are requests to individuals. By using
an if-clause, the speaker accounts for the possibility that the addressee cannot
hear the message. With this, the operator underlines that she knows that this
message might not have been heard by the individual addressed. By making

the message public, a wider audience is indirectly addressed too. Neighbours or friends might have listened to the announcement and may tell the direct addressee about it. With this, operators show their knowledge of the PAS, its limitations, possibilities and how to deal with these in public 'private' messaging. Moreover, a common sequential order is observable. Speakers refer to the addressee (name, section, or UN number),[15] the activity (usually going somewhere), the locality (where the person is expected to go) and the time. Concerning the time, it is important to notice that temporal adverbs are repeated usually in order to emphasise the urgent and significant character of the request. These characteristics can also be found in the other public private messages:

> In section 3, Naw Yoa Thoe's husband, listen! Somebody wants to talk to you on the phone. So, if you hear the information go directly to the phone shop, now (*12:00 a.m.*).[16]

> Naw Tha Ka's mom, come directly to the hospital, immediately. They can't wait for you any longer (*1:00 p.m.*).

> 01076, Hsae Kla Htao, Saw Goy Noy Wah, house number 128 house number 128 and UN number 007013, 007013. If you hear this, come to the information centre right now.[17]

The repeatable usage of temporal adverbs re-emphasise that the loudspeaker announcement system is used because of the urgency of the messages and that the operators take account of this urgency by using temporal adverbs. The following message represents the reach that the loudspeaker system has. Even visitors from other camps are called:

> Listen up. If you cannot catch the exact words, just listen to the house number. 40, 40, UN number 1001468. He lives in camp X. We don't know whether he has worked here or not. Someone wants you to come back to camp X. (*Message is repeated.*)[18]

A similar announcement was made when two teachers from another camp were visiting a friend. On Monday morning they were called to come back to the school of the camp to teach their classes. When they heard the announcement, they were visibly ashamed and immediately went back to the camp they lived in.[19] This reaction demonstrates how much social pressure these announcements can place on individuals and how effective they are in making people react immediately and how the PA system functions to discipline addressees. All the announcements cited show that urgency plays a central role in use of the system. This urgency, however, is not usually explained in detail. People try to retain a level of privacy and underline the urgency by using temporal adverbs such as 'now', 'immediately', 'directly' or 'right now'.

In the following message, we see that explaining the content emphasises the urgency in itself and puts social pressure on the addressee who is asked to perform the action.

> Section 4, Mae Soy Da Pir. If you hear this from the information centre—we are calling you to bring some water and other things for your child right now. Section 4, Mae Di Say Par, if you hear the information centre calling, bring some water and other things for your child right now. Thank you![20]

In this message similar information is given to the messages introduced above: the addressee and some details to help identify the person, in this case, the home locality and the individual's name, is shared as well as the call for activity, the time and the locality. However, in contrast to the other messages the operator shares more information than necessary concerning the activity: 'bring some water and other things for your child.' This added information creates social pressure for the woman and establishes an even stronger form of discipline. Everyone who listened and heard this announcement assumed that this mother had not taken care of the most essential needs of her child, who must stay in the hospital likely because of serious sickness. With this added information, the operator places pressure on the mother to do what has been announced but also indirectly on other people, who know this woman, identifiable by name and section. This deviant message is notable because in it, private information is made public. A discreet handling of the information is disregarded in favour of creating social pressure. Involuntary listeners are also indirectly called to react to the announcement. More than the other examples, this message demonstrates the indirect inclusion of involuntary listeners.

In sum, ordinary people use the PA system if messages are urgent and if addressees are not available. All messages introduced previously are very urgent and immediate reactions are expected. As the announcements are disturbing, everyone potentially hears the announcements and with this, social pressure and discipline not only by the addressee but also a wider public is created. The fact that the addresses are individuals, means that there is a social pressure towards the operators in making these announcements quick and straight to the point. This can be shown by the documented announcements: operators are economical with words; they try to keep the messages short; they avoid giving too many details, paraphrasing or mentioning personal issues and further explanation. Moreover, the announcements make clear that operators protect privacy and are discreet in avoiding forwarding more content than necessary to the public. By using the if-clause regularly, operators show that they are aware of the limitations of the PAS. It has also been demonstrated that the system is not simply a replacement for interpersonal communication or face-to-face interaction. Users are also aware of the potential of the system. Announcements not only demand a response, create social pressure and discipline from the direct addressee but also invoke the potential responsibility of indirect listeners, thus the camp public. Indirectly, a wider public is addressed, establishing social pressure and discipline to everyone to react. Here, the power of loudspeaker announcements for creating public camp orders becomes evident.

AUTHORITY, KNOWLEDGE-POWER
AND SELF-GOVERNANCE

While the private messaging addresses individuals, the following type of message refers to activities related to local governance issues and makes local governance public knowledge. It is not private people who are addressed but people in specific positions, specific members of groups or residents of particular sections. All in all, sixty-one (of eighty-four) of this public form of message were documented, which thus represent most announcements. Thus, loudspeaker announcements functions as a means of introducing and maintaining the self-governance system, membership, time structures, power-knowledge nexus, communality and reciprocal control among camp residents. Additionally, like the private-public message pressure, discipline and urgency are founded and maintained by these announcements. The public messaging can roughly be subdivided into three types: (1) section or camp-related events such as the ration distribution, (2) section and camp governance and management and (3) behavioural camp codes. The last type of messages is different in character. They produce a sense of communality and function as the camp alarm system.

The distribution of rations takes place around the twenty-first day of every month. This fixed time-structure exists and people know and are aware of it,[21] regardless, the supply of rations is announced via loudspeaker several times a day. Each day people are called to pick up the specific items that are distributed and, similarly to the private messages, the urgency and the need for immediate action is emphasised.

Section 6A, listen. One person from each family needs to come to the store. They must be older or the oldest, or younger people must be older than eighteen. Don't let very small children come to the store. Section 6A in this morning, listen. The ration leader will give the main ration in section 6A. So, if you get this information, you should all go to the store right now and take the ration books.

Everyone from the organisations or section workers. If you all hear this from the information centre, come to the store right now.[22]

The distribution message announced at the beginning of the day gener-ates, and at the same time introduces, spatial and time orderings for section residents as well as distribution rules. First, specific camp members are ad-dressed, namely those who live in section '6A'. Second, it is emphasised that one person from one family should come and not everyone, in order to avoid crowds at the warehouses. The background of this is that usually one family, which might consist of more than seven family members, who live in one household share a ration book, in which ration obligations are documented.[23] Moreover, the calling of a person specifies the characteristics of the person who is allowed to pick up the rations—they need to be a certain age. Third, again to avoid crowds, the speaker asks people not to bring small children, which we will see in chapter 5 is not realized in practice. Fourth, the 'ration leader' is addressed as the one organising the distribution and even as the authorised person calling for the event to begin. This also underlines the rel-evancy and significance of the 'ration leader' as the person who is responsible for the distribution event. Fifth, the ration book and its significance are ad-dressed, as well as the relevance of bringing this document to the warehouses. Sixth, the announcer addresses another group of people, those who are 'sec-tion workers'. The calling of 'section workers' makes it public knowledge that they are obliged to be present and to help during the distribution event. This gives announcements another element of social control directed to sec-tion staff. The public is made aware of their obligations and able to observe during the event whether section staff fulfil their obligations or not. Other relevant membership categories for section governance and administration are regularly communicated in these distribution messages, such as 'people who work in the section', 'family members', 'everyone from section XY' and 'distribution leaders'. In announcing them regularly these structures and categories are maintained among the camp public. The following distribution message was announced during the day:

One person from each family, if you hear this, come to the warehouse right now. And people who work together in the section have to come to the warehouse as well. This is for all the people who live in section 6A. Come to the warehouse right now.[24]

This announcement refers to 'one person from each family'. By using this description, the operator cites the rule again that not everyone should come to the *store*[25] but only one member of each family. Section staff members are addressed as well: 'people who work together in the section'. By recalling section staff members, the operator underlines section staff obligations. At the end, the operator re-emphasises that this announcement is addressed to 'all the people who live in section 6A' and again communicates the expectation of an immediate response. There are various examples of this kind of announcement, with minor variations. The following message is a common example of a distribution announcement by the end of the day when the distribution event is nearly at an end:

> People from section 3, who haven't got any rice yet, please go to the camp office now. We don't have much time left. Thank you.[26]

This announcement is a reminder for ordinary people who have not picked up rations yet. The urgency is emphasised by making clear that there is not 'much time left'. These kinds of announcements functions as reminders for camp residents. On behalf of the section staff, these distribution reminders function also to minimise their own workload, considering the time-consuming and laborious nature of the distribution events. Hence, distribution announcements are made five to ten times a day. Section staff members want to make sure that rations are picked up on one day due to organisational issues. During distribution times, the *store* needs to be arranged in a different way depending on what kind of ration item is being distributed. With the announcements, they stress the relevance and importance of picking up the ration item on that specific day. In this way, section staff communicate not only urgent time structures, but also that their authority over temporality concerning the distribution event: 'we' (as section staff members organising the distribution) 'don't have much time left'. Time orders are announced again and again even though the event takes place on a regular basis. Using this loudspeaker system to announce time structures or immediate points in time on a regular basis maintains the idea that the distribution can change or be postponed at any time. People know that it is arranged on the twenty-first of each month and they also know the chronological order, but they wait until the distribution event is announced before they go to the *store*. Section residents are made to depend on these time announcements.[27]

These distribution announcements make the organisation of the distribution and the respective regulations and rules audible to everyone who is present and listening. Self-governance structures are communicated and maintained as public camp knowledge. The camp public becomes aware of the idea of being self-administrated. While section staff set up time orderings, ordinary residents are able to control the work of section staff members. Through the PAS camp representatives' obligations becomes public knowledge.

The following type of announcement refers to camp and section governance and management staff beyond the distribution event. These kinds of messages demand an immediate response. Similarly, to the distribution announcements, these announcements are used systematically and on a regular basis. This maintains the argument that established interim structures of the camp are encouraged by the loudspeaker system. The next message explicates the idea that section staff are a privileged group of people who are regularly called to attend meetings and have access to camp knowledge that ordinary residents do not have. This resonates in other announcements regarding camp management.

> Hello, hello! Pläbolu Area. Every ration leader. If some of you want to know something come down to Thara Law house. Hello! Pläbolu area. All ration leaders. If you want to know something, please come to Thara Law house. At 12:00. The meeting is at 12:00. Thank you![28]

In this case, individuals are not addressed; rather, the speaker addresses a group of people that go along with certain attributes such as gaining access to knowledge. 'Ration leaders' are members of a group that have access to specific knowledge ('something'), which people who do not belong to this privileged group do not have. Added to this, the speaker mentions the locality where the information will be offered. As in the previous examples, the locality is personalised. The message demands specific knowledge, namely that the 'leaders' know where 'Thara Law house' is located. The operator expects the direct addressee to know where the house is located. In this way, the message is designed for ration leaders only. A typical characteristic in messages referring to the section governance and management structures is that immediate (re)action is expected. It is exceptional that a time is given at the end, which other examples demonstrate:

> Section 3, all leaders who are working in section 3 have to gather at the warehouse right now. Section staff of section 3 come to the warehouse now.[29]

> Everyone in section 2. One person from each family has to go to the warehouse because the section leader is going to convene a meeting for all people, so go and attend this meeting now.

> Hello, hello! Section 3 section leader, if you hear my voice please go to the camp office immediately. Wherever you are and whatever you are doing, if you hear me go to the camp office immediately because it is important and also bring your report with you when you go.[30]

Similar to other announcements, addressees are mentioned, as are the activity, the locality and temporal adverbs. The rule of being economical with words is followed. Only essential information is shared. Paraphrases, further

explanations and emotional issues are avoided. Only in the second announcement does the operator ask for an immediate response and gives a short explanation of why everyone in section 2 should come: a section meeting is to be
conducted. Moreover, these types of messages share an imperative style. The
direct addressees are again asked to react immediately. The announcements
are not only requests that are demanding, but operators also expect a prompt
response to the request. The expectation of a rapid reaction is most strongly
emphasised in the last message than in other announcements: 'wherever you
are and whatever you are doing', and 'if you hear me go to the camp office
immediately'. In this message, the addressee holds a public post. As there is
only one 'section leader' in each section, this is very precise information for
the public and everyone knows who is addressed.

The following example differs from other less emotional announcements
because the operator communicates his anger about non-attendance at previously announced meetings for section staff members:

> Sections 2 and 4, water workers if you hear the information come down to the
> information centre right now. Why don't you come directly to the information
> centre, where have you been? Sections 2 and 4 water workers if you hear the
> information come down to the information centre right now. Other people are
> waiting for you. Sections 2 and 4. If you are those people's neighbours, please
> if they come back tell them about the call from the information centre to come
> right now.[31]

This announcement is an answer to an open request for action. The 'water
workers' have not come to the meeting in time even though it was announced.
Moreover, the operator even addresses the addressees' neighbours, and
requests that the neighbours give this information to the addressees. Even
though this announcement is a deviant case, it makes us aware of the rule—do
not be emotional while making an announcement—but also of an important
characteristic of every public announcement. Announcements have always
a direct and an indirect addressee. General announcements are directed to
the wider public, even though this is not necessarily desired by the operator. Everyone is responsible for checking at the beginning of the announcements whether they are addressed or not. The direct addressees are usually
mentioned at the beginning of an announcement. Indirect addressees (the
public) are not mentioned but are addressed by the PAS. Indirect addressees
are everyone potentially listening to the loudspeaker announcement. They
are indirectly encouraged to let the directly addressed person know about the
message because the messages are usually urgent and important. Based on the
responses to announcements, people also react though they are not the direct
addressees: they search for their friends when they are announced and may

tell people about the announcements.[32] The message introduced previously is different because the indirect addressee is explicated and asked to take action: 'if you are those people's neighbours . . . tell them about the call.' The operator even calls for body-to-body messaging.

In sum, camp governance and management-related messages make clear that operators try to exert authority not only over time but also over knowledge and information. Regularly announcing that section staff members should attend meetings or go somewhere to get information creates authority in terms of the governance, management and administrative system of the camp. Only specific groups of people, for example, those with public posts, have access to specific kinds of camp knowledge. Sensitive information and issues are not announced via loudspeaker. Although the message is addressed to section staff, who are more sensitive towards the loudspeaker announcements in general,[33] residents are also able to hear these section-organisational announcements. Through the announcements, the section staff show their relevance for the section/camp, the self-organisation of the camp and section membership categories. This makes people aware of the self-organised administrative system, but staff obligations are also made public, become public knowledge and thus put pressure on the work of section and camp representatives. Residents get an idea about how this section is organised but can also observe section staff members: Are they doing their job, for example, go to meetings when they are called? New arrivals also learn from these public announcements regarding section/camp related issues and basic organisational issues. They learn about the membership categories in the camp: 'ration leaders', 'water workers', leaders who are 'working in section 3' and 'section leaders'. With these announcements the organisation of the camp is constantly created and maintained. Using the public address system alone is not enough to maintain an authoritative style. As the system is used frequently, regularly and is part of everyday life, the urgent and immediate response of the messages needs to be emphasised. This brings us to another important aspect: the announcements are used to call residents to go somewhere and to attend the events that regularly take place. These announcements support the idea that camp members make use of the loudspeaker system because of the lack of regular attendance times or *jour fixe* meetings, for example. There are established organisational practices (long-term regarding time and localities) that are not fixed in time, or, to be more precise: there may be fixed time schedules but they are not put into practice (short-term, regarding the time). Long-term permanent time structures are not systematically put into practice and with this an established interim space is created and maintained.

PUBLIC SANCTIONING, COMMUNALITY
AND ALARM SYSTEM

The last type of public message is announcing codes of behaviour. A distinction is made between announcements (1) where general long-term codes of behaviour are communicated and (2) those known as 'alarm messaging', where short-term behaviour prohibitions are signalled. Here announcements function as a warning system.

Long-term codes of behaviour and requests address a camp public and are characterised by having a strong educational undertone. Immediate responses are not expected but a general change in behaviour is. Operators of these messages also do not follow the rule of being economical with words. These kinds of messages are much longer than announcements introduced previously. These messages create or at least aim at creating a self-responsibility and a form of communality.

> Everyone in Lopuam area, everyone please listen to the information centre. Also, for those who are raising animals. Listen. We have to deal with water carefully because we have to share the water with everyone, equally. We have seen that water is being poured outside carelessly without regard for this water. Don't let such things happen, because we want everyone to use water without any problems. (*Repeated.*)[34]

Everyone in one area of the camp is addressed, but additionally a specific group of people should listen and follow the announcement: 'those who are raising animals'. The operator asks people to follow the code of behaviour—be careful with water—the reason for which is explained: to guarantee the equal sharing of water. The operator uses the we-form repeatedly, which creates a sense of communality. This also reduces the operators' authority and establishes the idea that 'we are all on the same level', 'we are a community', whether as someone telling you how to behave, the section staff responsible for water, people who have animals, or someone just listening to this announcement. These methodical ways of creating communality are performed by section leaders in section meetings as well. Added to this, the operator refers to observations 'we' (referring to his co-workers or his co-observers) have made, namely that 'water is pouring' due to carelessness. He is not addressing or blaming individual families or making individual households responsible for this but opens a problem that concerns everyone and calls everyone to watch out for such behaviour ('don't let such things happen'). This is a call for control and a request to everyone not to accept this behaviour from others. Finally, he makes the call for a sensitive and careful way of dealing with water reasonable: 'we want everyone to use water without any problems'. Another example establishes elements of communality and self-responsibility as well, but in addition the operator calls for people to control each other more explicitly.

> Hello! Hello! This is for everyone! For everyone! There is rubbish all over the place, so don't throw the rubbish next to your house or in the street. Everyone must clean his or her own place. Cleaning keeps our community healthy. This is really true. If we don't clean up it is unhealthy for our whole community and also for our health. So, we would like to say, if you see someone throwing rubbish out carelessly, please tell him or her not to do so in the future. (*Repeated.*) Thanks.[35]

The addressee is emphasised by repetition, namely 'everyone' who might listen and hear the announcement. The operator introduces the problem immediately, namely that 'there is rubbish all over the place'. He adds different codes of behaviour and makes these codes of behaviour reasonable such as 'cleaning keeps our community healthy', referring not to individuals or families but the 'whole community'. In this way, he creates elements of self-responsibility and communality to the camp public. When everyone takes care and is sensitive to this issue, then everyone will profit from this kind of behaviour. After this positive description, he adds the negative side of not following these codes of behaviour. In case people do not take care of the rubbish, the camp public is affected and so is everyone's health. In order to create a feeling of communality, the operator also uses the we/our form (such as 'our community', 'if we don't clean up' and 'our health'). In the last sentence, he explicates further what exactly self-responsibility means. That is, not only taking care of one's own rubbish and keeping the streets clean but also social, mutual and reciprocal control. He calls on people to observe and control each other and to act if they do not behave according to the rules: 'please tell them not to do so in the future'. In this announcement, the membership categories used all refer to an idea of communality, such as 'everyone', 'we', 'our', 'our community', 'the whole community' and 'them', opening two categories: people who do not take care and people who do take care. He calls everyone to observe, control and to act. He even calls for a reaction and asks people to sanction other members of the camp public, to make sure that his stated rule or codes of behaviour are followed.

These long-term behavioural announcements make clear that section staff members are aware of the need for self-responsibility and taking care of public camp goods. Through these announcements, community, self-responsibility and reciprocal social control is asked for and established. These announcements differ from other announcements because the speaker paraphrases and gives a long account, an explanation and justifies the call. The consequences

of not behaving according to these rules are explicated. These kind announcements refer less to organisational issues but are a normative way of educating
and putting pressure on the camp public. The social pressure they use to enforce the rules refers to, and at the same time accomplishes, the idea of communality, self-responsibility and even reciprocal control. Thus, loudspeaker
announcements are also used to educate people or even to call for sanction
measures by the public.

The last announcement introduced refers to the camp public as well, where
a short-term behavioural prohibition is communicated, scheduled for the next
day. The background of this announcement is that the local district officer,
the *Palad*, had said he would be present in the camp the next day. This happens every two months or so depending on the season and the accessibility of
the camp. Thus, also these announcements are heard regularly in the camp.

> Announcement for Pway Baw Lu area! Tomorrow no vehicles are allowed to
> travel outside or in the camp area, especially motorbikes, cars, boats and others.
> (*Repeated*)[36]

Although only people in this specific area are addressed, it can be assumed
that this announcement is made in other parts of the camp as well. This is a
not an immediate but a short-term ('tomorrow') prohibition, an imperative
regarding the driving of vehicles. The operator uses the term 'no . . . are allowed', which is strong and demanding. The zone in which this prohibition
refers to is explicated, regarding travel 'outside or in the camp area'. Moreover, the term 'vehicle' is defined more precisely. Besides the repetition, no
further methods are used to re-emphasise the importance of this information.
The announcement is economical with words; the message relates to short-
term behavioural prohibitions with no further explanation to justify the prohibition. The content of this message is enough to stress its significance for
camp residents. The significance of these announcements is understandable
when looking at camp residents' responses to the announcements. People
react to this message and hide their motorbikes and cars. Additionally, although this is not explicitly addressed in these announcements, people also
close their shops on these days. People are called to behave, and do behave,
in a different way for a short period. In this context, the announcement is
extremely important because the visits of district officers are not scheduled
but are simply announced beforehand, usually only a day in advance. People
change parts of their normal behaviour on these days to enable them to make
the local legal/"illegal" system possible (see chapters 6 and 7 on economy
and mobility). These responses demonstrate the extraordinary relevance of
this announcement and how important the address system is for the function
of public camp orders. In this way, the loudspeaker is also used as a warn-

ing system. Information is spread quickly through the camp, not because of the methods used by the operator to stress authority but simply through the content. Not everyone in the catchment area might have heard this announcement, but face-to-face interaction or body-to-body messaging functions well when it comes to important and significant information such as visits of the local district officer.[37]

PUBLIC CONTROL AND TIME STRUCTURES

When looking at the announcements made in the camp environment, the PAS is not reducible to a non-direct response, mass-communication channel, as might be the case in other contexts where loudspeaker systems are used. The messages are made public and everyone is indirectly addressed; often, though not always immediate, interactive (re)actions are expected, usually resulting in social interactions among physically co-present people or at social gatherings. Most announcements are a call for immediate co-presence. The private messages made public demonstrate the lack of alternative communication channels in the camp environment. Private messages would not be made public if other forms of technical communication were available. The private messages made public demonstrate that the PAS, as a communication technique, is accessible by the public and not only used to address the public. This strongly contrasts other contexts where the microphone is in the hands of authorised personnel alone. In this way, ordinary residents are part of the public announcement system that is not used only by authorities to demonstrate their power and their authority. Using the PAS puts pressure on people, as the messages are made public. The public can hear the announcement and the activities that specific people are asked to perform. Private information is made public and, in this way, is an instrument used to discipline people through making private messages public. The pressure is not only put on the individuals who are directly addressed but also on the individuals surrounding them, because of the indirect inclusion of third-party addressees. By presenting private messages to the public, the public is disciplined as well. The public messages demonstrate that the PAS is also an instrument used to order public camp life. But the loudspeaker announcements do not discipline only ordinary camp residents, but also section and camp staff members. Time structures or meetings that are to be conducted immediately are regularly communicated. Moreover, the section, as a relevant social unit for camp residents, as well as their self-management and control structures, are produced and reproduced. The camp public learns, through these announcements, about the governance and management structures of the camp and the section and that people with representative positions have obligations to fulfil but also access to camp knowledge the public does not have. Through the PAS, social pressure is exercised on section staff members to fulfil their duties that, through the loudspeaker announcements, the camp public is aware of. Additionally, the announcements maintain the character of long-term temporariness in organising and managing camp life, because time orderings are continuously announced, but not changes of time orderings in general. The temporariness of the organisation of the section and the camp is communicated and hearable to the public. Permanent time structures might exist but are not realised, which is why section staff must continually announce the time of meetings. The loudspeaker announcements demonstrate that there are few established or realised time structures. Fixed meetings could supersede these announcements, for example a *jour fixe* for section staff meetings could be advertised on posters and bulletin boards, and only delays would need to be announced. But as the loudspeaker exists and staff can use it, these long-term structures, such as fixed meeting times, are not established and do not need to be. The immediate character and urgency are emphasised again and again. Hence, when looking at these local micro-practices of announcements we can speak of an established, organised un-structuredness with regard to time, which fits in with the concept of interim space that is performed and established through these loudspeaker announcements. Most importantly, the loudspeaker system is also used to establish codes of behaviour and aims to create a sense of communal identity. Also, the function as an alarm system is significant. It has been shown that the PAS in the camp creates a camp public as well as orders and knowledge of public camp life.

NOTES

1. It is primarily camp residents who work at the hospital as nurses.
2. (Field notes, loudspeaker).
3. (Registered announcement, WS 320379).
4. (Field notes, campus).
5. (Field notes, economy).
6. (Registered announcement, WS 320397).
7. (Field notes, section).
8. (Field notes, phone shop).
9. (Field notes, phone shop).
10. (Field notes, phone shop).
11. (Registered announcement, WS 302399, 15 January 2014).
12. (Registered announcement, WS 302399, 15 January 2014).

13. This announcement was made by the woman described in the second scene at the beginning of this chapter.

14. The idea of analysing production formats in terms of principle, author and animator is borrowed from Goffman (1981, 227ff.) and discussed in more detail in chapter 4 on section meetings.

15. UN numbers refers to numbers that are given by UNHCR to register camp residents.

16. (Reconstructed announcements, DCSF 3539).

17. (Registered announcement, WS 320485).

18. (Registered announcement, WS 320481).

19. (Field notes, Noa's house).

20. (Registered announcement, WS 320482).

21. (Field notes, distribution).

22. (Registered announcement, WS 320509).

23. The concept of 'public camp secret' is explicated in more detail in chapters 4 and 5.

24. (Registered announcement, WS 320490).

25. The warehouses or storage buildings, which residents call the *store*, is the main place where section work becomes visible to residents and where the practice of a section is carried out. This is discussed in more detail in Chapter Four (pg. 82).

26. (Registered announcement, WS 320382).

27. (Field notes, distribution).

28. (Registered announcement, WS 320448, January 2014).

29. (Registered announcement, DSCF 3540).

30. (Registered announcement, DSCF 4455, lines 179–83).

31. (Registered announcement, WS 320476).

32. (Field notes, loudspeaker).

33. (Field notes, loudspeaker).

34. (Registered announcements, DSCF 3537).

35. (Registered announcement, WS 320409).

36. (Reconstructed announcement, DSCF 3540, 1 December 2014).

37. (Field notes, Palad visit).

Chapter Four

Governance, Public Meetings and Camp Secrets

Based on a fine-tuned analysis of formal meetings between ordinary residents and refugee representatives, this chapter demonstrates the significance of the section as a local governance body. This chapter additionally shows how meetings represent a constitutive social form that are relevant for establishing social orders in refugee camps. It elaborates on the power of face-to-face meetings and the related communication acts as well as their significance for creating and maintaining public camp orders and camp stability. The participants of section meetings live in a certain camp territory—the section—which is the smallest administrative unit in the camp. Section leaders and section staff members, who are also responsible for communicating camp-related information and rules to ordinary section residents, officially represent the section. Around fifty to seventy camp residents and section authorities or section staff members attend these section meetings. Other stakeholders, such as Thai authorities or aid agency staff are not invited and do not participate in these meetings but become part of them as they are made relevant and are referred to during the events.

At the beginning, this chapter makes some considerations more theoretical in character on section meetings in camps. Afterwards, important functions of meetings for camp orders are specified based on the six ritual items section meetings consist of. The main body of this chapter is concerned with parts of a speech mainly given by a section leader where (1) the power of communicating external rules, (2) the making of common camp orders and knowledge and (3) the concept of public camp secrets is specified. The arguments made in this chapter are based on more than five hours video recording, transcripts and observation protocols made of ten section meetings in different camp sections.

THEORISING SECTION MEETINGS

Meetings are commonplace in all kinds of organisations and are defined as gatherings of more than three people who assemble to talk about organisational or group functions or purposes (Schwartzman 1989; Boden 1994). Meetings differ from casual encounters in the sense that they have an organisational purpose and are understood as communicative events that form an organisation, community or even society (Schwartzman 1989, 39). Schwartzman points out that meetings construct order as well as disorder in social systems, 'and so they must be conceptualised as occasions with both conservative (as sense makers and social and cultural validators) and transformative capacities' (40). These considerations are applicable to meetings conducted in camp environments. Section meetings represent a constitutive social form that are relevant for establishing social order in refugee camps. But section meetings are a mix of what Schwartzman more strictly and narrowly defines as meetings and what Goffman more openly describes as social occasions. Schwartzman defines that a meeting is composed of more than three people, who

> assemble for a purpose ostensibly related to the functioning of an organisation or group, for example to exchange ideas or opinions, to develop policy and procedure, to solve a problem, to make a decision, to formulate recommendations and the like. A meeting is characterised by multiparty talk that is episodic and organised in nature, and participants develop or use specific conventions for regulating this talk. (1989, 61)

While some characteristics described by Schwartzman fit section meetings in camps, others do not. Section committee members, ordinary residents and especially the section leaders, hold a speech or give an address[1] that is prepared beforehand about diverse topics, regulations, changes or rules related to camp life. Yet, multi-party talk, for example, is limited during section meetings. Camp residents participate primarily as listeners. Since 'section meeting' is a term used by participants, this expression is also used in what follows, although the definition of a meeting given by Schwartzman cannot be properly applied to section meetings. Section meetings are more open, vague and tentative. Therefore, they can be understood more as a social occasion accomplished and created by its participants, and a practical achievement on the part of participants in which we will see the social order of the camp is produced and reproduced. The social occasion, according to Goffman is defined as

> When persons come to each other's immediate presence . . . a wider social affair, undertaking, or event, bounded in regard to place and time and typically

facilitated by fixed equipment, a social occasion provides the structuring social context in which many situations and their gatherings are likely to form, dissolve, and re-form, while a pattern of conduct tends to be recognised as the appropriate and (often) official or intended. (1963, 18)

Hence, the social occasion refers to a lot of gatherings. Gatherings are defined as 'any set of two or more individuals whose members include all and only those who are at the moment in one another's immediate presence' (18), or a situation where people present themselves as willing to exchange and mutual vulnerability to social interaction (Goffman 1977, 301). In this way a gathering starts when the meeting begins.

It is the section leader who initiates a section meeting, usually based on previous meetings he has attended with camp committee members and other section leaders at the camp office.[2] If there is a section meeting in a particular section, often (though, not always) meetings have been conducted within the same week in other sections of the camp as well. Given this situation, it indicates that other 'authorities' push the organisation of section meetings and a top-down information channel where information from higher authorities is communicated to the last administrative level of the camp. This chapter elucidates how the speakers in section meetings not only pass on commands and rules from other authorities but have the power to communicate rules in specific ways and modify rules. They are even able to establish new rules that conflict with aid agencies or state authorities and, therefore, must be kept as public camp (or section) secrets. Section authorities' scope of action is wide enough, which is why they can be called not only representatives but also authorities. Moreover, the data makes clear that section leaders are not only the animators but also the principles of the talks. Additionally, section meetings also differ from one section to another. The length of section meetings varies from half an hour to three hours. In some sections it is the section leader who does most of the talking while in others all section committee members or residents speak to the audience.

The terms 'animator' and 'principle' are borrowed from Goffman (1981). He uses the term 'footing" to describe changing participants' alignments or people's roles in social gatherings (128). The participation role or status is defined as the relation between participants in a participation framework and utterances. With this concept, Goffman breaks up the notion of listener and speaker into more differentiated parts, which helps us to better understand the talks given by section leaders: participation framework and production format (227). Goffman does not simply assume that the speaker is an individual who speaks simply for (and from) him- or herself but identifies different kinds of aspects of the speaker. He breaks the role of the speaker down into three different production formats: animator (the 'sounding box' through which the utterance comes), author (who composes the words uttered by the animator) and the principle (the person or party whose viewpoints are represented). All three formats can originate from one person but differentiating them allows us to consider where the words spoken originate and whom it is that they represent. Goffman acknowledges the different participation alignments in which people are engaged in conversations and that footing can shift during conversations. He states that these categories are applicable to ordinary conversations, but other activities, such as political addresses or lectures, require other sets of categories, including actor and audience (138ff.). 'The various kinds of audiences are not, analytically speaking, a feature of speech events (to use Hymes's term), but of stage events" (140). To understand the different kinds of listeners, Goffman argues one must move from the conversational encounter to the social situation in which the encounter occurs (140). Goodwin also highlights the interactive character of these footings and the relevance of the nonverbal communication of the listener within a participation framework and argues that the talk of the speaker cannot be isolated from the simultaneous actions of the hearer (2007, 18). He highlights that listeners and speakers 'build meaning and action in concert with each other through their mutual participation in embodied sequences of talk and action in interaction' (39–40). Goffman's and Goodwin's considerations help us to understand the speeches and talks given during section meetings but also considering the meeting situation as such, which are examined in detail subsequently.

PERFORMING POWER RELATIONS AND COMMITMENT

Meetings are conducted as required but are usually performed once a month or at least every second month. Section meetings have locally established conventions that order and regulate meetings. These ritual features are arranged in a sequential time order that consist of five ritual items: public attention; seating orders and pre-gatherings; opening sequence; speeches and reactions; and closure and post-gatherings. The observations of these six ritual items appreciate the operational sequences of section meetings in camps and reflect temporal, spatial, as well as social camp orders. Additionally, these considerations indicate the significant functions of section meetings, which are applicable to camp meetings in general. Section meetings serve as events that disseminate camp information and knowledge. What precisely is disseminated goes way beyond information. If it were simply information being disseminated, the loudspeaker channel or bulletin boards could be used instead. Staff members and the section leaders offer and communicate interpretations of information and more elaborate knowledge. Interpretations of aid agency or state regulations are shared as well as insider knowledge and knowledge based on practical experience. Additionally, 'illegal' practices or practices which are formally punished can be indicated. Moreover, these events initiate discussing formats. The section meetings enable people to interact with other section residents and staff members about section and camp-related issues. These camp events enable people to respond to specific information and to discuss this with other participants. These meetings establish social control and intelligibility. In contrast to loudspeaker announcements or bulletin boards, the face-to-face encounters in section meetings accomplish a concreteness and definiteness regarding the fact that people receive what has been disseminated. In a meeting, the attention paid while listening is socially and strongly enforced. Not only can the section leader see that the persons present take cognisance of the information, but all participants of the meeting see that people are attending the meeting and listening to the speeches. Staff members and residents can check the attendance, auditability and comprehensibility of participants. The speaker, for example, looks towards the faces of the participants and may see, by interpreting their gestures, whether they understand the information he offers. Participants are able to look at each other and comment on the speech via gaze exchange as well. While there are no public disputes, (dis)agreements are made visible through nodding, gazing and other forms of nonverbal communication. The embodied presence establishes a stronger form of social control than created, for example, in loudspeaker announcements. People can refer to other people's presence in the meeting in future disputes or in criticism about communicated issues. Moreover, section meetings establish and maintain power relations. The spatial and communicative structures that constitute a meeting create and maintain power relations within a section. In section meetings, the differences between ordinary residents, section staff members and section leaders are worked out, made visible and through this are both created and maintained. Ordinary residents recognise their section leader but also section staff members and are able to observe their performances. The section leader, for example, presents himself as a leader and makes his work and membership visible, describable, observable, recognisable and accountable to section residents. Most importantly, section meetings are founding section commitment. They are the only events in camp life that force attendance on section residents by acknowledging each other as being camp and section residents. The here-and-now presence allows participants to observe, recognise and realise their shared and common characteristics, establishing a sense of connection and commitment. These meetings open opportunities for face-to-face encounters, gatherings and informal exchange, and in this way section residents establish a common public event in collaboration that serves as an additional tool for establishing a shared commitment among section residents. Sharing common characteristics, commitment and obligation is not only relevant for establishing a camp public but also for public camp secrets, as will be elaborated below. The embodied presence of residents in one event, at one time and place, is of great importance for ordering camp life.

Public Attention

As section meetings do not follow a reliable time schedule, section staff members must attract people's attention and inform residents about the start of these meetings. Thus, usually section meetings are announced via loudspeaker half an hour to one hour before the section leader's opening sequence:

> Everyone in section 3. One person from each family has to go to the store because the section leader is going to convene a meeting, so go and attend this meeting now.[3]

These announcements are the first part of a sequence where an immediate reaction is expected: a response by section residents and staff members alike. Residents are expected to be readily available; it is assumed that they do not have obligatory activities that they may currently be involved in. Attendance at the section meeting is communicated as the priority. In this loudspeaker announcement, section 3 residents are called to go to the meeting. The speaker specifies that only one family member, as a representative of the family, should attend the meeting. This contrasts with other sections, where everybody is called to attend these meetings. Additionally, the section leader is named as the initiator, and so as someone eligible to convene a meeting. A general acceptance is demonstrated of the fact that one specific person or position among section staff, namely the section leader, has the authority to schedule a meeting. In some sections, additionally, another type of communication channel is used shortly before the section leader opens the section meeting. Staff members make loud noises with bamboo or wood to get people's attention. While the loudspeaker announcements are part of public camp life, beating of drums is used as an exceptional technique to intensifies the social pressure to go and attend a meeting. In some sections staff authorities implement sanctions, such as paying a fine when residents do not attend meetings. Others do not sanction nonattendance. This again underlines the assumptions made at the beginning. Sections organise themselves in different ways. Nevertheless, section authorities expect attendance to section meetings by at least of one family or household member. In this way, residents are forced to listen to what section staff members have to say and are forced to receive information. This is a form of enforcement by section staff on residents when it comes to participating in the local self-organising section system. In case the parties concerned do not hear the announcement or the beating of the drums, are not informed by others or simply are not physically present in the section, they miss the section meeting. Notices about the time of meetings on public bulletin boards are not given. In this way meetings cannot be cancelled or postponed. The time of the meeting is not pre-determined, though the location is. The subject matter and length of the meeting remain unmentioned in the announcements. Some words to the locality of section meetings, as well as the distribution events discussed in a next chapter, are mentioned: the *store*.

The warehouses or storage buildings, which residents call the *store*, is the main place where section work becomes visible to residents and where the practice of a section is carried out. These public buildings become a central meeting and gathering point and are used by section staff members and ordinary residents alike. This public place is where the section office is located, where section staff members meet regularly and where, for example, guests who want to stay overnight must register. At least two security staff guard the buildings overnight. Among section residents, it is well known that the *store* can also be used for punishment. In case people commit an offence, one form of punishment is for their ankles to be locked in a piece of wood and for the person to be locked at the *store* for twelve to twenty-four hours.[4] However, section work and the practice of a section should not be reduced to the practices conducted at this locality. Rather the section work becomes visible to section residents as well as visitors, particularly at this public locality. But not only section staff and section members but also aid agencies are part of the creation of public section buildings. The leading aid agency introduced standards in the form of a warehouse manual, published by the United Nations' World Food Programme (Thailand-Burma Border Consortium (TBBC) 2005 Jan–Jun, 31). Still, warehouses are constructed differently in terms of architecture and arrangement. Staff members of the individual sections need to adapt these guidelines to the specific environment, and ground of the locality. The *store* usually consists of three to six bigger buildings. In front of these buildings, a large roofed terrace has been built with a big bench so that residents can sit down. While the roofed terrace is accessible to everyone, the buildings—where rations and documents concerned with the ration distribution are kept—are locked. The keys are held by the 'section leader' and the 'distribution leader'. The storage buildings are eye-catching not only because of their cement base and big roofed terraces but also due to the many posters that are pasted onto their walls. While the hand-written posters are produced by section staff members and deal with camp rules, others are colourful, professionally produced and manufactured to a high quality. The latter are produced by the international aid agency.[5]

The Seating Order and Pre-Gatherings

The call makes respective section residents set out for the *store* Section staff members usually arrive at these public places immediately after the announcement.[6] After some time, more residents arrive and search for a place to squat. Based on gender and section position, a mutual understanding of a fundamental seating order exists among participants; although the final seating order is based on exchanging glances. Residents wait in front of the buildings—outside the roofed terrace. Women and men position themselves separately from one another: men go to the right side, woman to the left side. There are only few exceptions to this gender order. In contrast, section staff members gather under the roofed terrace and position themselves independently of gender. Gender seems to be a less relevant category for the seating order among section staff members. The section leader positions himself usually at a place where everybody can see and listen to him. But in general, the seating order of section meetings also depends on the architecture of the *store*.

In one case, the pre-gathering phase was used by section staff members to set up a more formal seating order.[7] Following the request by the section leader, staff members put chairs and tables under the roofed terrace, prepared hot water and put sweets, betel nuts and leaves on one of the tables. Additionally, the leader asked section staff to put a larger table under the roofed terrace, where the leader placed some of his notes. After organising this rearrangement, the section leader invited meeting participants to position themselves under the roofed terrace. The men responded to his request. Afterwards, the leader also invited the attendees to eat and drink. Only after a third invitation by the leader did the men start serving themselves. These observations express a general politeness towards authorities but also show that these kinds of offerings were exceptional. In general, the device and attribution of the membership category of the spokesman becomes evident: it is again the section leader who is allowed to give orders in public to section staff and ordinary section residents alike. Additionally, the leader's performance makes him a host who has a domiciliary right to the storage buildings as well as the right to predetermine the seating order.

Usually, the section leader opens meetings officially only after one hour or longer after the loudspeaker announcement and the beating of the drums. Meeting participants make use of this pre-gathering time. Most importantly, the time provides small communicative event opportunities. People talk to their seat neighbours and small groups and gatherings are created. These pre-meetings are situationally accomplished among ordinary residents and section staff members alike and serve as a basis for exchanging news and gossip. Added to this, the gatherings and the number of people waiting at this public place invites people passing by to join in. Seeing other people waiting and gathering at the storage buildings encourages others to participate not only in the small gatherings and pre-meetings but also in the upcoming section meeting. Observations at the pre-gathering phase and the seating order establish differences between the section leader, section staff and section members. At the same times, these differences are re-created and re-emphasised in these meetings among the participants.

The Opening Sequence

The section leader decides when to start the meeting, usually by opening it with a greeting, a welcome or another form of short introduction. But this can take up to one and a half hours and again demonstrates the power of the section leader in setting up people's time structures. Mostly, this opening sequence is quickly mumbled without much emphasis. There is no prayer, singing or anything else before the leader starts talking, demonstrating that this is business as usual and part of the everyday working activities for those who reside in the camp. Religion plays a central role in the camp, but it has not been integrated into section meetings. The meeting is not performed as something special or extraordinary that would require a special performance.

Speeches and Reactions

The section leader heads the section meetings. The section leader does most of the talking. Only occasionally do other section staff members speak to the audience. Infrequently, the leader asks participants questions or for their opinions and views. This contrasts to other sections where residents are more involved and comment on the leader's talk. Correspondingly, section authorities as well as section residents give longer speeches that were agreed upon beforehand. Usually, during speeches, participants are quiet and listen. Attendees sitting near speakers do not usually talk during meetings. Participants who have positioned themselves further away from the speakers whisper to each other occasionally. The distance allows people to break the rule of listening and staying silent during these meetings. Nevertheless, the implicit agreement by the listeners to be silent during the talks produces and maintains respect for the speakers and the legitimacy of these meetings. Topics that are addressed during these meetings range from internal organisation issues (how to organise section work, how to organise a cultural event) to bureaucratic procedures (questions about different registrations in the camp or resettlement options), news and changes (why the hospital is being closed or a new aid agency is working in the camp), as well as general camp rules and regulations (that no alcohol is allowed or the possibility of having a driving licence for the camp created by the KRC). Also, letters are read from other camps or community-based organisations, usually requesting donations in emergency cases such as the aftermath of flooding and fires that are regular occurrences during the rainy season (June to August) and the dry season (February to May) respectively. One part of such a speech is analysed in detail later in this chapter.

Closure and Post-Gatherings

As with the opening sequence, not much attention is given to the closing. Through the closing, the section leader again performs his (higher) status in the section by exhibiting his power and duty to close the meetings. After the leader closes the meeting, some participants leave the *store* while others stay for a while in order to talk about the issues and topics that were addressed. After the meeting, the section leader is available to the attendees and he usually stands in a group of people (not only section staff members but also section residents) and discusses issues raised during the section meeting and further informal meetings are established. The end of a section meeting also provides small communication opportunities. It is accepted by the participants and the section leader that there will be certain issues that are difficult to address during the section meetings and that need alternative formats, such as these post-meetings. Controversial or heated debates or disputes are usually not part of these public section meetings but are observable in more informal gatherings.

The power of communication and section authorities as well as additional functions and characteristics of section meetings are explicated in the following part, based on the speech of section leaders.

THE POWER OF COMMUNICATION AND CAMP REGISTRATION

After the section leader has opened the meeting and provided a short introduction, he steps down next to his secretary and asks him to take over. The secretary starts his address by explaining changes:

SECRETARY. I have three points to say. The first one is that new born babies have to undergo an interview before they register with the UN. From now on new born babies won't be able to register with the UN automatically when they are born. They have to undergo an interview even though their parents have a UN registration. The interview will be conducted on the 15th. After the interview they might have to take photos for the registration.[8]

The secretary refers to a change in the registration system. In the past, children were registered with an IOM/UNHCR caseload automatically when they were born, in case the parents registered with IOM/UNHCR and informed the responsible person of the UNHCR about the birth. This registration policy changed. From now on, parents must participate in an interview with the baby and a photo of the baby is taken. The secretary communicates the change in the system of registering as if it is one of many. Otherwise, the change could have been emphasised in a more obvious way. The information is given briefly, without further explanation. He communicates the change in a very formal way that comes close to a loudspeaker announcement. Additionally, the announcement is recipient-designed. The concept *recipient-design* is borrowed from Garfinkel and refers to the fact that communicative behaviour is adapted to the addressee. The use or non-use of specific abbreviations or technical terms depends on whom you are talking to (Goodwin 1981, 149; Sacks, Schegloff and Jefferson 1974, 727; Garfinkel 1967). We encounter this practice regularly in all talks and interactions. The speaker expects the respective listeners to know how to interpret the information and the meaning of it. The secretary assumes, for example, that people know that there are parents with UN registration and parents without UN registration, and that this information refers only to people with a UN registration, which means that these families are registered in the official MOI/UNHCR caseload. The speaker assumes, moreover, that there is common knowledge regarding administrative formats of registration and what it means to be interviewed and by whom. The term 'might', which he uses at the end, makes clear to listeners that he does not have precise and clear information considering this aspect. Then he goes over to a change in another registration processes:

> The second point is, there are kids who were born between August 2008 and August 2010 and that have Thai documents, right? For that Thai document, they haven't signed with their finger-prints yet. Now they will make sure about this, so you have to bring your kids on the 13th of March 2014, 1 p.m., for the finger print as well.[9]

The second point the secretary speaks about refers to children that were able to receive Thai registration documents. This is again communicated in passing and as if everyone understands what he is talking about. The information is given as if the secretary simply must communicate information to the people. Many questions remain open, in fact, for example, why fingerprints are necessary now four to six years after Thai birth certificates were given to newborn babies and what will happen if the respective people are not available on this date. Where the fingerprints are to be taken is also not mentioned. His way of providing information to participants is like the way people make announcements via the loudspeaker and as if he does not have much knowledge about the exact procedures.

Plural Camp Registration Systems

These two messages refer to parallel camp registration systems that create different administrative categories of camp residents. To understand these a short excursus on the camp's plural registration processes follows. Different registrations constitute, for example, a division between officially registered populations, as provided by official caseload (MOI and UNHRC), and the feeding caseloads published by the international aid agencies based on registers produced by camp representatives. In Thailand, the decision to register 'displaced persons fleeing fighting' was not a legal but a political decision made by the national government in 1999. Until 1999, it was the camp leaders of individual camps who took care and produced records, including the registration of new arrivals, deaths, births, weddings and departures, not Thai authorities. These registrations were necessary for gaining access to the ration items provided by aid agencies. In 1999, the first snapshot of the camp population was taken by Thai authorities. The decision to conduct such a registration was made by the Royal Thai Government (RTG), but district authority personnel conducted the interviews and provincial authorities made the final decisions about rejecting or accepting people. This highlights the strong involvement of local authorities. After registration in 1999, the progress towards an ongoing and systematic refugee registration by state officials has been very slow and opaque. Reception centres were built in many camps where district officials conducted interviews with new arrivals and made a pre-decision that was sent to the established Provincial Admission Boards (PAB). Asylum seekers had to wait in reception centres until the PAB made the final decision regarding whether they met the admission criteria or not. The formal policy of the PAB, as well as the district officers, was that only families that were fleeing fighting, and not the effects of fighting, would be included in the caseload (TBBC 2000 Jul–Dec, 2). The decisions of the PAB took a long time and were inconsistent; it remained unclear under which criteria a person or family was to be accepted or rejected. Moreover, the interviews in reception centres were conducted only sporadically. These problems and the high rates of rejection caused tensions in the settlements. Many newly arrived people and families started to avoid presenting themselves for interviews in the overcrowded reception centres. These unsystematic registrations since 1999 created different kinds of registration categories for the camp population, because camp leaders and refugee representative organisations continued to register new arrivals and updated their own camp records continuously. This is another example of non-regulation: a local solution was found by refugee representative organisations that was tolerated and even supported by the Thai government. Meanwhile, aid agencies continued to use the camp representative records as a basis for their calculations for aid support ('feeding figures'). Additionally, UNHCR got involved and did not accept all the decisions made by the Thai authorities. UNHCR regularly appealed against the decisions of PABs (BBC 2000 Jan–Jun, 5). During the PAB meetings, UNHRC was supposed to have an observatory role, but this was not always put into practice. UNHRC and PAB/MOI did not fully agree on common registration practices. Thus, people were registered with UNHCR but not in the official MOI/UNHCR caseload. Finally, in 2002, the Thai policy changed from accepting 'persons fleeing fighting' to 'no new arrivals'. The PABs and the reception centres were no longer used and were closed. The MOI instructed aid agencies only to support residents that were registered in the official state caseloads (BBC 2002 Jan–Jun, 5) and camp leaders were put under pressure not to register new arrivals (BBC 2002 Jan–Jun, 5). In practice, however, new arrivals were not forced to return to Myanmar, aid agencies supported non-registered families, and camp leaders continued to register new arrivals as they had always done. These parallel registrations led to a division between officially registered populations as provided by MOI/ UNHCR and UNHCR caseloads and the feeding caseloads published by the international aid agencies based on camp records.

In 2004–2005, the MOI and the UNHCR began a new registration procedure in order to renew the official caseload from 1999. Only the people registered in 1999 were re-registered, plus the births of these registered people recorded by UNHCR and the people who were admitted through the PABs between 1999 and 2002. According to these MOI/UNHRC numbers, there were around one hundred and twenty thousand officially registered refugees plus around twenty-three thousand people that were registered by UNHCR (TBBC 2005 Jul–Dec, 10), who registered cases rejected by the PABs as well as unrecognised residents. Newly constituted PABs were asked to consider the new arrivals and holding centres were built in the camps to process the unregistered camp population. In these established holding centres, new arrivals and unregistered refugees were processed, as well as people who were registered with the UNHCR between 2003 and 2005. But people who approached the camps after 2005 were considered 'slip holders' and were not allowed to register. The background of the re-registration in 2004–2005 was the RTG had recently allowed third countries to offer resettlement to the populations that were included in their official caseload. People who were officially registered in the 2004–2005 re-registration, and those subsequently approved by the PABs, were allowed to take part in this programme. The registration in 2005 was the last official registration. Newborn babies of registered parents were registered and systematically added to the MOI/UNHCR database (TBC 2013 Jan–Jun, 20). Until 2015, more than 103,257 people resettled to a third country (TBC 2015 Jan–Jun, 10). In 2014, the MOI, together with the UNHCR, conducted a census (not a registration) in all camps from January to April 2015. People were asked to hold number cards and pose for photos by Thai authorities. Thai authorities issued smart cards with a serial number and with information contained on a data chip to all camp residents older than eleven years (TBC 2014 Jul–Dec, 13). According to the TBC, the verification process has been inconsistent: reports were made about re-registration, removals of ration lists and temporary school closures (TBC 2014 Jul–Dec, 12). The MOI/UNHCR 'Verified Population Census' registered 109,035 people (TBC 2015 Jan–Jun, 6). According to the TBC 'Verified Caseload', in 2015 there were 110,307 people living in the camps (TBC 2015 Jan–Jun, 6).

In his talk in the section meeting, the secretary addresses another additional registration process, which serves as another good example for how state regulations are dealt with in camp contexts: in 2008, the Thai Civil Registration Act came into operation, stating that all children born in Thailand are entitled to a birth certificate, including camp residents. Regardless of status, all children born in the camps and regardless of their parents' status, have the right to be issued a birth certificate by the RTG. Consequently, in 2009, the MOI launched a pilot pre-screening process to address unregistered camp residents. MOI-trained staff conducted these interviews. The results of these interviews were submitted to the MOI. However, the process was never finalised (TBBC 2009 Jul–Dec, 6). The process of issuing birth certificates to children of unregistered parents went very slowly and was unsystematic[10] and, finally, completely stopped in 2012 (TBC 2013 Jan–Jun, 20).

The previous considerations show that Thai regulations and policies concerning the registration of displaced persons have not been very consistent or systematic, but other forms of registration by other organisations have been established to deal with these inconsistencies. The registration and the production of different camp resident numbers exemplify what has been argued earlier. Different organisations produce different numbers due to different aims and interests. Now, it is the task of section representatives to communicate and explain these ongoing changes and complex registration processes to camp residents that they need to understand.

To return to the third point the secretary refers to, the speaker refers to the principle of the information he is announcing in order to distance himself from them.

> And then we always make a comment about this point. If you go to the forest to cut bamboo and wood . . . they again gave us a warning when we attended the meeting. But now, there are not a lot of people doing that. We hope you don't go to the forest to cut bamboo and wood again.[11]

He starts his third point by saying that the subject matter—cutting bamboo and wood in the jungle—is regularly mentioned by 'we', referring to himself and other section representatives. He makes listeners understand that the group he is referring to as 'we', namely, section authorities, have been given a warning by 'they'. For the first time in his address, he refers to an event ('the meeting') where he got information from others. His message highlights a hierarchical communication chain. The 'Nebwe' and the section leader (the two who regularly attend meetings with other camp actors) get warnings from other authorities ('they'). Who exactly the source of the warning is remains unclear—Thai commanders, aid agencies, Thai village leaders—but section authorities have to pass on the information to ordinary camp residents ('you').

In contrast, in the second part of the message, the speaker performs a break with the communication chain and shows the blurred character of Goffman's production formats. First, he uses communicative methods to distance himself ('we' as section authorities) from the principles of this warning 'they again gave us a warning', highlighting their role as a 'sounding box'. He does not perform that he represents the rules. Second, he does not use communicative methods to give a warning to his listeners. Instead, the speaker passes on the warning in a very reduced form by questioning the necessity of mentioning this rule (saying that not a lot of people are breaking this rule in reality). Lastly, he communicates the warning not as a warning but as a reminder or recommendation of action: 'we hope you don't go to the forest'. Within the communication chain, a warning is transformed into a recommendation of action.

Though the speaker claimed to have only three points to address, he goes on with a fourth point that is related to camp boat owners. This issue is not communicated as a recommendation of action but as a respective request.

> The next point is for those who have a boat. I think there are several people who have a boat in section 3. Boat owners have to attend the district meeting. Representatives are not allowed to go. Boat owners have to go on their own because when they have issues, they are going to take action. So, you have to go when they call for a meeting.[12]

In this sequence the Nebwe addresses a group of people, namely 'boat owners'.[13] He explains that boat owners must attend 'district meetings', referring
to meetings with Thai district authorities, and emphasises that the embodied
presence of the 'boat owners' themselves during those meetings is necessary. This rule is communicated more strongly than the rule on bamboo and
wood. The message is passed on as a given condition and a necessity not put
into question. The speaker communicates the issue as if he alone were the
principle, identifying himself with the rule strongly ('have to attend', 'are not
allowed', 'have to'—repeated two times). We could argue the communication chain has been successfully implemented. Conversely, this rule shows
that the communication chain is occasionally broken. Section residents in
specific positions ('boat owners') need to be present in particular meetings
with state officials on their own, and section representatives are not able to
act as *intermediaries*.

In conclusion, camps are organised based on communication chains that
occasionally break down. Moreover, different subject areas require different
communication performances. The speaker uses different communication
methods to make rules become definite or to create a distance to rules, the
'speakers' and through this also the role of the 'animator' or 'sounding box'.
The first three issues the speaker does not communicate empathically or
with a great deal of effort. This leaves the impression that it does not matter
if these recommendations or rules are followed. Particularly, communicating the 'warning' as a recommendation for action shows the power of the
'animator' communicating and the smooth transition from simply being an
'animator' to becoming a 'principle'. This argument is confirmed when looking at the section leader's speech. By reiterating, strengthening and adding
information on the registration processes mentioned by the Nebwe, the section leader emphasises the significance of registration processes rather than
the prohibition of collecting natural resources in the local area.

SECTION LEADER. I want to strengthen one point. Babies who are younger than
six months don't get rations. Still, register your new-born kids in time please.
(*Pause.*) I also want to ask you one thing. For kids who were born in 2008, 2009,
and 2010, do they need to be born in August? (*Pause.*) It is between August
2008 and August 2010. Those who have UNHCR ID have to go and register and
sign with the fingerprint. There are kids who haven't signed with their fingerprints, right? So, they have to sign. Is it for new arrival or people with UNHCR
ID? It is just for people with UNHCR ID. Do you remember the date that you
have to go? I am going to remind you again. It is on 13th of March 2014 and it
is from 1 to 4 p.m. The venue will be the UN office. (*Pause.*) If there are new
arrivals at your home, please submit their names as well. In 2014, they won't
accept the new arrivals anymore. So, please submit the name of new arrivals.[14]

In this part of the speech, the section leader addresses three different aspects of the complex registration processes. At the beginning, he states that babies should be registered because when they are older than six months, they are entitled to rations but only get them when they are registered with the aid agency ('register your newborn'). In his section point, the section leader highlights and adds additional information to the second issue his secretary addressed previously. He underscores the timeframe children need to be born in (even by using a rhetorical question) and the necessity of their parents having UN identification. These two characteristics are the condition for being able to receive, or already having, a Thai birth certificate and only these people need their fingerprints taken so that the registration is complete. He uses a rhetorical question to highlight the exact registration date and adds additional information the secretary did not mention: the opening hours and the venue. At the end, he refers to 'new arrivals' who should go and register their names as well, because, to his knowledge, after 2014 new arrivals will no longer be accepted. He does not go further into this aspect, such as the question of where new arrivals must go to register, who in this specific context they are, whether new arrivals are to be registered with the aid agency or the MOI/ UNHCR caseload.

In this part of the speech, the section leader makes the section meeting become a space for establishing clarity and transparency in the confusing camp registration systems. He neglects aspects his secretary mentioned, such as the warning, but puts a lot of effort into making listeners understand concrete registration procedures. In comparison to the secretary, the section leader gives listeners clear instructions and talks to the listeners directly. He makes use of certain methods to avoid ambiguities and misunderstandings of relevant information. These methods include asking (rhetorical) questions and giving answers to them, using very clear formulations, making repetitions of the statements, explaining the reasons for the registration, even addressing the consequences of not registering. Still, issues remain open that again show that the section leader's talk is recipient-designed. The speaker expects listeners to have common knowledge of the registration processes in the camp.

There is another communication method that both the secretary as well as the section leaders make use of during their speeches. Both speakers make use of the pronouns 'we', 'they', and 'you' in their speeches. Either 'you' or 'we' are categories that include participants in the concrete situation of the section meeting who are in attendance. In some sequences, speakers distance themselves from the listeners in the meetings—ordinary section residents— and make use of the pronoun form 'you'. In other sequences, they use the 'we' form to highlight either the common character of listeners and speakers as section residents or camp residents, or 'we' as section staff members. The vaguer personal pronoun 'they' is used to refer to other authorities that are absent from the situation. The speakers distance themselves from 'them' several times. A more precise introduction about who 'they' exactly are seems to be unnecessary. Speakers assume that listeners know that 'they' are usually state authorities or aid agencies. To give examples from the talks given by the Nebwe and the section leader introduced previously:

they will make sure about
they again gave us warning
when they have issues, they are going to take action
they won't accept the new arrivals

The usage of the pronouns by the speakers accomplishes and re-establishes both meeting and camp orders such as knowledge differences and power relations between residents and section staff members or camp representatives. Additionally, by using the pronoun 'they', the communication chain is highlighted, the fact that speakers pass on information by other authorities and that speakers act as information operator/mouthpiece for other authorities or animators. Still, what has been shown is that even though it appears as though speakers are only animators, a closer look at the way speakers pass on information to ordinary residents is necessary to understand their communication power. The speakers make use of techniques and methods that demonstrate their power of communicating camp rules and issues as more or less important, such as communicating warnings as warnings or as recommendations for action. While the secretary mentions warnings by other authorities only in a diluted form, the section leader does not go into this topic at all but strongly emphasises the registration process. This demonstrates the power speakers have to communicate rules, information and messages.

Another method of making rules common knowledge or giving heed to a rule is to communicate specific rules consistently, and again and again, in section meetings. The repetition method is systematically applied in all section meetings that have been observed. A section leader explicitly refers to this method in his opening sequence:

I think we can start now. Just to let you know, there is one new rule that we are going to discuss. For the rest of the rules, how can I put it, some of you follow them but others don't follow them. It is about old issues but they are like new ones because we have to remind you again and again. [15]

The section leader underlines in his opening sequence that there is only one new rule to be introduced. Other rules he needs to reiterate to remind section residents about those rules. Referring to 'the rest of the rules' is a way of accounting for these established rules. Organisational issues about fire prevention, the ban on alcohol,[16] or, as mentioned in the previous part, the ban on logging became common camp knowledge through the ongoing repetition in section meetings. These rules are new and differ from pre-flight rules and behaviour. The 'reminders' produce well-known rules and thus established knowledge among camp residents. In this way, a (new living) space with an established rule catalogue has been created for an undetermined and long-term period.[17] It is clear how speakers in section meetings use their power to communicate camp rules and how they make use of specific methods and techniques to underscore, neglect or underline rules given by other authorities.

MANUFACTURING A SECTION PROBLEM

The following considerations are about the performance of a section leader in the way he convinces his listeners to not follow the changing rules made up by the aid agency. The section leader explains the changing rules and regulations, the massive disadvantages for the section and his suggestion on how to deal with this problem. The different ways the speaker communicates and the extraordinary timeframe (almost forty-five minutes) he spends with this issue shows that the section leader has an interest in making listeners understand the problem. In comparison to other communication formats, the leader puts an extraordinary effort into explaining because he is reliant on the complicity of section residents. Additionally, he wants to make sure that people do not misunderstand and misinterpret his suggestion, assuming, for example, that he himself or section staff members falsify documents to enrich themselves. To stress the importance of this meeting and the issue discussed, he even changes the seating order at the *store* in the pre-gathering phase of the section meeting. At the very beginning, the section leader turns a financial section staff problem caused by the aid agency into a problem for all the section residents.

> First of all, I am going to talk about the rations. For the ration, we are going to discuss it. You won't have much idea about the situation within the section because it does not really matter to you. For us there are a lot of issues that matter. We always have small expenses.[18]

This sequence presents the listeners with the overall topic that is discussed in the following speech: the rations and the expenses section staff members have in general. Added to this, the speaker establishes a difference between listeners/residents ('you'), who do not have knowledge ('ideas') about the section, and section staff members ('us', 'we'), who have 'a lot of issues that matter'. These issues are not formulated in detail except that 'we always have small expenses'. This introduction aims to sensitise listeners to problems that section staff members and other residents must deal with.

> Time is fickle. It changes all the time. Because of the ongoing changes of time and the situation we might be confused about some issues. Previously, they kept the accounts for the rations in a different way. This year they changed the style of the ration book again. For that reason, we have some kind of problem. We have a problem. Everyone is responsible for letting each other know about the situation. We have to let each other know and we also have to understand each other.[19]

The speaker describes changes and unstable times and situations as confusing, relevant for all meeting participants ('we') and the camp public. He includes himself in the activity of being confused rather than excluding himself from it. While in the previous sequence he makes up a difference between ordinary residents (who 'won't have much idea about the situation') and section staff, in this part he equalises himself with residents, creating a common distance to the aid agency's change. Afterwards, he introduces the documenting change (accounts) that was made ('again') by 'they'. The speaker contrasts 'we' (including every section member) with 'they', referring to or assuming a common knowledge about who this is (the organisation that is responsible for delivering the rations). The changes and confusions that are communicated are connected to this vague, unspecified pronoun 'they'. The speaker distances himself from both the aid agency and from responsibility for the changes. Added to this, the speaker differentiates between causing a problem ('aid agency') and having a problem ('section residents'), highlighting the differences between the membership categories again. Due to the changes caused by 'them' the speaker establishes a (generalised) section-residents problem (including ordinary section residents as well as section staff members) by highlighting a common problem in repeating: 'we have some kind of problem' and 'we have a problem' Depending on the context, the speaker emphasises or omits differences between section staff and ordinaries. The 'we' pronoun is established by the speaker in the upcoming sentences to a greater extent when highlighting the mutual responsibility and understanding among all section residents. Until now, the speaker has not offered a lot of information to listeners but gives a longer introduction into a matter that introduces the change and aims to establish unity and solidarity among section residents (against the one who causes the changes—the aid agency): the aid agency caused the problem because they changed the system and now all section residents have to deal with it (section staff members and ordinary section residents alike). He continues by going further into the situation:

You already know about the rations. If we want to know about it, we can check
the objectives, rules and regulations of TBC on the cover of the ration book. . . .
Well, this is how they designed the new ration book. If you have this amount of
people, you will get that amount of ration. They designed everything for that.[20]

The speaker assumes that a common knowledge about rations exists among
listeners ('you'). He adds that everyone ('we'—all section residents) can
read the regulations and rules concerned with ration items because they are
stated in the 'ration book'. In this regard, he re-emphasises that these rules
are made by the aid agency. Although he does not explicitly say what changes
have been made, he refers to the relationship between section staff and the
aid agency, emphasising that 'they' are the ones that make the rules and
explicate how much ration items residents receive. After this, he distances
himself and section staff members from the changes: 'they designed the new
ration book'. Referring to the book, he emphasises the fixed, objective and
unchangeable character of the changes made by the aid agency. The number
of rations people receive is fixed by the aid agency and is in the ration book
and, hence, transparent to every section resident. The emphasis is placed on
changes that have been made by the aid agency. In a next step he finally explicates the formal change:

In sum, we won't be able to use the old system because the amount in the ration book and the account that we have to send them has to match. If they don't
match, they will say that we are wrong. After that they will say we are not allowed to use the leftovers. As I previously mentioned, we[21] are in a situation
such that we always have some expenses for distributing the rations, and you
won't be able to pay if we collect these small expenses from you. It is not appropriate to collect it from you. We also don't want to do that.[22]

In this part of the speech, the section leader explains what exactly has
been changed by the aid agency as well as the consequences for the section.
The change is that the ration book (usually in the hands of section residents)
and the ration distribution register (usually in the hands of a section staff
member) must match. Formerly, the match was not controlled by the aid
agency so that 'leftovers' (for example, when someone did not pick up rations) could be used for the financial system of the section. 'Leftovers' are,
for example, given to newly arrived people who are not entitled to the aid
agency benefits yet, for security staff members who take care of dead bodies
who are not buried yet, for cars that need to be rented for section necessities
or for the purchase of the walkie-talkie system. He explains that based on
the change section staff members are forced to collect money from section
residents to compensate these expenses. Thus, the speaker transfers the section staff problem to a general section residents' problem. Additionally, he

demonstrates his power over section residents and again re-establishes the differences between residents and staff members by having the authority to collect tax-like contributions. However, he immediately distances himself from this practice and communicates this as an unwanted practice. With this, he performs his understanding of, and solidarity with, residents and shows that he represents their interests and not those of the aid agency. The section leader creates a collective, communal section residents' problem in his speech. As noted, the speaker clearly uses the pronouns 'you', 'we' and 'they' as a method of (un)doing differences, similarities and shared communality. With the common section problem, he underscores and re-establishes camp orderings, in which section residents must stick together (staff members and residents alike) in opposition to the aid agency. He establishes the rule that section residents share the same problems (section staff members = the whole section = ordinary residents) that must be seen as common problems and dealt with in collaboration ('we have to let each other know', 'we also have to understand each other'). Solidarity and strength within the section as an opponent to others, such as aid agencies who change rules, which do not fit to local section-related circumstances. Developing the shared problem, stressing the necessity of commonality and unity of ordinary residents and section staff members and doing differences to others (such as aid agencies) is part of the responsibility and challenge of section work and establishing these character-istic section orders. The following part demonstrates how the section leader is plausibly presenting the usefulness and necessity of falsifying documents.

GOOD ORGANISATIONAL REASONS
TO FALSIFY DOCUMENTS

For the ration distribution now, different sections use different strategies. As I mentioned, different people have different perspectives on this. When I asked and talked to other people about the way they do it, they replied to me that they reduce the amount of rations for those who did not pick up rations in time. They still put the full amount of rations in the account that they have to submit. So, I told them when they come and check, this will be a problem for you when you tell them that you use it for the good of the section. Then they said, if they have a problem with that, we will just ask them to come and distribute rations them-selves. But we will also have a problem if they come and distribute the rations themselves, right? Because all people who are about eighteen years old should be present, if not they won't get any rations anymore. If they use their system it will affect everyone. Am I right?

M. Yeah.[23]

In this part of the speech the speaker emphasises first that different sections and respective section authorities or representatives have different points of view regarding handling the problem of the change. Presenting that he discussed other solution-oriented options with other section staff members of other sections in the camp makes him appear as someone who is considering carefully the options to deal with a problem. To underline this, he also elaborates the problematic consequences of these other approaches. He uses indirect speech, underlining that he is reporting an 'original' exchange with staff members of other sections that makes him and his speech appear to be faithful and honest. In his indirect speech, he presents himself as someone realising and pointing out the difficulties, namely that the aid agency will realise that the documents do not match. The speaker introduces the response of other section staff members to his objection. They argue that if the aid agency recognises this and has a problem with the discrepancy, they should 'distribute the rations themselves'. The speaker insists that this would further disadvantage the camp residents, relating to another rule laid down by the aid agency, which is not realised in the camp: 'if they use their system it will affect everyone'. This sentence highlights not only differences between aid agency rules and the local realisations of these rules by section staff members, but also two distribution rules. In so doing, the speaker highlights the power and possibility of section representatives creating separate distribution rules. This means that public camp secrets already exist and are systematically applied in camps. For example, residents know that everyone over eighteen should, according to aid agency rules, participate in the distribution event. However, according to camp representatives this rule is not feasible. To avoid crowds at the *store*, section staff members systematically call only one member of each family to pick up rations (see chapter 3 on loudspeaker announcements). These public secrets are not only observable in relation to aid agencies but also towards Thai authorities (see chapter 6 on camp economy and chapter 7 on camp mobility). The section leader performs the fact that he deals with the problem based on well-grounded, thought-out and careful deliberation. By referring to other approaches and their disadvantages, the speaker makes his considerations and his decision-making process transparent to his listeners. Additionally, he integrates listeners with rhetorical questions, using this to perform their active role in the decision-making process. He even refers to existing discrepancies between aid agency rules and the local distribution system. All these preceding explanations are used for justification for the upcoming sequence where he presents his way of dealing with the problem and the advantages for the financial system of the section, and thus all section residents as well as absent section residents. He creates a new public secret, that he also communicated to other section leaders.

And then I told them that I am not going to do it like them. I will mention about it in both: the ration books and the account that we have to submit to them. So, we can use the extra rations for the good of our section. This is how I am going to do it now. Regarding that issue, I want to say that those who are able to be present will get the same amount of rations as usual. But we will not give rations to those who are not able to be present. So, I want to ask you not to be angry with us if you are left out in the ration distribution. You might say that we left you out, so we have to mention this in the ration book. If we mention this every time in your ration book, TBC might cancel your name permanently for getting rations. They already announced that.[24]

He clearly separates his approach from other section leaders' approaches by using the pronoun 'I' several times, which he has rarely used during the speech. At the same time, he demonstrates in the first sentences his power to make decisions independently. Most importantly, this shows how the section leader performs himself as a paternalistic opponent to other section leaders and to the aid agency rules. He states that he will record the full number of rations as picked up by absent section residents so that the records and the ration book matches and the discrepancy becomes invisible in the documents. Additionally, the speaker highlights that there are no changes to be expected for residents present during the distribution event. Residents who are not present will no longer receive ration items. This is the change made up by the section leader in the section distribution system and his solution to the problem. By using the indirect speech, the speaker again tries to get people involved in his considerations. He even indicates listeners critical interpretation of his approach openly: 'You might say that we left you out, so we have to mention this in the ration book'. But immediately turns listeners' attention to the disadvantage of recording absent residents. In this case the TBC would take their name off the list for receiving rations permanently because the rule is that people must be present in order to receive rations. He even emphasises the realisation of the rule by stating that 'they already announced that'. With this line of argument, the leader creates his approach as an advantage even for absent residents and continues explaining this:

In our section, there are some people who come for the rations but who stay outside the camp. Some people stay outside the camp around three to five months. If we mark this information in the ration book, they will be in trouble when they come and check it. They might cancel your name permanently after being away from the camp two to three months. Therefore, you will be in trouble as well.[25]

He explicates that there are people in the section who 'come for the rations but who stay outside the camp'. Who stays outside the camp is known by section staff members but not known by aid agency staff members. This is another example of a public camp secret even though the aid agency might be aware of and identify it as a problem which must be contained through more bureaucracy, control and presence of the aid agency. The section leader refers again to the disadvantages of recording the discrepancy for people who stay outside the camp 'when they come and check it'. In the following parts of the speech the section leader restates that section staff members will not report absent camp members so these people are not dropped from the distribution system permanently. In return, residents accept that their ration books are marked as if they had received rations. Furthermore, he argues that as soon as these people, who are staying outside the camp, return, they will be able to receive rations as usual. With the 'leftovers', section staff members are able to cover expenses in the context of section work. In this way, section work becomes dependent on absent section members and wrongly documented ration books.

THE CREATION AND BASIS FOR PUBLIC CAMP SECRETS

Until now, the section leader explains his approach of handling the problem of the change in the ration system and the necessary background ('for the need of our section').[26] By sharing his approach and the plan to falsify documents openly in the meeting, he is creating a new public secret. During his speech, the aid agency is depicted as a threat from the outside that has the ability to make changes and intervene in the section world. However, the section leader shows that he knows how to deal with these threats for the good of the section and its residents: establishing a public secret. In this way, he performs both the power of the section leader and a powerful section system. The public secret demarcates the section system to the aid agency system. But at the same time the shared, public secret is based on a necessary communality and solidarity among section residents that the section leader strongly needs to highlight and refer to at the end of his speech.

> No matter how we operate in our own section, there will be no problem if we are united and understand each other. If we don't understand each other and do as we want, we will certainly have a problem. Therefore, we have to understand this situation. If you don't understand and if you are not satisfied with this way of doing it, we can discuss it now. I don't want any complaints after we agree on this. Complaints can hurt others. Now, how do you think? Is it the right thing to do?
>
> M. I think it is the right thing to do.[27]

In the last part of the speech the speaker introduces his listeners to a general moral order, namely that section residents must be 'united and understand each other'. He highlights the identification with the specific section system ('in our own section') and states in a more general way that an absent moral order of understanding causes problems. Only after this introduction does he express the nuance of the situation, explaining that he wants listeners 'to understand the situation', referring to the solution of the problem, sharing a public secret explicated previously. He again indicates possible critique and disagreement to his approach by the listeners and opens it up for discussion. Next, he delegitimises retrospective sanctions after an agreement has been made and asks listeners for their comments and opinions. Even though the speaker acts as if he wants to discuss the issue with the participants, involving them in the decision-making process and opening it up for critique, he seems to expect agreement. Listeners' responses are limited but people are nodding, and one listener confirms his suggestion. It is important to notice that in this way the section leader shares the responsibility of the public secret with all participants of the section meeting. Everyone agrees with his approach and he no longer carries the secret alone. Still, the option and chance of immediate response and discussion shows that meetings as a specific communication setting provide these possibilities. On the one hand, they involve people in the understanding process and allow speakers to observe whether section residents have understood the discussed issues or not. On the other hand, it is possible to discuss and argue in public, even though this is not done yet. Only at the very end of the speech does the leader get a more elaborate response from a section resident. The response is an agreement of the solution provided by the section leader. Still, the responder makes clear that he has understood the section leader's idea by repeating the public secret. In general, listeners do not tend to verbally participate in the meeting, however, that does not mean that they are passive, replaceable marionettes.

This chapter demonstrates that section meetings have the character of a social event and help to sustain the unity of the section and the camp by validating the current order and its rules. Moreover, they serve as a space for making sense of the camp and its orders for camp residents. The face-to-face presence of section members serve as a basis to disseminate camp information and knowledge. Section meetings (re)establish social control and power relations but also intelligibility among section residents. The meetings found section commitment. Moreover, the speakers at section meetings are not only 'sounding boxes' or 'animators' instructed by other authorities. They do not solely function as mouthpieces or intermediaries. Knowledge of certain rules regarding the section and the rules of the camp are created and maintained in section meetings by speakers. During the meeting analysed here, the speaker establishes the power of the section system by communicating in public that it is reasonable for section residents to falsify documents issued by other camp authorities. However, this needs a detailed and substantiated justification. The section leader requires the support of ordinary residents. In this way, the power of the section system is established and maintained and requires not only motivated section leaders and staff members but also the commitment and agreement of ordinary camp residents. With this, section staff can successfully use their power to practically create, maintain and change administrative section structures for the good and maintenance of the section and the camp. The ability to establish a public secret makes the power of the section residents visible. The public secret establishes an entity in opposition to other sections and the aid agency. Sharing a secret moreover establishes unity and solidarity. But this is also the case vice versa. Unity and a shared solidarity among section residents make it possible for the section leader to present such an approach: cheating the aid agency in public (Bochmann 2019). In these two ways, the power of the section is maintained and accomplished. Simply communicating these 'cheating practices' in a public event shows how powerful not only section leader can become, but also the solidarity of section residents. Obviously, it is not possible to communicate such a complex issue via loudspeaker announcements or to put it on bulletin boards. It needs the presence of section residents in the form of face-to-face meetings. Thus, another important function of the section meeting has been identified. The function of a section meeting is to create and maintain communality, also in reference to others, other sections (who follow other approaches) and the aid agency (who change the distribution system, to the detriment of section residents). The section as an administrative order becomes a moral and social order, and an entity with which residents identify. In this way, the section leader establishes a shared public secret and presents or communicates the moral order as a solution to a practical and financial problem with the maintenance of established section structures—section work. In establishing the public secret, the section is maintained and accomplished as an autonomous governing body within the camp system that has the power not to implement new rules but to make up its own rules.

NOTES

1. The term 'address' refers to an event where a person speaks to an audience.
2. The camp office is positioned in the middle of the camp, where camp committee and staff members conduct their work.
3. (Reconstructed announcement, DSCF 3538).

4. The section leader, the social leader and the security leader investigate cases together and make joint decisions regarding whether a person is to be punished or not, and how she or he will be punished (interview protocol, section leader 1).

5. It is noteworthy that the leading aid agency agrees to zero 'visibility', that is, not to display aid agency posters in the refugee camps, signs or stickers as requested in the guidelines by the MOI (BBC 2001 Jan-Jun, 55). However, the omnipresence of aid agencies is made clear by the presence of posters in almost every corner of the camp. This is again another example of the different regulations and the gaps in local realisations.

6. (Observation protocol, meeting 1).

7. (Observation protocol, meeting 2).

8. (Video transcript, DSCF 2526, meeting).

9. (Video transcript, DSCF 2526, meeting).

10. Based on numbers of births in 2011, in the camps there was a significant back-log. In 2011 there were around 3,900 births in the camps (according to the numbers given by the camp committees), in the beginning of 2012 only around 2,960 birth certificates had been issued by the RTG since registration began in 2008 (TBC 2011 Jan–Jul, 16).

11. (Video transcript, DSCF 2526, meeting).

12. (Video transcript, DSCF 2526, meeting).

13. This category is an important one in the camp, as these are the people that have permission to enter and to leave. Boat owners run a daily and quite reliable camp public transportation system (see chapter 7 on mobility).

14. (Video transcript, DSCF 2526, meeting).

15. (Video transcript, DSCF 3609 to 36011, meeting).

16. These two rules were mentioned in all observed meetings.

17. While punishments for breaking these rules do exist, they depend on the section committee members or other authorities and their way of enforcing particular rules.

18. (Video transcript, DSCF 3610, meeting).

19. (Video transcript, DSCF 3611, meeting).

20. (Video transcript, DSCF 3611, meeting).

21. He refers to section staff members.

22. (Video transcript, DSCF 3611, meeting).

23. (Video transcript, DSCF 3611, meeting).

24. (Video transcript, DSCF3611, meeting).

25. (Video transcript, DSCF3611, meeting).

26. (Video transcript, DSCF3611, meeting).

27. (Video transcript, DSCF3611, meeting).

Chapter Five

Public Bureaucracy, Examination and Panopticon

Like other refugee camp constellations in the world, in Burmese refugee camps in Thailand, ration items and their delivery are financed by Western donors, and international aid organisations develop rules and regulations on how rations should be distributed. Still, it is not only aid organisations that are involved in the distribution system. Multiple actors constitute the distribution chain. First of all, aid agencies must cooperate with district and provincial authorities. They also must instruct Thai organisations to organise the delivery of the rations, hire drivers to bring the ration items to the respective camps and manage the huge warehouses outside the camps. Moreover, refugee representative organisations such as the Karen Refugee Committee (KRC) and camp committees are involved and take care of documentation and records. At the end of this distribution chain, section authorities are responsible for the practical and final distribution of food items to ordinary section residents. As this end of the distribution chain is an important event of public camp life and local camp orderings; it becomes the focus of this chapter.

This chapter starts with an introduction to the distribution chain, how residents become entitled to receive rations and the relevant documents used during the process. Next, the relevance of the distribution event for public camp orders is explicated. Corresponding with the function of loudspeaker announcements and section meetings, the distribution event structures camp time and space but also creates specific camp membership categories. Next, the chronological order of distribution events is presented. The main body of this chapter explores the public order of the distribution events, showing that the final distribution of rations is not solely in the hand of the aid agency machinery but is managed and established in collaboration with different participants of the event. Camp residents control each other's collections and make clear to each other that their collections are legitimate. Section residents generate the distribution event as a form of a public bureaucracy in a strict and practical sense and perform public miniature examinations—witnessing each other, and examining the work of section staff and their documentation in the respective records provided by aid agencies. Added to this, material objects such as documents and scales are important in realising the events' characteristics. This chapter is grounded on over seven hours of video recordings of different distribution events in different camp sections. Moreover, different distribution events have been observed where different kinds of food rations have been distributed such as rice, fish paste or charcoal. Event orders vary from section to section and specific types of food items necessitate different kinds of management. People adopt their practices to the types of rations and the spatial ordering of the warehouse. Nevertheless, the overall findings are applicable to different distribution constellations and warehouse architecture.[1]

CHAIN, DOCUMENTATION AND ENTITLEMENT

As outlined earlier, the Consortium became responsible for providing food and shelter in the camps. The leading agency finances these rations through donations from international donors and gets permission to deliver the rations at the national level. The Thai Ministry of Interior allows aid agencies to support the camps under their given regulations and guidelines. In addition, the Consortium has to organise permits for delivery from local and district Thai authorities, which according to TBC staff is a very sensitive topic.[2] Practically this means that aid agency staff have to negotiate with local authorities, deal with bureaucratic barriers put in place by local authorities to access supplies and offer a care programme to the camps (Burma Border Consortium (BBC) 1996 Jan–Jun, 5). The deliveries involve complex bureaucratic procedures and require paying fees to respective local state authorities, and thus vary from district to district. When a new local district officer is appointed, aid agency staff have to reopen the debate about the overall conditions for delivering rations.[3] Since 1997, aid agencies started to recruit Thai nationals to help them deal with Thai officials (BBC 1997 Jan–Jun, 10). Moreover, a local Thai organisation, employing truck drivers, is under contract with the Consortium and delivers the ration items. This Thai organisation also manages the huge warehouses outside the camp, located near bigger Thai towns from where the delivery trucks set out. During the dry season, most supplies are delivered monthly (exceptions are salt[4] and soap[5]). During the rainy season, the camps located in more rural areas and where field research has been conducted, rations must be stockpiled up to six months prior to the rainy season, as the roads are impassable for the delivery trucks during that time. Ten-wheel trucks, which have a carriage capacity of 400–500 kg of rice, transport the different ration items. For safety reasons, the trucks travel in a fleet. When the transporters arrive at the camps, they stop at the checkpoint. Camp staff members check the overall amount being delivered and sign the documents stating the number of rations that have arrived at the camp. There are small offices at the entrance of camps where quality checks of the ration items are occasionally made. However, in general, these first checks are done in passing. The responsible staff do not weigh the vast amounts of rations or check every single rice sack or fish paste container.[6] After this pre-check at the entrance, the truck drivers bring the rations directly to the respective warehouses, from where section authorities take the rations to put them in the section warehouses. It is part of a section's work to receive the rations from the trucks and put them into the respective *store* buildings. When section staff notice that the trucks are arriving, they call all section staff over the loudspeaker. Before introducing the practical delivery of rations to camp residents some background information on the question of who is entitled to receive ration items are detailed.

As noted earlier, in the 1980s and the beginning of the 1990s, the aid agencies mainly worked through the refugee committees that sought to represent the refugee population because state regulations did not allow permanent aid agency staff in the settlements. State authorities tolerated refugee representative organisations setting up their own office facilities near Thai towns, enabling them to coordinate relief assistance from outside the camps and to organise the delivery of rations in the individual camps by representatives such as section staff members. The governance, administration and jurisdiction structures, including registration, food distribution, sanitation and camp security were solely in the hands of refugee representatives (Bowles 1998, 12). The needs of camp residents were counted based on monthly reports on population statistics and records given by refugee and camp committees (BBC 1991, 10). They also conducted the administration process for these goods, performed quality checks of the supplies and decided about the entitlement of ration items (BBC 1992 Jan–Jun, 36). The Consortium only arranged and organised the transportation of the supplies, including the necessary permits from local Thai authorities. As a result of an evaluation by the European Commission Humanitarian Office (ECHO) in 2004, the aid relief programme underwent major changes.[7] The Consortium reviewed the warehouse designs, for example. Originally, warehouses were individually built and rebuilt, and were community established and non-standardised. After the evaluation, the leading aid agency implemented standards referring to the Warehouse Manual published by the United Nations' World Food Programme (Thailand-Burma Border Consortium (TBBC) 2005 Jan–Jun, 31, 2010 Jan–Jun, 132). Warehouse management teams were formed and the weighing of rations in camps was made obligatory. Traditional measuring tins were banned to ensure accuracy and transparency. According to the report, a formal inspection by aid agency staff each month became obligatory (TBBC 2006 Jul–Dec, 86) but in practice these are conducted only occasionally.[8] This change was based on international norms but does not represent decisions made by refugee representative organisations or regulations introduced by Thai authorities. While, until 2007, the aid agency's feeding numbers were based on numbers given by the camp and refugee committees. After 2007, the Consortium started to develop its own database to determine ration needs. Finally, in 2008, they conducted their own baseline survey in 2008 based on the UNHCR database, not the MOI/UNHCR database (TBBC 2007 Jul–Dec, 32).[9] Since then, until new arrivals get rations, they have to conduct interviews with TBC staff members and photos are taken, and in this way, they become part of the feeding figures and the aid agency bureaucracy. These developments show that aid agency mechanisms came to be involved in the administration of ration goods that beforehand were in the hands of refugee representatives. Still, after a family or a person arrives at the camp and wishes to stay and to receive rations items, they first have to speak to and register with the respective section leader. It is the responsibility of the section leaders to find a house for the respective person. Usually, they know where empty houses are, or know people who have resettled or left the camp for other reasons and are selling a house. A real estate market has been established, especially since the resettlement programme started. After the talk and registration with the section leader, new arrivals must wait until the next round of interviews for new arrivals is conducted at the camp office. Camp staff members conduct interviews every two to three months. When new arrivals pass these interviews, as most interviewees do, camp committee members present the information to TBC staff who follow the earlier mentioned procedure.[10] The registration with the aid agency can take up to six months. Section staff members, however, usually give new arrivals basic food immediately after they arrive, depending on their financial condition.[11] This is one example given by the section leader why tax-like contributions collected from section staff members are necessary. These and the following observations make the plural involvement, but also entanglement, between the different camp actors very clear: according to the camp leader, it is the aid agency that decides who is entitled to receive rations or not.[12] According to TBC staff, ration distribution is mainly in the hands of camp committee members who decide whether people can become part of the aid system or not.[13] But the analysis of section meetings shows that section leaders, section staff members and the camp public, are also part of this decision-making process (see also chapter 4). At the same time, aid agency staff argue that distribution policies, such as that only people who personally show up receive supplies, 'is conducted in a very strict manner. We control this regularly.' [14] These ostensibly contrasting statements by aid agency staff occur also in their reports that, on the one hand, claim that refugee representative organisations oversee reception, storage and distribution of food and non-food items, and on the other, report that they check two warehouses per camp each month in order to see whether they meet the guidelines based on the World Food Programme (TBBC 2012 Jan–Jun, 135). Aid agency staff ostensibly check ten parameters of the ration delivery, including:

> ration calculation, measurement and delivery; usage of ration books; and the presence of ration posters, monitoring feedback information and comments post-boxes. It looks not only at the ration received, but also at possible causes of why a ration may not be received as planned. This includes identifying any systematic errors in weighing (e.g. defect scales), calculation mistakes, non-use of ration books, recipients being uninformed of the correct ration, and recipients having no means to voice distribution problems or injustices. (TBBC 2009 Jun–Jul, 57)

These control mechanisms remind us of the Foucauldian idea that every possible action can be controlled and monitored. However, the practical realisations of these mechanisms are very different. No systematic and detailed control on the part of aid agencies was observable. Checks are conducted only occasionally for very short periods during the final distribution in a section. In cases where aid agency staff members are present, usually for around twenty to thirty minutes, they conduct interviews with respective section committee members and have a closer look at the relevant documents. But during the rainy season (from July to October), some camps are not accessible to aid agency staff at all. Even though checks are irregular, a standardised warehouse management and bureaucratic system has been established by the aid agencies that should not be underestimated. According to the aid agency reports, this system was developed with camp representatives (TBBC 2012 Jan–Jun, 135).

One part of this management system, which is visible and comes to be justified during the distribution event, is the general 'ration distribution register', in the hands of section staff members, and the 'ration books' that every family holds.[15] These two documents are relevant objects that do not only keep the distribution procedure going but are an important part of the process of making the distribution procedure accountable, rational, reliable and bureaucratic. Both documents are provided by the aid agency and are also given back to the aid agency at the end of the year.

The 'ration distribution register', also called the 'record' by section staff members, is a list of all section families or households that hold a ration book, where every month the distributed rations are documented. This record is only used by section staff. During the distribution event this document is usually in the hands of the 'monitor', the distribution leader or the section leader. At other times, it resides in the *store* office or the home of the 'monitor'. The ration distribution register is given to the camp committee at the end of the month, bringing the distribution registers of all sections into one document. These numbers are then given to the KRC district office, who hands these documents over to the aid agency, which controls the numbers and publishes the numbers in their reports. As explicated in the following, during the distribution event the 'ration book' is much more relevant than this 'record'. In contrast to the ration distribution register, which is in the hands of section, camp and KRC staff, the ration books are mainly in the hands of section members. The ration book is a document that belongs to an individual household. Ration books are distributed by the 'distribution leader' and her assistant (who receive the books from the aid agency staff members) to residents at the beginning of every year. At the end of each year the ration books are given back to the aid agency. During the distribution events are ration books put in the hands of section staff members. The ration book entitles camp residents to collect rations for themselves and their household members (or more precisely: the people who are supposed to be household members, according to the ration book). The document legitimates residents as rice collectors. People's entitlements are noted and residents can refer to them. This gives people a sense of reliability but at the same time excludes those who are not registered with the aid agencies and do not have these documents. The amounts residents are entitled to receive are visible and accessible for individual families, and during the distribution event, are visible to the respective section staff members and, as we shall see, also to other section residents. Currently, the ration book is in English, Burmese and Karen. This was not always the case. By the time responsibility for the distribution had been placed in the hands of the camp and section leaders, in 1993, the register was solely in Sgaw Karen language.[16]

TIME, SPACE AND MEMBERSHIP

Before we go into the details of the distribution event itself, its general relevance for ordering public camp life will be detailed. Moreover, the sequential time orders of the event are introduced. As with the loudspeaker system and the section meetings, ration distribution events accomplish time orderings, make different camp memberships visible and create spatial orderings. The distributions structure the time of camp residents and induce them to do certain activities in regular, temporal patterns. Each family who shares a ration book must organise themselves such that one family member is present and able to pick up the ration goods at a specific moment. Although it is known among camp residents that the distributions start on the twenty first of each month, as explicated in chapter 3, distribution times are announced several times a day, on the day of the supply, via loudspeaker by section committee staff. The announcements reinforce the strict time management that the distribution event produces. The distribution of all items lasts three to four days. First rice is distributed, which takes one to two days. The next day 'Asia remix,[17] beans and oil, are given out. After that, fish paste and charcoal are distributed. Occasionally, the distribution days of specific foods vary, for example, when certain products arrive late. Soap is distributed by another agency every two months. Twice a year people also get salt. Other items that residents receive are not registered in the ration books. Once a year, usually in November or December, each person gets one piece of winter clothing and a blanket. Before the rainy season starts, everyone can collect a mosquito net. Newborn and breast-feeding babies and pregnant women get additional support. Water is usually available from taps in most households. These ration items are distributed to everyone without control mechanisms that evaluate whether a person is really in need of these goods or not. An exception is the distribution of bamboo and materials to repair or rebuild the bamboo huts. Housing material is distributed only once a year, usually after the rainy season. Whether a family receives bamboo and leaves for the roof depends on the condition of the individual hut and is based on a decision made by shelter staff members of the section and section leaders. Aid agency staff are not involved in these decisions. There are also households who count as 'self-reliant', these households are not entitled to receive ration items at all. Thus, the distribution system creates and maintains different section memberships categories, such as shelter staff or distribution leaders, and makes them visible in public. The delivery of ration items addresses most of the people in the camp. Almost everyone who arrives at the camp, who registers with the camp administration and is accepted by the TBC is entitled to receive these benefits.

But there are also camp members who are excluded from these benefits, such as residents who are self-reliant, who are not registered with aid agencies, visitors and *Or Sor* members. There is no one central place in the camp where the supply is distributed; rather, the distribution is organised according to the spatial partitioning of the camp; the camp is divided into sections. As noted, each section has a building where the rations are delivered, stored, and distributed: the warehouse, or, as it is called by camp inhabitants, the *store*. The *store* is a central public building for each section, where the rations are stored (see also chapter 4). In this way, the distributions establish stable, constant and public buildings in the camp where, for example, the section meetings are conducted. Additionally, the events for supplies forces most residents to be present. Indeed, there are sanctions for people that do not pick up rations. Section leaders may give warnings in oral and written form to people who do not pick up rations or threaten residents to record non-attendance with the aid agency. The aid agency rule is that residents over eighteen that are not present during the distribution event are not eligible to receive rations. According to this rule, after two months of not attending the distribution event, residents lose their entitlement to receive rations. However, section leaders do not usually report non-attendance because several practical reasons do not allow them to abide by this aid agency rule (another example of a public camp secret). First, section staff members prefer only one or two family members present at the warehouse to pick up the rations to avoid crowds during the distribution event. Second, not all family members are present and available on these dates. People are involved in other important kinds of activities (see the various working activities in which people are involved explicated in chapter 6). Picking up rations or becoming part of the distribution event is time consuming and laborious.

Distribution events are like section meetings in terms of having performance features arranged in a chronological and strict form of organisation. The following sequential ordering is grounded in observed data and consists of five characteristic elements. In contrast to the section meeting, the order here is based on the path of rice collectors. First, the loudspeaker announcements attract public attention to residents and people entitled to ration items. Afterwards, rice collectors go to the *store* and become part of the public order of the event. Third, rice collectors wait until their names are called. Only then do they enter a zone of discipline and examination where they receive rations, an area where their behaviour is keenly observed and certain behaviours are expected. Fourth, they leave the place as a joint accomplishment. The last element should not be neglected. Especially during the rice distribution, residents often need help from others in order to carry the heavy rice rations to their homes. The rice rations can be very heavy—a person who picks up rations for a family consisting of five adults over eighteen years old must pick up 60 kg of rice and transport it home. People often must climb up hills to reach their homes.[18] However, the following video sequences focus on the distribution of rice rations and the practices observable at the second, third and fourth element: becoming part of the distribution order, waiting and the zone of panopticon.

BECOMING PART OF DISTRIBUTION ORDERS

The loudspeaker announcements show that collectors do not have a fixed appointment. There is a general understanding that specific households are supposed to come in the morning and others in the afternoon, people do not always follow this rule. When people arrive at the *store* they see a lot of people gathering together. In fact, the ostensibly chaotic goings-on over-whelm anyone attending the event for the first time. That is why a structural problem with the event, in general, is, on the one hand, establishing and making visible a fair treatment of the rice collectors and, on the other hand, organising this event in a sequential order.

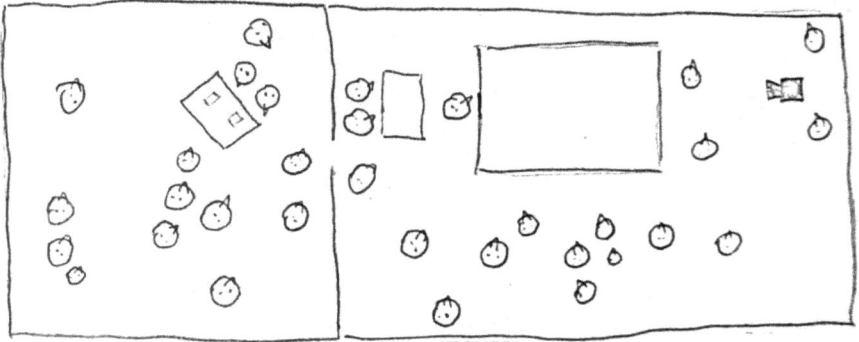

Layout of the *Store*

The minimalistic drawing shown in figure 5.1 gives an overview of the spatial layout of the *store* building and place where the following scenes take place. As can be seen, there are two stations, occupied by section staff—here called 'admins', where rice collectors hand over their ration books. The practices of people conducted in the entrance area where station one is positioned is focussed upon the following.

A woman with a purple headscarf (*1*) is standing in front of the admin table, obviously waiting. In her hand is a robe and the green ration book. Next to her is a man with a green shirt (*2*), holding a rice sack. A man with a purple longi (*3*) enters the entrance area and walks to the admin table, standing next to the waiting woman (*1*). The man with the green shirt (*2*) starts walking around, also walking behind the admin table. All three people are standing near the admin table and try to hand over their books to the admin. The admin documents in other rice collectors' ration books. Another man with a pink headscarf (*4*) walks to the admin table and stands there as well. Finally, the woman with the purple headscarf (*1*) and the man who just arrived (*4*) start talking. She makes gestures with the ration book. Another woman with a pink blouse (*5*) arrives, goes to the admin table directly, and wants to put her ration book, without looking at the other people who are standing there, on the admin table. The admin hinders her from doing so (*verbal interaction that we cannot hear in the video*). She is probably sanctioned by the admin because she is not following the rules. The admin avoids an accumulation of ration books on the desk. The woman im-mediately takes the book back and stands in front of the table like the woman with the purple headscarf (*1*) who arrived before her (*5*). She makes clear to the admin and the other people that she wants to become part of the distribution ordering. The admin probably tells her to wait and to hold on. The woman does not look at the other women, nor does she ask or talk to the other people around her. The woman with the purple headscarf (*1*) still has her ration book in her hands and is waiting. Another woman with a white scarf (*6*) enters the scene and walks straight to the admin table as well, but first looks at what is going around her. She starts talking to the woman with the purple headscarf (*1*). Finally, the woman with the purple headscarf (*1*) (*who arrived at the admin table first*) hands over her ration book to the admin because he looked at her. Besides this woman there are (*at least*) six people observe what the admin calculates and writes down.

When the admin has finished writing in the ration book, the woman (*1*) leaves her 'waiting space', straight after getting her book back. She goes to the door, takes off her shoes, and enters a building next to the admin's table (*03:26*). The woman (*1*) has been waiting more than three and a half hours for this documentation act by the admin. After the woman (*1*) has left, the woman with the pink blouse (*5*), who was sanctioned by the admin, looks around to find out whether it is her turn or not. She is looking at the other people who are standing at the table, nods her head and tries for a second time to give the ration book to the admin. The admin is looking at her and the book, showing her that he accepts her action. Even though the others have been standing near the table longer than her (*5*), it is accepted that it is her turn. The woman with the white scarf (*6*) leaves the scene. The man with the purple longi (*3*) who until now has been standing near the admin table, starts to walk around. An-other woman wearing a white t-shirt (*7*) arrives at the admin table. She starts talking to the woman with the pink blouse (*5*). The admin puts the ration book on the desk, so that the woman with the pink blouse (*5*) can take it back. This occurs without them looking at each other, so the expected action is apparently clear. The admin has finished the registration. She immediately takes her ration book and like the other woman directs her body to the entrance of the build-ing, takes off her shoes, and enters the warehouse building, where the second station is located. The woman with the white T-shirt (*7*) puts her book on the admin's table, a glance from the admin lets the woman know that it is her turn.

Obviously, it is not the other people's turn yet (*2, 3, 4*), because they do not show any attempt to give their documents to the admin yet.[19]

There are three women in the scene, who arrive at the place and go directly to the admin's table and signal with their activities that they want to become part of the sequential, bureaucratic order. Their movements are geared towards the order of the sequential distribution procedure. The scenes clarify that the procedure is organised according to the rule of 'first come, first served' and additionally, 'one at a time'. The latter rule gives the whole procedure a sequential organisation. Order of arrival seems to be the normative basis for this form of waiting, which renders an unscheduled service. It is not organised like a classical queue, such that one party or individual occupies a place in the queue and with that makes clear whose turn it is. A queue is not observable. People do not make it explicitly visible whose turn it is, rather attendees' position in the invisible line must be locally negotiated. Additionally, there are also people present who do not show an interest in becoming part of the formal procedure immediately. In an ordinary queuing situation this would cause irritation, frustration and sanctions, or at least provoke questions. Here we observe that the right moment for putting the ration book on the admin's table must be negotiated via gesture, gaze, or verbal communication. There is an invisible order and those rice collectors who arrive need to discover this order for themselves. The woman who arrived and put her book on the table is sanctioned through rejection. Most people who arrive first try to find out about the ordering and see whose turn it is mostly through verbal or non-verbal communication. By handing over her ration book to the admin, the admin recognises that the rice collector is present and available to pick up rations, and documents this in the ration book. Admins are recognisable by their positioning (usually in front of a table), the objects (ration books, pen) they have in their hands or that are positioned on the table and their practice of writing numbers in the ration book. The admin at station one counts and registers the amount of rice the collector is entitled to receive. The admin oversees the ration distribution register, which contains a list of the people who are officially registered as entitled to benefits. The person checks whether the numbers registered in the ration book (handed over by the rice collectors) match the distribution ration register of the section and tick off each family in this document in order to avoid abuses. Participants may copy ration books, and in this way are prevented from coming twice or more. Besides this, the admin calculates the exact rations the rice collector is entitled to and writes the full amount in the ration book. The ration book documents only detail the entitlements of the individuals of the household or individual family members, but section staff need to calculate the whole amount that the household is entitled to receive. When the admin is done with the registration and calculation, he puts the ration book back on the table. Rice collectors then take their ration books to the second station. In this way, some rice collectors become part of the bureaucratic distribution procedure immediately.

As noted earlier, other participants become part of the distribution order but not the bureaucratic procedure. They are present at the *store* but do not attempt to hand their ration books over to the admins immediately. In the described scenes, four people described do not hand over their ration books to the admin or give the admin any sign that they intend to do so. They prefer to walk around the entrance hall, observe the procedure, examine what the admin is documenting or interact with other participants. All of them carry a rice sack and the green ration book. They are prepared to become part of the bureaucratic procedure but look as if they aim to become part only at a later stage; they do not seem to have time concerns. How do they become part of the distribution order? Their acts show the first step of making the distribution event and the bureaucratic acts public. Participants can and do observe what the admins are documenting, how much individual households get, if ration books match with the record and if admins are calculating correctly. The creation of this public bureaucracy is also possible through the spatial arrangement, where participants are able and allowed to position their bodies behind the admin to see what he calculates and documents. These examining and observing practices are socially accepted.

QUEUING DOCUMENTS AND WAITING

Rice collectors who immediately become part of the bureaucratic procedure also have the time to produce the event as a public bureaucracy.

> After handing the ration book to admin 2, the woman with the pink blouse (5) leaves the building again, puts on her shoes, leaves the entrance area and goes outside. She has some time to kill; she needs to wait until her name is called, enabling her to enter the rice zone.[20]

After station one, rice collectors must, and usually do, immediately hand over the ration book to station two. Participants give the ration book to the second admin so that lines of individual bodies are not required; the books queue on behalf of the people. The queuing does not require immediate bodily presence because the books form a queue on the table at station two, representing present rice collectors. Participants may have a vague knowledge of how long they will have to wait for their names to be called, for example, by estimating the time through looking at how many ration books are on the table at station two. The commitment to being present and within earshot is the basis of this queuing system. This system allows the respective rice collector to fulfil other obligations or become engaged in other activities, such as observing bureaucratic acts conducted during the event, for example, in the entrance hall or inside the building where people enter the rice zone. This is the point where people who become part of the bureaucratic procedure immediately observe the event, and thus potentially make bureaucratic acts public. Some people may also get involved in other primary activities such as drinking tea or eating something near to the storage buildings. Nearby a small café is located, and people sell fast food such as rice noodles and other snacks only available during the distribution events. There is time to exchange news and information, to gossip, and to simply talk to participants. In this way, the distributions become also social camp events. However, the announcement of participants' names reminds ration collectors of their main activity, namely picking up their ration items. As follows, the bureaucratic procedure is determined through the books and the calling of names. The calling of the names forces people to react immediately. Rice collectors stop their secondary activities right away to go into the building where station two is positioned.[21]

THE ZONE OF PANOPTICISM

People with different participation status are present at and near the rice zone: admins, the scale inspector, rice collectors, staff helpers and observing participants. Only those who have been called can enter the secure, controlled and less crowded area.

The admins are positioned behind the scale inspector and update the ration books. They call the rice collector's name and the amount of rice she is to receive. She enters the rice zone and starts to take rice with her hand and places it in one sack. Thus, in this scene three male helpers and a female rice collector are in the rice zone. The helpers assist the woman and fill another sack with rice. The first sack is on the scale. Helper 1 puts some rice, using a small metal box, into the sack. A second later he takes the rice out of the rice sack because the scale shows that the sack weighs more than it should. The scale inspector makes a move with his hands. Similar to helper 1, helper 2 positions his body in a way so that he is able to perfectly see the display on the scale. The female rice collector watches the scale display while filling another sack with rice. The scale inspector also keeps a very concentrated eye on the needle of the scale. Then without speaking and in the same moment, many things happen simultaneously. Helper 1 takes the last addition of rice out of the sack. When this ephemeral moment has passed, after the scale has shown the exact and correct amount of rice, the rice collector turns her eyes back to her action of filling the rice sack. Helper 2 also turns his eyes and his body away from the scale and goes back to a sitting position. Altogether, five people look at the scale, stop at almost the same moment and go on with other activities. In the meantime, two women (*outside of the rice zone*) position their bodies in such a way that they can see the scale and observe the scene as well, even though their gazes are not focussed on the needle of the scale. The scale inspector repositions the scale and helper 2 helps him without being asked. The female rice collector puts the next sack in position and waits for helper 1, who then puts the rice sack on the scale. Helper 1 again needs to fill the sack with some more rice and the woman moves next to the scale in order to prop the sack open. The scale inspectors' gaze is again focussed on the needle of the scale. A man enters the warehouse, and one more woman positions herself in the doorway. She keeps an eye on the scale, together with the woman next to her. The woman sitting left of the scale, a little way off, also focusses her eyes on the scale. More people enter the warehouse. Again, there is too much in the rice sack so the scale inspector himself stands up and takes some rice out of the sack with his own hands. During this time, seven people look at the needle of the scale. The inspector squats in order to the see the scale display properly. For a second time many people glance briefly at the display while in the next moment all of them seem to be involved in other actions (the helpers start chatting, the woman near the entrance goes somewhere else, the scale inspector looks somewhere else). After the fleeting moment, when the amount in the rice sack is correct has passed, the rice sack is put aside. The whole procedure is undertaken with barely any verbal interaction. During the procedure, another helper, who is sitting next to the scale inspector, laughs[22] and the scale inspector says once: "put more in."[23]

Two admins sitting behind the scale inspector are calling people, allowing them to enter the rice zone. The admins also call out the amount the rice collector is entitled to receive, which again everyone nearby can hear. Additionally, they document the amount of rice the collector has received. The scale inspector, sitting behind the scale and behind the admins, is checking the weight that the scale displays. He is positioned in a way that allows him to check the scale and the correct amount of rice properly. Occasionally, the scale inspector puts the scale back into a proper position so that the scale can also weigh the correct amount. This practice re-emphasises his position, demonstrating that his actions and behaviour are absolutely focussed on the correct function and display of the scale. This further supports the argument that participants are engaged in making the procedure rational and bureaucratic and shows how seriously they take this; making it visible to the other participants as a publicly accessible procedure. The scale, together with rice bags, creates a boundary, a space and an area that hinders rice from being spilled. These markers underline an enclosed section that not only stalls the spread of rice but restricts people from entering this area without legitimate purpose. Only recognised helpers and people who are called by the admins at station two can enter the rice zone. This makes it possible to maintain over-sight of the situation regardless of how many participants are in the building. In contrast to possible actions and behaviour in the entrance area and in the building where the rice zone is located, behaviour in the rice zone itself is strictly organised and no other practices are allowed. Within this area rice col-lectors and helpers are forced to behave in restricted ways. Their orchestrated, routine activities must be carried out in an exact sequential order. These prac-tices are: rice collectors go into the rice zone, scooping up together with the helpers the rice from the floor, filling the rice sack with the correct amount of rice, putting the rice sack on the scale, casting a glance at the scale, checking the correct amount of rice, modify the amount of rice if necessary, and leav-ing the area with filled rice sack(s).

The spatial layout of the rice zone and the controlled actions make this area manageable and publicly accessible for the audience. Additionally, most of the communication in the rice zone is undertaken non-verbally. During the event it is very noisy, but within the rice zone silence dominates; not much verbal communication is required. During this situation, participants do not negotiate about the amount of rice they are entitled to receive, and nor do they make any complaints. What is verbally communicated and audible to ev-eryone is the loud calling of the names and the amounts of rice people are to receive. The ration book and the scale have the last word on how much people are entitled to receive. The use of the public scale is an instrument that makes the amount of rice that the collector receives appear accountable and rational.

The scale is an instrument for control used by participants. This is observ-able to everyone, but there is also a mutual expectation that everyone will agree on this procedure. The ration book (observed by rice collectors) and the handling of the scale have a deep relevance for making the event publicly available and for the sense of its being controlled by the public. The objects legitimate and decide about the amount of rice participants receive. No other procedures decide on who gets how much, but the amount of rice, based on the numbers documented in the ration book, is checked with the help of the scale. This makes the procedure become rational and bureaucratic. The ration books and the scale could even be understood as participants of the event themselves, but one that must be made relevant by human participants. It is not assumed that objects act by themselves, as suggested by Latour (2006, 485ff.), but objects may become participants when human participants in the event situate them. The social meaning of an object, as well as its function, is achieved in the process of using it in a situation (see Garfinkel, Lynch and Livingston 1981). Objects do not have the competences required to make themselves relevant but need human actions to become participants of situations. It is not only these objects that structure the sequence and create rationality but also the meticulous gaze.

The moment of glancing at the display on the scale in concert makes this procedure not only public but also accountable, rational and systematic. This meticulous gaze, as well as the procedures beforehand, is very typical of the distribution event for other items that are distributed, as well. The meticulous gaze by many attendees checking the amount of rice on the scale comes not only from those in charge but also from other participants; it shows how people establish, encourage and support each other in not only this very bureaucratic and rational way but also in a public event—hey perform a collaboration that goes beyond formally expected documentation and distribution according to aid agency rules. The scene also shows that different people occupy the available space and by doing so signal their intentions and make them visible to everyone. In principle, everyone sees and knows where to go and where to stand, and when someone enters the rice zone everyone know what practices are expected and performed. The facility's layout places constraints on what kinds of activities are possible and in what space. The spatial layout of the setting, the arrangement of objects (rice sacks, the scale) and bodies, the open door and walkways, allows participants to observe the whole procedure. Participants in the event can check the work of the admins and enter the distribution hall regularly (including myself). They enter the hall and observe the procedures behind and in front of the scale. The methods of handling the scale, the rice sacks and the 'rice zone' itself are relevant for making these kinds of public distribution possible: the scale is positioned in such a way that people who enter the distribution hall are able to see the display on the scale immediately. It is not only the people who oversee the distribution procedure that are able to see the display on the scale, but also a maximum number of other people.[24] The practices in the context of the rice zone is evocative of the panopticon (Foucault 1979, 91), established not solely by architecture but in collaboration with the participants.

Discussed were the different participation statuses, the spatial layout, the role of the objects and documents as well as the collaborative gaze that make the event public and rational. These accomplishments additionally make the equal treatment of camp residents continuously visible and comprehensible. The event is the performance of a reasonable and logical procedure that plays out according to locally generated rules (gaze exchange). The investigative stance (Zimmerman 1969, 332), which focusses on obeying bureaucratic rules, is made visible to everyone. People constantly control each other and show each other that they are obeying the rules. Through their performance they confirm that no one is cheating by behaving according to the rules and making visible that they are competent enough to not be cheated; for example, through the investigative glances at the scale as well as the looking over the shoulder of the admin. The performance of this investigation is achieved through exchanging gazes and in the ways that people look at each other, at the documents and at the artefacts. We can observe how humans organise themselves in a public, accountable and rational way. In this way a public truth, or a public accountability is accomplished.

STRICT SEQUENTIAL ORDER, CONTROL AND RULES

In the following scene, the focus is on another distribution event at another warehouse. The scene highlights how participants, ordinary residents and staff members alike, collaboratively remind each other of the strict sequential order and rules of the event.

> While the male rice collector fills his rice sack, the admin calls out loudly for the next rice collector to enter the rice zone (*two rice collectors are in the rice zone*). A female rice collector arrives with her child. The woman enters the zone but helper 1 makes a gesture with her arm and hinders the child from entering the rice zone as well. The child (*pre-school age*) reacts immediately and does not enter the rice zone but walks along the boundary, which is built up of rice sacks. The female rice collector starts to fill her sack with rice.
>
> The male rice collector fills the sack positioned at the scale together with helper 3. Again, in collaboration everyone looks at the scale and inspects the amount of rice. The male rice collector puts some more rice into the sack. He wants to put some more in but the scale inspector stops him with the words: 'weli, weli', which means 'finished, finished'. He checks the scale again and puts his rice sack on the boundary of the rice zone. Someone from outside comes and helps him to carry the rice sack. He almost leaves the rice zone but is called by admin 2: 'Here, take your ration ticket! After you take the rice, take your ration ticket'.[25] The rice collector steps up to the rice sack boundary, closes one of the rice sacks, and talks to a man standing outside the zone, ignoring the admin. Admin 1 reminds the rice collector again and points with her pen (*five times*) to his ration book and says, 'Take your ticket',[26] in a strict tone, 'Here, take your ration ticket! After you take the rice, come and take your ration ticket'.[27] The two men are still engaged in closing the sacks. Finally, the man picks up his ration book and leaves the scene with his friend.
>
> In the meantime, the child (*who wanted to enter the rice zone as well*) walks along the 'rice fence' and tries to sneak in from the other side. But helper 2 observes the child. The child plays a little with the rice, still at the boundary. Then the child steps into the rice zone and is not hindered by anyone, but eventually goes back to the boundary. The child again steps into the rice zone and receives

a strict look from helper 2 and some words (*not audible on the video*). Another person from outside (*who can't be seen in the video*) says, 'You should bring the rice packet with you at the same time!' (*to the person who came to pick up the rations*).[28,29]

Two aspects of this scene are particularly noteworthy. First, the male rice collector is reminded to behave according to the proper, fixed procedure of the ration distribution procedure. The admin insists that the rice collector takes the ration book before leaving the rice zone and repeats her demand three times. This scene shows that there is a rigid sequential order that is maintained, for example, by calling people's attention to the upcoming sequence. The people in attendance show each other how to maintain this strict order. No other practices are allowed (such as the chatting between the two men). A ration book needs to go with the particular body in order to fulfil the requirements of the procedure. Thus, the basic procedure might be seen as a mutual integration or incorporation of those present into the bureaucratic course of events, and people support each other in order to integrate themselves and their practices into this procedure. Demands by the admin help to accomplish this. But the call from outside shows that, additionally, ordinary rice collectors encourage each other to remain integrated in the process. Apart from this, the rational and formal character of this procedure allows people to behave in a different manner. A woman giving an order to a man in public in this strict way is not usual but is observable at the distribution events. The bureaucratic procedure dominates, thus allowing another kind of gender order in public.

Second, we need to pay attention to the situation with the child who is prevented from entering the rice zone. A child breaks the rule by entering the rice zone and helpers use the rules by referring to them. The rice zone is reserved for certain bodies that have been called in advance and certain restricted practices: filling the rice sack, putting the rice on the scale and not for socialising. The rice zone is a zone of discipline and children are not permitted to enter; but this must be accomplished, performed and shown again and again. No other practices are allowed and not everyone is allowed to cross the boundary into the rice zone. It is a different physical space, there are other social practices that are carried out and there is a different kind of social power in this zone.

THE PUBLIC MINIATURE EXAMINATION AND BUREAUCRACY

The observations make clear that with the help of bureaucratic elements, camp residents generate a public bureaucracy in the strict sense of the word.

The bureaucracy is public because rice collectors and distribution authorities perform a bureaucracy that is visible and accessible to everyone. Moreover, the event speaks to an elaborate, bureaucratic and institutionalised system that is strongly dependent on participants' public involvement. The procedure is highly structured, and people constantly show each other, verbally and non-verbally, how it works and how the procedure should be undertaken. The public spatial ordering, the public positioning of the scale, the public regis- trations in the documents and the public collaborative meticulous gazes, for example, make the proceedings bureaucratic, according reliable, transparent and publicly accessible procedures. This arrangement allows all rice collec- tors to become involved in making the bureaucratic event public. Participants actively encourage and support each other in creating and maintaining this characteristic procedure. The work of distributing rations accomplishes a form of public bureaucracy with various practices that make the equal treat- ment of refugees visible and comprehensible. Distribution participants con- tinuously make it clear that the distribution is being performed in an account- able way. These practices make the distribution not only accountable and rational but also 'relaxed', since there is a high degree of predictability to the procedures. The rigid and sequential order hinders and prevents people from questioning others. Everyone knows that they will get the number of rations that are documented in the ration books and the public practices make the equal treatment of every rice collector visible and, in so doing, also absorbs criticism. This is further suggested by the fact that people remind each other of the procedure and maintain the it in collaboration. In general, few conflicts during the distribution procedure were observed. The public bureaucratic procedure makes the event more relaxed, because everyone knows that they will get the amount of rice that is documented in the ration book, and people see that everyone is treated fairly and according to the documents. The ar- rangements also speak in favour of the interest of camp residents in making distribution practices transparent, rational and visible to the camp public.

However, these practices do not eliminate nepotism and favouritism be- cause many aspects are nevertheless negotiated in other contexts, such as section meetings or more private backstage meetings (cp. with chapter four). But what the event establishes is the appearance of nepotism having been eliminated as, for example, the section leaders' wives participate and perform as ordinary rice collectors as well.[30]

The relaxed character of this event that is, at the same time, very much con- trolled and ordered was disturbed for a moment when an admin made a joke:

> The admin calls the rice collector's name and he comes to the rice zone and wants to enter it, but the admin adds in a serious tone, 'your name is already in America'. The rice collector looks at the admin and stops moving, before

entering the rice zone. At the same time the admin and the people who hear this comment start laughing. It took some time for him to realize that it was a joke, but after a while the rice collector also started laughing and finally entered the rice zone. I did not understand the situation and asked a student who I knew who was standing next to me waiting for his name to be called. He explained that the person whose name was called got his date for resettlement in two weeks or so, so everyone is laughing about this fact.[31]

Even though the procedures and activities at the distribution event seem to be relaxed, the joke more explicitly shows how the described distribution order is actually based on mistrust among the participants. Is this exactly the amount of rice documented in the book? Is the rice collector entitled to receive the benefits? Are section staff members not cheating?

When entering the rice area, people actually go into a miniature exam situation for the camp public that is about ratifying one's status as a reasonable member of an ordinary distribution event who is entitled to benefits (Bochmann 2019). As has been shown, no rice leaves the rice zone without being registered by the event participants and their meticulous gaze. Thus, the procedures are based on uncertainties or even mistrust—otherwise these specific public practices would not be necessary. Equal treatment needs to be performed in public, which turns the distribution into a public examination. There is an examination of the documents, the artefacts and people's bodies. The documents are investigated and updated twice during the procedure and it is noted that the person is entitled to receive the benefits. The public registration of the ration books also allows every section and camp member to check and examine the section staff who fill out the books. The artefacts are checked through a collaborative gaze of the weight of the rice sack on the scale, which makes visible that this is the exact amount of rice that the person is entitled to receive. Moreover, bodies undergo an examination. Participants enter the rice zone, and with this, others legitimise them and the household or family as registered and accepted section and camp members. Thus, when entering this public bureaucratic procedure, collectors are immediately introduced and exposed to a monthly public miniature examination ratifying their status as an acknowledged section or even camp member. This is done every month, not by aid agency staff, but via collaborative practices among camp residents. The event as such, but particularly the collaborative practices in the rice zone, reminds one of a small disciplinary institution or even a panopticon (Foucault 1979, 91) established not solely by architecture but by the participants themselves. The case shows how power emerges from local arenas of concrete action and practices where microstructures (in this case, forms of control and discipline) are produced and reproduced by camp residents themselves.

These findings from observing the distribution event, where public transparency, accountability and rationality is accomplished, may seem to contrast with the public secrets that are also part of the distribution event—such as the good organisational reasons that are given for falsifying the documents. We encounter these public secrets also in contexts of economic behaviour and camp residents' mobilities, to which the following two chapters are dedicated. But the contrast is destabilised because public bureaucracy is not directed towards aid agencies but towards the people who are present: camp residents. The performance described is not for the aid agencies but for the section members, and thus, primarily directed towards the camp public.

NOTES

1. This chapter is grounded on six video recordings of more than seven hours of different distribution events in different camp sections. Moreover, different distribution events have been observed where different kinds of food rations have been distributed such as rice, fish paste or charcoal.
2. (Interview protocol, aid agency 2).
3. (Interview protocol, aid agency 2).
4. Salt is distributed twice a year by the TBC.
5. Soap is distributed every two months by Malteser International.
6. (Field notes, distribution).
7. In this year the name was also changed from BBC to TBBC (TBBC 2004 Jan–Jun, 7).
8. During the period of field research this was not the case. I observed only occasional visits by aid agency staff members.
9. Chapter 4 introduces the different registration systems of the camp population.
10. It was only in 2012 that criteria were developed and documented for these kinds of interviews.
11. (Field notes, section leader 3).
12. (Interview protocol, camp leader 2).
13. (Interview protocol, aid agency 2).
14. (Interview protocol, aid agency 2).
15. The term 'family' is used in this context because families tend to share one ration book. It is rare for an individual to hold a ration book.
16. (Interview protocol, section leader 3).
17. Asia Remix is a mix of different flours.
18. (Video, DSCF 4666, distribution).
19. (Video, DSCF 4632, distribution).
20. (Video, DSCF 4632, distribution).
21. (Video, DSCF 4632, distribution).
22. (Video, DSCF 4648, 05:10, distribution).

23. (Video, DSCF 4648, 05:30, distribution). Behind the camera we see more people who sit and speak (you can hear their conversations in the video). During these scenes, I am not behind the camera but outside the building.

24. The scale could be positioned somewhere else, for example by the wall, so that the scale inspector would be able to overview the warehouse and would not have people behind him. Besides this, people are allowed to and do enter the distribution hall (even me, with my camera). This was sometimes restricted to people who are called and allowed to enter the rice zone.

25. (Video transcript, DSCF 4666, lines 85–89, distribution).
26. (Video transcript, DSCF 4666, line 93, distribution).
27. (Video transcript, DSCF 4666, lines 85–89, distribution).
28. (Video transcript, DSCF 4666, lines 78–80, distribution).
29. (Video, DSCF 4666, 12:35–14:05, distribution).
30. (Field notes, section).
31. (Observation protocol, distribution).

Chapter Six

Normality, Anomy and Economy

Working activities in camp environments have been called 'income generating practices' (Werker 2007; Horst 2006; Jacobsen 2005). But this may indicate that working activities function only as improvement of people's livelihood or income generating. In what follows, the term 'working activities'
is preferred and used in order to emphasise another important and relevant
quality, namely producing normality and ordinary camp life. A presumption
regarding the state of normality or ordinariness is that it is something produced, situated and ordered in people's practices. In accordance with Sacks
and Goffman, this chapter shows that normality is a locally accomplished
state or condition in refugee camp environments and the preferred interpretation or performance of even troublesome situations (Sacks 1984, 419ff.;
Goffman 1974, 339ff., 353ff.). As a result, working activities in the camp are
important to generate camp normality.

This chapter focusses on the open camp economy in Burmese refugee
camps. The first part overviews the various working activities in the context
of Burmese refugee camps in general. Second, a big grocery store, its history,
networks and linkages beyond camp and state borders, as well as the various
working activities that are connected to the store are introduced. The main
body of this chapter explores interactions at this store. Two sections divide
the main corpus of the chapter. The first section shows how in ordinary shop
interactions camp normality is achieved. The second section presents the
ways local actors perform the exceptional character of the camp and how 'illegal' camp practices become visible. Afterwards, practices are presented that
show how residents deal with these ambivalences and embed troublesome
situations in normalcy. The main part of this chapter is based on the analysis
of more than ten hours of video recordings at a big camp grocery store and the
transcripts of interactions produced by translators and me. Additionally, ex-

tensive observations have been conducted in the camps and the Thai-Burmese borderland in the context of economy. I accompanied, for example, travels by boats and Jeeps of Thai and Burmese vendors, camp residents and other migrants and refugees who conduct business in the borderland.

SPECTRUM OF WORKING ACTIVITIES

Although camp residents receive aid, this does not prevent them from being active in diverse working activities. Neither the difficult camp environment nor the difficult political and legal status of camp residents prevents them from becoming engaged in working activities. According to the national guidelines, displaced persons and camp residents in Thailand have neither the right to work nor to move freely. They are also not allowed to open bank accounts nor can they be granted state licences that allow them to legally conduct business in the camps. Additionally, the camp environment where the main research has been conducted is situated a great distance from towns and markets, is isolated from other business people and lacks proper infra- structure. Apart from the fact that residents' statuses prohibit them from owning vehicles during the dry seasons, the route to the camp and to local towns is a difficult four to five-hour car drive. During the rainy season, it is almost impossible to access the camp by car. These restrictions and obstacles do not stop camp residents from working in and outside the camp and do not stop them from leaving and returning to the camp to carry out business. People's working activities depend on skills, knowledge, experience and social networks, partly from their pre-flight lives and partly from what they have acquired during their stay in the camp. Working activities carried out in the camp are as diverse as people's skills. They range from the simple to the more professionalised and are short- or long-term.

The following overview demonstrates the range of working activities in which people are engaged in contexts of Burmese refugee camps in general. People work for refugee representative organisations at the section, camp or regional level or for aid agencies. Residents become teachers, nurses, nurs- ery-school teachers or social workers. Although it is also forbidden, residents go to the jungle outside the camp to collect bamboo, plants, leaves, flowers and other natural products and sell these natural resources in the camp. People fish and farm, depending on whether they have the land to grow on or not. They produce and sell snacks or dried fish. Others grow vegetables near their houses if space allows. Some residents can get hold of land near the camp to grow vegetables and rice or raise animals—mostly chickens and pigs. Camp residents offer services to others, such as repairing houses, repairing and producing jewellery, or health services such as herbal treatments. People weave clothes, tablecloths or curtains and open small shops to sell them. Residents repair electronic products, produce and sell traditional clothes and there are several tailors in the camp. In computer shops, residents offer different services as well. Some women offer hairdressing services in their houses or open beauty salons. There are many traders and restaurateurs. Residents own generators and sell electricity to households. There are different religious institutions where people become involved in organising, implementing and managing religious ceremonies. Residents run libraries and a small cinema. A public transportation system has been established by boat owners and drivers. Primarily, men work as boat drivers, who have established and continue to maintain a public transportation system that connects the camp with other Thai as well as Burmese villages and towns. People are shop, café, and restaurant owners, or work as waiters or cooks. There are a lot of small shops in the camps, especially along the main roads—almost every second house on the main roads have been converted into shops. Most of the shops sell snacks and food items. There are also bigger shops that specialise in plastic products, household necessities, clothes, or books and magazines. The bigger shop owners offer bank services as well, such as borrowing money or exchanging currency. Since the resettlement programme started in 2005–2006, camp residents have received remittances from their relatives abroad, which has led to more and more shops and restaurants appearing along the main roads of the camp, and people starting to own motorbikes and TVs. Scholars researched this phenomenon in other regional contexts as well (Horst 2006; Jacobsen 2005; van Hear 2003). The remittance procedures are conducted with the help of local Thai nationals, because camp residents are not usually allowed to have bank accounts. There are a few Thai-Karen people living in the camp (with Thai registration cards) that offer to send, receive and bring remittances to other residents. Some camp residents also have relatives in local Thai villages. In this case, they deal with remittances together with their relatives with Thai registration documents. In this way, Thai nationals also get involved in the camp economy. There are even bamboo buildings in the camp provided by aid organisations reserved for Thai nationals, enabling them to open shops—but these buildings were not used and stood empty at the time research was conducted. Indeed, there are several Thai nationals who come to the camp regularly to sell products, mainly fresh food items such as fish, meat and vegetables to shop owners and camp residents. Moreover, Thai nationals are also engaged in camp residents' businesses, such as transporting products from Thai towns to camp shops. Men from the nearby Thai town come to the camp selling ice cream. Since the resettlement started, primarily female Thai villagers opened the so-called phone shops near the camp. Internet and telephone networks are prohibited in the camps, but Thai nationals are given licenses to run these shops. Besides offering phone and internet services, the owners of these shops are additionally engaged in sending and receiving remittances on behalf of camp residents. They hire female camp residents to run the shops on a daily basis. Additionally, there are job opportunities for Burmese refugees and migrants, especially in the border area but also in the bigger Thai cities (Brees 2008, 391). Working as an English teacher offers good pay and sometimes even legal status in Thailand. Burmese people working without proper documents in Thai-Myanmar border towns and villages is a phenomenon that people, in general, and local Thai officials deal with daily, as in other regional contexts (Betts et al. 2014, 16; Werker 2007; Horst 2006; Jacobsen 2005; Kibreab 1993). Brees argues that in Thailand refugees, 'illegal' immigrants or people with precarious statuses make a significant contribution to the host economy (2008, 390).

A variety of working activities are introduced in which camp residents and Thai nationals living near the camp are engaged, from short- to long-term working activities in and beyond the camp. This rough overview demonstrates that camp residents are engaged in ordinary working activities despite the aid items and packages they receive, the restricted legal framework in which they live and the diverse difficulties they must deal with, such as restricted communication channels and the remote and difficult-to-access area they live in. Based on these working activities, people establish themselves in the camp. Social relations are established on a long-term basis. Particularly those who open grocery stores or restaurants must plan on a long-term scale when it comes to their resources and investments.

SOCIAL NETWORKS AND CROSS-BORDER RELATIONS

The grocery store described here was established by a family who had come from a smaller town in East Myanmar, where they also ran a grocery store. Together with a friend, the oldest daughter of the family left Myanmar in 2002 and came to the camp. She attended the camp high school and, in parallel, opened a small shop in the camp. After her high school graduation, she opened a bigger shop together with her parents and her sister, who followed her to the camp in 2008. The family got their products from a small Thai town, a two-hour boat ride away. The father of the family had relatives in this town and went there by boat to buy products twice a week. In 2009, the middle daughter married Sola, a camp resident with Thai registration. A year later, the oldest daughter resettled in the United States. Sola's Thai registration made ownership of a van legal and with the financial support of the resettled daughter, the family was able to buy a van in 2011. In all the camps there are residents who own motorbikes and some even own cars, but state officials do not allow them in the camps. That is why refugee representative organisations issue traffic rules and licences for motorbike and car drivers, which camp residents do not receive from Thai authorities.[1] These documents allow residents to legally drive in the camps. This is an example of non-regulation to which local solutions are found by refugee representative organisations. This, too, is another example of the kind of ambivalent regulations that exist in camp contexts, which impact everyday life. National policies do not allow refugees to possess driving licences, while in the camp itself driving licenses are necessary and are distributed by local camp authorities. Meanwhile, the Thai registration card allows Sola to legally commute between the camp and bigger Thai towns three times a week to buy Thai and Burmese products for the shop. Still, Sola must hide the Jeep when the camp commander or the military from Bangkok visits the camp (cp. chapter 3, pg. 74).

According to the shop owners, around 30 per cent of the shop's products are originally from Myanmar while 70 per cent are from Thailand. Basic food items are available at the shop such as sweets, snacks and vegetables. Apart from food, the owners also sell betelnut, cigarettes, medicine, hygiene products, torches, knives, sticking plasters, all kinds of tiger balms and toys for children. Tobacco is sold as well, which, according to the mother of the family (Antu) is not allowed. That is why they put the tobacco at the back of the store so that it is not visible when entering the shop. It is not only tobacco—other products are also not taxed and are put at the back of the store. But *Or Sor* members, local state authorities present in the camps, also buy products from the shop. This 'shop culture' strongly differs from the shop opposite the grocery store. Mrs White, an older Burmese woman (that is, of Burman ethnicity), goes to Yangon, the capital of Myanmar, once a month and buys products there. Her shop is specialised in all kinds of non-food and non-clothes products, such as Burmese magazines as well as DVDs, jewellery, clocks and other Burmese products.

The shop is located at the front of the house on the main road, while the back of the house is furnished as a living space. During the shop's opening hours, the work and living space tends to merge. But usually, customers do not enter the back unless they are invited. This is a common use of work and living space, but an ordinary practice observable in the camp as well as in Thai and Myanmar villages and towns. Antu and the middle daughter mainly manage the shop and its finances. Other family members help in the shop daily such as Antu's husband, the youngest daughter, Sola's cousin who is a Thai national from a Thai village nearby and the father's cousin from a village in Myanmar. Sola's parents and siblings who live nearby are engaged in the business too, as their home serves as storage for the grocery store.

Most of the store's customers buy products in family-sized packs and then sell the single products in their own small shops. The store's other customers are immediate neighbours and camp residents living in sections nearby. Some customers are Thai locals who come to the shop to buy products that are not available in their villages. Also, local Thai authorities buy products at the shop and even order products from Myanmar because they are not available in Thai villages or towns. Yet the shop is not only a place where people buy products. Since the store is located near the river, where a port-like locality has been constructed, traders or visitors from Myanmar and Thailand can easily access the camp and the shop. This condition that has enabled the establishment of long-standing transnational business interactions between shop owners and these merchants are discussed later. Merchants and other vendors from Myanmar or Thailand come to the shop to sell products. Local villagers from the Thai or Myanmar side of the border, which is nearby, sell products such as fish to the owners, especially in December and January, as well as fresh vegetables and other food or non-food items. In this way, the shop serves as a sales market. Camp residents also sell homemade cakes and snacks which the shop owners resell. In addition, several Thai vendors come by Jeep to the camp and sell fresh vegetables, meat and fish to the big shops in the camp very regularly. Shop owners are also engaged in working activities other than selling and buying products. Sola, for example, regularly leaves the camp, sends packages as well as letters to the post office in the town, and takes people to the villages and towns he is passing on his way. Interactions connected to this issue are introduced below as well. Shop owners offer services such as lending money, exchanging currency, help with receiving remittances and taking orders from Thai towns. Residents or Thai villagers order products from catalogues such as tricots for the school uniform or the school soccer and volleyball team. Antu gives medical advice as well. Among neighbours she is known for having knowledge on both Western and traditional, herbal Burmese medicine. Added to this, the family owns a generator. Although national regulations make clear that generators are only permitted for community buildings, the family sells electricity, as the generator brings power to more than ten households.

The history of the grocery store and the driver's working activities show that this business is based on long-term expectations and a sense of security rather than from fear of trouble with Thai authorities. The long-term expectations include not only the shop owners but clients, vendors and merchants as well. The shop and its success are based on pre-flight experiences and were not established in a biographical vacuum. We will come back to these pre-flight contacts when they are made situationally relevant in an interaction at the grocery store between a merchant and the shop owner. The family had a shop in their hometown, and the experiences and skills they developed in the past enter the present situation. Added to this, social ties and networks that go beyond camp borders and engagement in a wider economic context are important. The store is embedded in a transnational, even international, network and provides job opportunity for relatives abroad. The shop is established because camp members can leave the camp and are able to buy products outside. This highlights the phenomena of mobility as an important aspect of camp life. Thai and Burmese vendors enter the camp to conduct economic relationships with camp residents. Hence, the camp is also an opportunity for local villagers to engage in working activities. These different aspects show that the term 'camp economy' tends to be misleading because it indicates an economy inside the camp. The camp economy is not closed but rather based on its local and international surroundings and regular mobility and contacts beyond camp and state borders. Thus, we should speak of an open camp economy, in which not only camp residents but also Thai authorities and people living near the camps and beyond are engaged.

ACHIEVING CAMP NORMALITY

Clients of the grocery store such as merchants, vendors and customers—including *Or Sor* members or Thai vendors—show each other in their interactions that they are involved in a normal and ordinary business. The business is not categorised or perceived as "illegal," a black market or smuggling opportunity, including the work of the Thai vendor. In public camp life, it is not perceived as exceptional when someone does business in the camp. Rather, business activities are made to be ordinary, such as that someone opens a shop and sells products, but also locals and camp residents alike commute between camps and local towns and villages in both states. How this camp normality is achieved is shown in the following ordinary interactions at the grocery store. The majority of interactions and practices in the grocery store relate to buying and products, where the ordinariness of the seller-buyer interactions and practices are produced. With these typical buyer-seller interactions, which last a few seconds or minutes between customer and shop owner, the participants of the situation show each other and make each other observable, visible and accountable, such that the shopping situation is normal. Ordinary shop conversations are about the price and the number of products, but also about the availability and the quality of products. The following interaction exemplifies one of these ordinary shopping interactions:

C. For how much do you sell the noodles? (*In Karen.*)

ANTU. We have Mah Mah for five and six baht. Do you want noodles for six baht or five baht? (*In Karen.*)

C. What? (*In Burmese.*)

ANTU. We also have five-baht noodles. (*In Burmese.*)

C. I'll buy the noodles for six baht.

ANTU. You will take the noodles for six baht?

C. It doesn't matter whether it is five baht or six baht. I'll buy twenty packs of noodles.[2]

Most conversations do not refer to characteristic camp structures or phenomena, but ordinary seller-buyer interactions that appear in other shop environments as well (Sheth 1976; Cannon and Perreault 1999). Shop-related conversations also include orders for specific products from Thai or Myanmar towns and questions about how to go about this. Apart from these ordinary seller-buyer interactions, the grocery store serves as a space where it is possible to talk with the shop owners about other topics in order to establish, maintain and negotiate relationships with each other and, of course, to exchange news and gossip with neighbours. Daily interactions include complaining about the weather, cars that drive too fast down the main road located in front of the shops, or talking about friends, neighbours and relatives. But most of these everyday talks do not refer to specific camp structures or camp life as such. Occasionally, people talk about the resettlement programme and people and relatives who have resettled. The resettlement programme is even integrated into the selling strategies of merchants from outside the camp, as the following example will show. Merchants from Myanmar are a more unique category of customers, but even in interactions with non-residents it can be demonstrated how ordinarily and routinely they run. As for the background of the merchants: the couple regularly commutes between a village in Myanmar and the refugee camps in the borderland and sells toys and other products to camp shops.

HUS.[3] You said this product here can really run right? (*Referring to an airplane toy.*)

M.[4] Yes, if you move it back, it will start going to America or Canada (*demonstrating the movement of the toy*). One airplane for 50 baht only.

HUS. Ha Ha. (*All participants are laughing simultaneously.*)

M. Take this one, with the flowers. There are different kinds of flowers (*refers to some headbands she has*).

(*Interruption.*)

Hus. Last time I bought this kind of product and I could sell it very quickly (*referring to the airplanes*).

Hus. You only brought these products again? This time you didn't bring much (*while looking through all the products*).

Antu. Are you making a video? (*To AB and performs in front of the camera.*)

Hus. You talk a lot that's why you sell your products quickly (*Hus to M and Antu and M are laughing together*).[5]

After negotiating the price of a product, the shop owner asks for more information on a specific product. The merchant explains that the airplane toy can 'go to America or Canada'. She brings the listeners in a figurative sense to the localities that are proclaimed by the resettlement programme. The toy is used as a metaphor for the situation of camp residents and the mobility possibilities people in the camp have or at least are associated with. She is selling people a vision, using the airplane as a metaphor for something that may become reality soon for residents. She recipient-designs the products in terms of the specific dynamics and topics relevant for camp residents who are the main customers in this grocery store. It is a sales pitch that works only for camp residents. The merchant shows with her sales strategy that she knows what is going on and what the relevant topics in the camps are. She categorises camp residents as having the opportunity to go abroad. The shop owners laugh about her account but do not go into the topic further. Her method of recipient-designing products for specific groups of people is a common 'sales strategy' (Clark and Pinch 1988). The encounter shows that these business relations, established between residents and non-residents in camp environments, are just business as usual. Business is done in the context of the target group of camp residents that are categorised as being able to move/fly 'to America or Canada'. The camp is a specific market where specific sale strategies are adopted.

The second encounter examined is a more detailed conversation between another merchant and the shop owners. The merchant sells products to this shop regularly. He lives in another camp located one to two hours walking distance from this camp. In contrast to the previous merchant couple, he is in the employment of shop owners in a city in Myanmar and sells products from them to camp residents. Thus, he regularly commutes between the camps and a city in East Myanmar. His aunt, who has a shop in the other camp, is Antu's friend. They were born in the same village in Myanmar. The shop owners usually speak Sgaw-Karen but this conversation is in Burmese because the merchant does not speak Karen. Antu's husband is ordering products from the merchants:

Hus.[6] And we want Sai Sai (*another kind of snack*) as well.

M.[7] I have only a very small amount of Sai Sai left but I still have a lot of other products.

(*Interruption.*)[8]

M. The one that I brought yesterday (*refers to Sai Sai*) has already gone? How can it be gone in just one day?

Antu. We can sell that one (*refers to Sai Sai*) really quickly. (*Laughing.*) That's why we ordered a lot and we still want to order more.

M. No one sells Sai Sai (*name of a snack*) except you, so you can sell it very quickly and everyone really wants it.

Antu. Hmm yes. But don't bring three packages, bring five.

M. I'll bring you five packages of Sai Sai. Actually, at first a lot of people from camp X[9] asked me for Sai Sai but I didn't give it to them. I gave it only to your shop.

Hus. Moe Htet (*another snack*) is a good seller as well.

D.[10] Yes, that one is good (*refers to Moe Htet*). So, you are going back tomorrow?

M. Yes, I'll leave tomorrow. I'll bring Sai Sai for you when I come back from Burma.[11]

Antu. If you come back bring M' Yway (*another snack*) and Moe Htet as well.[12]

The husband orders products and mentions a specific snack. The merchant answers that he only has a small amount left of this product but emphasises that there are other products available that he can sell. There is no response from his interlocutors, because a customer entering the shop interrupts the conversation. After the customer leaves, the merchant comes back to the topic that was talked about previously. He shows surprise about the fact that this specific product has been sold already, referring to an encounter in the near past ('yesterday'), where he already brought this product. Antu gives an account of this phenomenon by explaining that the product is a good seller that she wants to order and sell again. The snack's name ('Sai Sai') is also bound to a locality and there are difficulties in making it available in the camp. The product is unavailable in Thailand, which is why the shop owners must order this product from the merchant who commutes regularly between Thailand

and Myanmar. The merchant gives another account of the good sales figures for this product, namely that only this shop sells this kind of product. Antu does not go into his account. Instead, she makes an order, emphasising the amount. The merchant agrees and repeats the number of packages she has ordered but comes back to and re-emphasises the exclusive agreement he makes with the shop owners with this product. He excludes people from camp X but 'gave it only to your shop'. Through this exclusive order, he aims to establish trust, a close and long-term relationship as well as commitment. The shop owners do not seem to acknowledge this. Instead Antu's husband states that there is another snack that is a good seller, which is confirmed by the middle daughter as well. She wants to know when the merchant is 'going back' to Myanmar, assuming that he is leaving 'tomorrow'. The merchant confirms her assumption and adds that he will bring the product that has been talked about previously: 'I'll bring Sai Sai for you when I come back from Burma', referring to a future encounter. With this, he suggests that he will come back, but the specific date or time remains vague. There is no reference to a definite point in time of product delivery. Nevertheless, Antu orders more products from the merchant but she uses the if-form, indicating a flexibility of her order. Still, Antu assumes, referring to past experiences with the trader, that he will go to Myanmar and will come back to the camp and deliver her order. In a later part of the conversation, the merchant also points to the relationship between Antu and his aunt. The relationship between the two business people was established in the past in Myanmar. Saying that he sells the 'popular' product only to this specific shop maintains the existing relationship but also invokes a commitment between him and the shop owners. The relationship between Antu and the merchant's aunt may be the background of this exclusive agreement suggested by the merchant. However, making exclusive agreements with shop owners are not unique to the camp situation. Again, this encounter shows how ordinary camp residents do business, such as making exclusive agreements and ordering products from other countries, but also the way camp residents cross national borders with products and move in between camps to sell products from Myanmar. What is not communicated is the exceptional or difficult situation that being engaged in this kind of business in this environment represents. Still, the if-clause used by Antu might refer to unreliability and the particularity of the situation. The shop owner is not sure when exactly or if the merchant will come back again.

In the following transcript camp residents talk more explicit about mobility problems and difficulties they must overcome in order to leave the camp. The conversation took place shortly before Sola was going to leave the camp by Jeep. A neighbour came to the shop and started chatting with Antu for a while. The man indirectly demonstrated his intent to go with Sola. The conversation is interrupted several times because customers enter the shop asking questions to Antu. Before this conversation part, Sola explains to Antu that a boy from the neighbourhood wants to go with him and that he told the boy to ask his aunt for permission. Antu does not respond to Sola's comment but restarts the conversation with the neighbour, switching to the topic mentioned by Sola.

ANTU. Children don't feel carsick easily. But for me, I'm very lazy about going outside the camp because I get carsick easily.

N.[13] That's right. I also don't like to go by car.

ANTU: I feel very uneasy and uncomfortable when I go by car. I get carsick very easily.

N. (*Nodding.*) I think going by boat is better than going by car. We can breathe the fresh air in the boat.

ANTU. But going by boat (*Pause.*) . . . I'm afraid of the stones under the water. But it's ok if it's the Salaween River. There are not so many stones in the water.

(*Interruption.*)[14]

N. I think I'll also go and visit Thaw Lel Hta (*a small Thai village between Mae La Oon and Mae Sariang*).

ANTU. Oh, that's good.

(*Interruption.*)[15]

Antu. You said you would go to Thai village X? Do you have any children there?

N . Yes, I do.

ANTU. You do, right?

N. I have a nephew there.

ANTU. So, you don't have any of your own children there?

N. No, I don't have my own child there.

(*Interruption.*)

ANTU. How long will you stay there?

N. I think I'll sleep there only one night. But maybe I won't even sleep there but instead ask someone from there to bring me back.

ANTU. So, you only want to stay there for a day?

N. Yes, just one day.[16]

While the neighbour clearly shows through his behaviour that he wants to ride to the next Thai village, Antu instead gives an account of why she does not like to leave the camp. Antu makes a generalisation about children. After that, she explains why she does not go outside the camp herself: there is a personal individual boundary ('lazy') caused by an individual physical restriction ('carsick'). There are no complaints about legal or bureaucratic restrictions and there also seems to be nothing extraordinary about the activity of 'going outside the camp'. She expresses a physical restriction concerning mobility, in general, when driving the car. Laziness and body constraints limit her in carrying out the activity. The way she is using the terms to describe the activity of leaving a place, namely 'going outside the camp', she emphasises that her shop is in a special kind of environment. The neighbour states that he understands her concern, and expresses agreement. The neighbour adds something, not only agreeing on the physical boundary—he dislikes specific transportation systems. Antu agrees and restates her physical difficulties, in general, when going by car. The neighbour shows agreement through nodding and brings in an alternative transportation option: 'I think going by boat is better' and gives reasons for this ('breathe the fresh air'). Antu's response to this option is another concern. Going by boat has disadvantages as well, referring to geographical and environmental difficulties when using the boat ('stones under the water'). Then the neighbour introduces his interest and says: 'I think I'll also go and visit Thai village X'. This comment is understandable only in the context of the situation and Sola's presence in the situation. As noted, through his behaviour, the neighbour wants to make the shop owners indirectly understand that he wants to go with Sola. Although he agrees with Antu beforehand on the difficulties of traveling by car, he wants Sola to understand the previous sequence of the conversation with Antu that he wants to go with him by car out of the camp. He accounts for his desire to travel and makes sure that Sola understands his purpose. 'Visit' refers only to a short stay in the village.

After another interruption, Antu asks about the purpose and the length of the stay in the village. Having children, as Antu assumes, might be a good reason to shoulder the physical challenges of travelling that the two had agreed on beforehand. He answers yes, although he states that he has a nephew living there. Antu wonders: 'So, you don't have any of your own children there?' The neighbour answers the question in the affirmative. Again, the two interlocutors are interrupted. Antu refers to the talk after a while and asks about the length of his proposed stay in the village, assuming that he will stay there for a couple of days ('How many days will you stay there?'). He answers that he will stay there for one night or even return on the same day, in case he finds someone who is willing to bring him back to the camp. The term 'back' expresses a spatial orientation, explaining that he is usually in the camp and is leaving only on a temporary basis. Then he shows that he depends on other people's kindness, referring to people who stay at the village and are going back to the camp. Antu is wondering about two issues in his comment. First, that he goes there but has no children there. Secondly, she wonders about the short stay and restates her response in a question. She is not wondering about camp residents leaving the camp or having children in Thai villages. Her request shows that, for her, it is not usual to stay only one night in this village and even more unusual to return the same day. Many aspects of his travel are communicated vaguely and with uncertainty: who will bring him back, when, and how, none of this is clear. This, however, seems to be unproblematic for the neighbour and for Antu. Antu is concerned about the short duration he is planning to stay but not the fact that he does not know how, with whom, or when he will be able to come back. Moreover, she wonders why he does not have children living in the village which would justify the difficulties of the travel. In this conversation, camp residents discuss camp mobility. Its challenges are discussed not in terms of the legal or bureaucratic boundaries, but in terms of individual bodily restrictions as well as environmental problems. Besides that, it seems to be unproblematic that the neighbour is unsure about the drive back to the camp. What is unique or exceptional (an issue Antu is wondering about) is someone making such a long trip even though he does not have children in the village and staying there for just one day. Again, conversations about leaving and returning to the camp are normalised and not communicated as something extraordinary or exceptional and demonstrate how normalised these practices are. It seems normal and unproblematic for the interactants also to have children living in Thai villages outside but near the camp.

Most of my observations in the shop, as well as most of the conversations in the shop, deal with ordinary owner-customer or owner-merchant interactions. Even conversations about leaving the camp as shown previously are not referred to as something exceptional but as ordinary camp activities. People go to Thai towns nearby and leave the camp to go to Myanmar or Thailand on holiday, for business or working activities or for study and other purposes.[17]

NORMALISING EXCEPTIONAL SITUATIONS

Indeed, there are situations where the 'grey zone', the exceptional and extraordinary character of the camp environment, are visible. This is the case, for example, during the occasional visits of district authorities in the camp.

This morning I was really confused and worried because the roads were empty and all the shops on the main road were closed; no one else was around except me. Later on, people explained to me that the *Palad* is going to visit the camp. Contrary to my feelings, the shop owners were happy about being forced to close the shop on a regular working day. When I asked Antu how she felt about this (*closing the shop on a regular weekday*) she laughed at me and responded: 'These are my holidays. This is how we have to do it. Nothing to worry about.' The next day they open the shops and use motorbikes as if nothing had happened.[18]

These visits make residents become aware of the fact that the legal restrictions do not go along with the local practices in the camp. Antu's grocery store usually opens after sunrise and closes shortly after sunset and is closed on Sundays. But when state officials visit the camp, usually once every couple of months, the shop is closed on a weekday. The shop owners have to hide their working activities from these specific state authorities. As noted earlier, camp residents are given notice about these visits via loudspeaker announcement. During these times, residents know that they not only have to close their shops but also have to hide their motorbikes and Jeeps. It seems like that during these times the camp public performs a total institution (Goffman 1961). The camp leader gave me the reasoning for these announcements and the expected actions. He explained that he did not want the *Palad* to see the many big shops, motorbikes and cars in his camp in order to maintain the image of the poor refugee at least for (higher) Thai authorities.[19] Even though these official visits make the camp public aware that the shops are established in a grey zone with ambivalent rules, Antu's reaction of making it a holiday shows how they normalise the visits in their daily practises.

Two more examples of normalising exceptional situations are the 'offering of bribes' to local state authorities present in the camp regularly as well as the 'tax-like contributions' to section representatives. The terms 'offering of bribes' or 'tax-like contributions' could be used interchangeably. Shop owners pay no fees or taxes to these state officials, but the car owners importing products to the camp have to offer a bribe to the *Or Sor* members. These monthly payments allow them to travel and to pass camp checkpoints regularly with their cars. The fact that they pay these monthly fees and have regular encounters with such authorities reaffirms the businesses' grey zone that is established and maintained in negotiations between camp residents and local authorities: 'We know that we have to go there and pay, you know?'[20] In conversations I had with the shop owners, they emphasised that 'paying fees is normal when doing business in Myanmar and Thai villages or towns and so we have to pay here too.'[21] Also Thai vendors that access the camp regularly in order to sell products to camp residents pay monthly fees to the *Or Sor* to be allowed to carry out their business. People who access the camp with motorbikes, even though importing products, do not have to pay these tax-like contributions. As noted, shop owners do not pay *Or Sor* members but pay tax-like contributions to section staff members as mentioned in a section meeting.

> NEBWE. The next issue is if someone has a shop and they are selling around 5000 baht they have to give their name to him. If there are people who are selling things that cost 5000–10000 baht, they have to give their name to him.[22]

Some shop owners pay extra fees to section staff members so that they are not categorised as self-reliant. The leading aid agency responsible for the distribution system is aware of camp residents' working activities. They have a formal category for households or families who are especially successful in their working activities: self-reliant. These households or families should not be entitled to receive rations. Households or families with bigger shops are categorised as self-reliant and they are given signs by the aid agency to display in their shops that make passers-by aware that their household is self-reliant.[23]

These three examples demonstrate the paradox or ambivalent character of social camp orders and structures residents must deal with. (1) Legally, camp residents are not allowed to run businesses or to own motorbikes and Jeeps. Shop owners do not have official state licences that legalise their position or selling practices. Additionally, they must maintain the picture of camp residents (or refugees) as helpless and needy. (2) They must pay fees to local *Or Sor* members that allow them to perform their ('illegal') working activities as well as to local refugee representatives. (3) The aid agency formally recognises people who are especially successful in their working activities and have established the term 'self-reliant' for them. But actually, only people with big grocery stores are categorised as such. The aid agencies, therefore, include these local arrangements in their policies that residents pay local authorities to run a business that is the basis for becoming self-reliant, even though state policies say camp residents are not allowed to have work permits and are not allowed to regularly leave and return to the camp. One could argue that aid agencies recognise and support these 'illegal' practices but at the same time punish successful residents by refusing to give them rations. That is why residents try to avoid being categorised as self-reliant and tend to pay section staff members for not categorising them as such. These examples demonstrate that there is a specific and characteristic camp structure and constellation such that aid agencies, local authorities, section and camp staff, and camp residents are involved in establishing and maintaining a plural grey zone. Although these specific situations exist and make people aware of the "illegality" of their actions, the paradoxical nature of the situation shows how people normalise these situations in everyday life. The exceptional is made to be routine. In this sense, we could speak of a double production of a normality and temporal predictability.

In the following we look at more troublesome situations related to camp structures and how people communicate about these ambivalent situations in everyday interactions. In the first scene, participants talk about the obstacles car drivers have to overcome at the checkpoint in order to access the camp. This conversation takes place in Burmese; a merchant well known to Antu is present in the shop and does not speak Karen.

(A neighbour, and friend of Antu, enters the shop and looks at the merchant who organises his products he wants to sell to Antu.)

N. Where does he live? *(To Antu, in Karen.)*

(Antu is counting packages of snacks and probably has not heard the question. At least, she does not reply. When she finishes counting, she starts talking to the merchant in Burmese.)

Antu. It's very hard even to get one or two baht.

N. Does he live in village X? *(A small Thai village close to the camp, again asking Antu in Karen.)*

Antu. He lives in Mae Ra Moe. He has to come quite far to reach us here. As you know, we all have to struggle to survive and we don't have freedom to go in and out of the camp easily. *(In Burmese.)*

(Interruption.)[24]

M. In our camp, cars enter but they have to pay the Thai soldiers who are waiting and checking the entrance of the camp. *(In Burmese.)*

Antu. Yep, I'm talking about exactly that.[25]

The merchant is an unknown person to the neighbour and a common question posed to unknown people in the camp is usually where the person comes from. Antu, however, does not hear the question and the neighbour reformulates it suggesting that the man comes from a Thai village. The neighbour observes the way the merchant looks, his activities and the unknown face, and takes him to be someone from a local Thai village even though he speaks Burmese and not Thai. Her question and her reaction show that it is nothing extraordinary to find Burmese-speaking people in Thai villages from outside the camp but it is unusual enough to ask questions about the person. Antu answers the question appropriately, which shows that the neighbour's question, as well as her suggestion, is nothing to wonder about. Antu reacts ordinarily and is not surprised at the neighbour's question but answers more extensively than necessary. She explains and accounts for the presence of the merchant in this specific locality and even offers a legitimation. Antu accounts for his entitlement to be in the camp and his doing as necessary, relevant and significant work for camp residents in general. Moreover, with her 'we', the shop owner introduces her business partner, the merchant, as standing in a common category of participants in the situation, even though he is not a resident in this specific camp and is a stranger to the neighbour. With this, Antu shows that everyone in the situation belongs to the same category, which again legitimates the merchant's being in the camp. On the one hand, 'we all have to struggle to survive'. On the other hand, she makes clear that no participants, or camp residents, in general, have the freedom to move easily. In this way, she twice shows that the merchant undertakes a difficult task in doing business in this specific place, and furthermore, he accounts for his presence in the camp. This interaction shows two aspects. First, camp residents have a permanent local presence. It is legitimate to ask about the origin and residence of unknown persons. Second, Antu includes the merchant as belonging to them, as standing in a common membership category: difficult survival and no free movement. Staying outside the camp and being a camp resident does not represent a contrast, but instead is something that needs to be explicated. Antu says: 'We don't have the freedom to go in and out of the camp easily' either. The social boundaries of a camp may encounter a camp borderline, but clearly go beyond it in everyday interactions and practices. Camp residents work on and with the camp border and use it in legitimising their ways of living. Camp residents work with the categories of 'in' and 'out', which are indeed bridgeable (not 'easy', but possible). We notice that in this situation Antu talks to a resident of another camp, not to her neighbour, where only individual—physical (laziness, carsickness) and environmental (stones)—difficulties concerning leaving the camp are negotiated.[26] In this conversation, with a business partner, Antu puts more emphasis on the difficulties of leaving and entering the camp, in general.

The merchant specifies the difficulties a car driver encounters when passing the camp checkpoint in his response. The merchant first distances himself from the location and the people that are part of the here-and-now situation by referring to 'in our camp'. By saying 'our camp' he marks a difference between himself and his residence, and the people who are part of the here-and-now situation. Antu and her neighbour are part of another camp and hence belong somewhere else. He makes clear that he is not a member of this camp, but a resident of another camp, where things might work in a different way. With the term 'there', using another indexical expression, the merchant assumes that it is common knowledge where he lives, explaining that 'there are' people with cars 'who enter the camp'. He is thus not assuming anything about camps, in general, but relates his comment to the camp where he is from. Moreover, using the phrase 'enter the camp' shows that the environment is specific. As noted, this comment would not usually have been made in reference to a village. The verb 'entering' refers to a (camp) border or checkpoint, or a territory where people must bridge an obstacle.[27] In his short comment, the merchant moreover makes use of two different membership categories: 'Thai soldiers' (*Or Sor* members) and people with cars who enter the camp. The membership category 'Thai soldiers' goes along with the category-bound activity of waiting and checking. The membership category 'car owners entering the camp' goes along with the category-bound activity of paying money. This is common knowledge and a normal perception. Everyone understands what he means when he says, 'paying money'. Only people who know the local system can enter the camp with a Jeep. Antu's response to this comment—'Yep, I am talking about exactly that'– shows she is aware of and confirms the practices described by the merchant and his critique of the practice. With her response she also refers to a statement she had made recently regarding the difficulties of doing business in the camp due to certain restrictions and the local system of paying. This example underlines how these exceptional camp structures are talked about and negotiated between the interlocutors. The following scene shows how shop customers complain about the unavailability of products.

C. Don't you have cigarettes?

(*Antu shakes her head.*)

C. Haven't you ordered the products from Mae Sariang yet?

ANTU. I have, but I don't think the boats are allowed to travel at the moment.

D. But yesterday, I saw Pah Day Kyaw (*a boat owner*) travelling by boat and he brought products. I'll ask him about that.

C. Is it Pah Day Kyaw who owns the boat? I think it's allowed if he is travelling (*to D*).

D. Yes, him. I'm not sure about whether they are allowed to travel or not, that's why I wanted to ask him when I see him. But I haven't seen him yet.

ANTU. I don't have cigarettes. How many cigarettes do you want?

C. I want to buy two packs of cigarettes.

ANTU. I don't have packs. I have singles for one or two Baht.

C. Really? Hmm. (*Pause*) Oh, I think this jiggery looks really delicious (*looking at the jiggery*).

ANTU. Yes, it's not jiggery but cane sugar with coconut milk. It is very sweet because it's mixed with coconut milk. Isn't there anything else you want to buy?

C. I don't think I want to buy anything else.

ANTU. The cigarettes haven't arrived yet. We have ordered them but the traders can't enter the camp now.

C. When will they arrive? Do you think the products will arrive this week?

ANTU. Are you asking about the noodles *(which they talked about before)*, or the cigarettes? For the cigarettes, I've ordered them, but I still have noodles.[28]

The customer is interested in a specific product that is unavailable. The customer demands a reason for the unavailability of the product and suggests immediately, asking whether the shop owners failed to order the product in time. Antu defends herself by stating that she did order the product. She immediately gives an alternative explanation for why the product is not available. There are restrictions on boat mobility. Antu's daughter enters the conversation and brings in her observation, which contrasts with Antu's account. She saw one boat owner travelling by boat. At the same time, she says that she wants to ask the boat owner she saw for more detailed information concerning the issues. The customer, however, seems to know this boat owner as well and assumes that this specific boat owner might be able to travel (he probably has Thai documents that would allow him to travel, while other boat owners might be restricted). The daughter refers to her uncertainty regarding specific information and talks about asking this specific boat owner soon. She uses the 'they' form, referring and including all boat owners. The conversation then returns to cigarettes. At the beginning of the conversation, the neighbour asked for cigarettes and Antu said, 'I don't have cigarettes'. At the same time, she is interested in the number of cigarettes the customer wants. She responds by saying that she would like to buy two packs. Antu admits that she has cigarettes but only a small number. The customer then becomes interested in another product and the shop owner tries to motivate her to buy something else or at least to think about it. She reacts and is sure that she is not interested in buying anything else. Again, Antu explains that the order has been placed, as usual, meaning that the shop owners have done their job properly but the traders who come in and out of the camp with the products have difficulties entering the camp. She again accounts for the unavailability of the products: 'traders can't enter the camp now'. As before, she uses the phrase 'enter the camp'. The category 'trader', however, differs from the category 'boat owner', but both groups are restricted in their activities. By using the temporal adverb 'now', Antu shows that this remains a temporary problem. She does not go into the question but reformulates it. The exact reasons why they are not allowed to enter are not talked about; it might not be negotiated because it is a problem residents face on a regular basis. This is a form of remaining silent about certain issues. They do not talk about the reasons and so the situation cannot be exceptional. A sense of normality is preserved: it is assumed that the products will arrive soon. Hence, it is a common assumption that there are restrictions on the movement of boats as an interim phenomenon that will last for a few days and will be over soon. It is not talked about or interpreted as something unusual, it is treated instead as an annoyance. Usually, boats are a reliable transportation system, importing products on time, but there are occasional restrictions which people have to deal with. Even in the worst-case scenarios discussed here, where interlocutors talk about the boats that are not allowed to travel, the border remains open in the talks themselves because the restrictions are discussed as a temporary, situational, short-term phenomenon. The restriction on boat travel is interpreted as a temporary state. The examples show that the ambivalent situation is normalised in daily practice and in people's interpretations of the situation, because people know and rely on their knowledge that this situation is temporally restricted. In people's interactions it remains an exceptional restriction. These are part of camp structures, which are embedded in everyday interactions and interpreted as normal.

INCORPORATING ANOMALY AND AMBIVALENCES

Camp economies are strongly based on the camp's surroundings, such as social networks and family ties, and reliability of mobility beyond the camp and even state borders. Many people are involved in, profit from and maintain economic activities inside and outside the camp including local state officials. Shop owners, for example, make themselves self-reliant and even generate job opportunities for non-camp residents from Myanmar and Thailand. This service is done even though many of these activities are necessarily embedded in a legal grey zone. The structural and legal framework is marked by ambivalence that residents are aware of and deal with. The case of the grocery store clearly shows how shop owners are required to disobey state prohibitions in order to be able to buy products, to leave the camp and conduct their business. Additionally, they are forced to make their shop and their working practices invisible in specific situations such as during Thai military visits. When Thai officials visit the camp and people close their shops and paint a picture of an enclosed and economically poor camp, this becomes part of the public order, which integrates the ambivalent governance and jurisdiction structures into ordinary life. People incorporate the ambivalences into everyday life and find ways of dealing with them. Additionally, in public camp life, working activities and running businesses are not performed as something "illegal" but as something ordinary. This is also possible because of paying tax-like contributions to local state authorities as well as section and camp representatives. In collaboration with others, camp and non-camp residents, as well as state authorities who are involved in these working activities, produce the normality of these specific (ambivalent) camp structures in public camp life. Again, public secrets are established but in this case in collaboration with local state authorities. Based on interactions, it has been shown that the local system for handling and incorporating these ambivalent legal frameworks is normalised by camp residents and non-camp residents alike. Troublesome camp-related situations exist, but camp residents prefer to normalise these situations in everyday conversations. The ambivalent character of camp structures, such as temporary prohibition on mobility that is not complied with, is embedded and normalised in people's interactions and practices. Camp residents tend to keep these ambivalent structures secret and try to avoid talking about them within ordinary working practices. In this way, they perform a normality that creates and develops public camp life. The particularity and exceptionality of the camp situation is normalised by the camp public.

NOTES

1. (Field notes economy, photo: Sola's driving licenses issues by KRC).
2. (Video transcript, DSCF 4306, lines 252–61, economy).
3. Husband.
4. Merchant.
5. (Video transcript, DSCF 4305, economy).
6. Husband of Antu.
7. Merchant.
8. Conversations in the shop are regularly interrupted because customers have questions about products or want to buy things.
9. Camp X is the name of the camp where the merchant lives.
10. Antu's middle daughter.
11. As noted in chapter 3, camp residents and people living along the Thai-Myanmar border still use 'Burma' when referring to their country, despite the official change of name to Myanmar.
12. (Video transcript, DSCF 4306).
13. Neighbour.
14. The conversation between those two people stops and restarts later. Antu is talking with the customer.
15. Again, the conversation between the two people stops and restarts later. Antu is talking with the customer and other people in the shop also start talking.
16. (Video transcript, DSCF 4457, lines 221–37, economy).
17. (Field notes, mobility).
18. (Field notes, economy).

19. (Interview protocol, camp leader 2).

20. (Field notes, economy).

21. (Field notes, economy).

22. (Video transcript, meeting, DSCF 3611, lines 571–73).

23. (Field notes, economy).

24. A small part of the conversation was not audible because a motorbike with a loud motor passed by.

25. (Video transcript, DSCF 4305, economy).

26. (Cf. Video transcript, DSCF 4457).

27. This assumption was discussed with two translators extensively. The term 'entering' is usually not used in the context of villages.

28. (Video transcript, DSCF 4307).

Chapter Seven

Mobility, Architecture and Border Regimes

National regulations in Thailand state that camp residents are not allowed to leave the camp and expatriates as well as visitors are not allowed to enter.[1] Accordingly, the infrastructure surrounding the camps establishes a picture of immobility and closeness. Border objects visible through their white and red markings are positioned at the entrances of every refugee camp along the Thai-Burmese border. Additionally, a barbed-wire fence surrounds all camps. Likewise, aid organisations confirm the picture of the camps as enclosed spaces. The strict border control by Thai officials and the forced immobility of camp residents is depicted as the basis for the strong involvement and support of aid agencies (Thompson 2008, 26ff.). These camp characteristics are confirmed by people's narratives and accounts:

> We are not allowed to leave the camp.[2]
> We are restricted in mobility.[3]
> Maybe you understood this wrong. You have to understand that refugees were never allowed to leave the camps.[4]
> Camps are always closed, and residents are never officially allowed to travel in or out.[5]
> Refugees are not allowed to leave the camps.[6]

These statements represent the way people talk about camp mobility restrictions. What dominates in these perspectives is the narrative of an enclosed character of the camps. Thus, camps are expected to be an area of enclosure and the image of camp residents as not being allowed to travel or to be mobile is maintained through regulations, discourses and oral narratives. These interpretations from different angles and perspectives lead us to expect the camps to be enclosed spaces, which should be also visible through examination of local camp practices. We expect to observe a strict border regime. But the previous chapter already indicated diverse fractures from that perspective. Indeed, differences exist between regulations, discourses, and narratives concerning the closeness of the camps and practices observable in public camp life. This chapter shows that when we observe aspects of camp mobility in more detail, we recognise, that diverse aspects of permeability in this intended confinement are possible. The supposedly enclosed space is not an enclosed space with small openings, but instead seems to be an open space with only some points of closure. In the following, I analyse the complexities of camp mobility, camp borders and how these closed/open borders are negotiated in public camp life.

This chapter is divided into three parts. The first looks at camp checkpoints. At the beginning the checkpoint architecture is described, which highlights the enclosed character of the camps. These static object descriptions are followed by a comprehensive analysis of the incorporation into people's practices. Practices of border guards as well as the ongoing entering and leaving practices of ordinary pedestrians, motorbikes and vehicle drivers are looked at in detail. The second part of this chapter focusses on the camps' public transportation systems. The reader is introduced to how camp residents have accomplished a local public transportation system in collaboration with local host and home state authorities in the borderland area. The third part of this chapter answers the question of what happens when camp residents travel beyond the camp environment in the Thai-Myanmar borderland area. Here, linkages to Western countries and their role in strengthening local systems of mobility come into play.

The considerations made in the first two parts of this chapter are primarily based on video sequences chosen from about five hours of audiovisual data recorded at checkpoints and ports. In addition, field notes, informal conversations and interviews, for example, with state authorities and other audiovisual data outside the camp areas was used. The last part of this chapter make clear that when understanding camps, it is necessary to conduct ethnographic research not only in camps and their direct environments but also beyond. That is why I followed camp residents and their mobility practices and conducted research in the borderland area, around Thai border cities and villages.

ARCHITECTURE: EXCEPTIONALITY AND CLOSENESS

What all camps in Thailand share is the fact that these areas are marked as divergent from other localities. Barbed wires and checkpoints create a picture of entering an exceptional and enclosed zone. While some camps have a lot of checkpoints, such as those located along main roads, camps located in rural areas have only a few. All checkpoints share a similar layout. The very first object that makes the camp zone visible is an entrance sign, which differs from typical village entrance signs in this region, in terms of form and the size, the languages used and the information written on it.[7] The sign is very large, printed in black and white, and presents a Thai emblem. This makes the sign difficult to miss. The information on the sign is given in three languages (Burmese, Thai and English), which leads to the assumption that people are entering a territory where different languages are addressed. By using three languages, the official character of this area becomes apparent and thus marks a boundary. The entrance sign uses a format that mentions not only the name of the locality but also characteristics of the location: 'Camp X Temporary Shelter Area'. With this sign the area is fabricated as a place, which is temporally restricted and characterises certain kinds of housing conditions. The term shelter indicates that people who live in this area are seeking refuge or need to be protected from something. The term 'shelter' also points to a duty to assist. Additionally, the checkpoint is characterised by a red and white infrastructure. Marking objects in these colours suggests managing or limiting access to certain areas by preventing vehicle and pedestrian traffic from accidentally entering a dangerous or different territory. The ordering of these colours let people know that this is an enclosed area where access is regulated, or where a zone begins where one needs to pay attention or exercise caution. The barbed wire, the wooden fence and the red and white gate emphasise and maintain the idea of entering an enclosed space.

Moreover, the way the objects and entities appear allows lengthy temporal continuations to become visible: the objects are not new but have been neglected or ignored by the people who want to produce this space as enclosed or as exceptional; they are dirty, partly broken and have been unprofessionally rebuilt at times. Nevertheless, the posts and the entrance area have been built for long-term use. Additionally, signs with camp rules, in Thai, are positioned in the entrance area. Only the Thai (and Thai-Karen) *Or Sor* members and local Thai-Karen villagers can read Thai. This brings up the question of whom this sign is meant to address. A language boundary is underlined. The use of Thai may highlight that even though exceptional, this is Thai territory. In contrast, the rule sign is headlined 'Camp X Temporary Shelter' to resemble the entrance sign, though it adds 'Special Control Area'. It seems to be important to accentuate, in English, the protection that a specially controlled area may provide. Hence, the sign is not directed at non-Thai-speaking residents or visitors clearly. The rules re-create a stable, orderly and controlled zone, but this contradicts the language used because the rules address visitors and residents alike. The rules state that entry to the zone is restricted and

Chapter Seven

highly regulated; here authority is defined as a spatial zone, documents are necessary, temporal limitations are made and people's behaviour is regulated. Moreover, a small black and white extra sign stating the 'opening hours' supports the assumption that the architecture of the area aims to demonstrate again a controlled and regulated territory. Opening hours are temporal limitations on access to certain territories—again a method that creates an enclosed space or at least a space where access is temporarily impossible.

After entering the gate, passers-by are again confronted with red and white objects and there are characteristic Thai checkpoints signed with 'Checkpoint. The 7th Volunteers Defence Corps Company, XY District'[8] The sign indicates the function of the red and white coloured hut: 'Checkpoint'. Moreover, it references a locality that represents the controlling aspect of entering this territory, also representing the instruments used to put the regulations at the entrance into practice and to realise the signalled control. Also, the sign refers to the name of the local district. Besides the Thai language used on this sign, there are usually national symbols fixed at the hut, the national flag and a poster of the Thai King, highlighting again that we are still in Thai territory.

The described architecture creates a space through the symbols and the languages that we are in an area where international and Thai actors merge. The objects and layout of the entrance area aim to highlight entering an enclosed, controlled and permanently fenced-off zone. These static descriptions on the architecture of the border checkpoint are limited and lack the incorporation of these spatial orders into people's practices. As discussed earlier, objects and infrastructure does not only speak or act for themselves, they do not simply represent social orders but need human actions to become participants of situations (cp. chapter 5. pg. 120). How is this infrastructure used and incorporated in people's practices? Are people controlled and regulated as suggested by the architecture?

ACTIVE NON-REGULATIONS AND CONTROL NEGLIGENCE

Many people are passing the checkpoints. Drivers with vehicles and motorbikes enter and leave the camp area. But there are also border guards stationed at the checkpoints. The following descriptions are based on one particular checkpoint of a camp located in a rural and difficult area to access.

The Border Guards

Two different groups serve as border guards at the checkpoint: the territorial defence volunteer corps, the paramilitary group, or the Thai camp security personnel—called *Or Sor*—and the omnipresent camp security.[9] Members of the *Or Sor*, who are Thai citizens and often also Thai-Karen, are under the authority of the camp commander *Palad*. Some of the *Or Sor* members have been working in the camp for more than twenty years, and most of them speak the same language as camp residents. The *Or Sor* members live at the checkpoint during their stay in the camp and spend two weeks on duty and two weeks off duty. Consequently, relationships between *Or Sor* members and camp residents have been established; some of the *Or Sor* members are even married to residents of the camp. The *Or Sor* members are not always present at the checkpoint; they prefer to stay in their huts, which are located behind the checkpoint in a fenced-off area. The building next to the checkpoint where camp security members reside is always occupied. Camp security observes the goings on at the checkpoint. In contrast to *Or Sor* members, the camp security personnel live in their respective homes within the camp, and the building at the checkpoint serves only as a workplace. A short excursus on the camp security followings because they have an outstanding role for camp orderings.

The camp security is responsible for and takes care of establishing and maintaining security in the camp. The camp security at the border checkpoint consists of section security staff members from different sections of the camp. Formally, staff members are under the jurisdiction of their respective section leader and the security leader. Each section must provide section staff for duty at the camp checkpoints. Security staff members do not only guard the camp entrance but also guard the *stores* and the ration items for the whole night and record visitors from outside the camp who want to stay overnight. Moreover, they are present during all kinds of public events happening in the camp. One security leader and, depending on the size of the section and its population, between five to ten security staff work in one section. There are specific rules for camp security. The existence of exclusive rules for security staff highlights their relevance and extraordinary position among other section staff members.[10] Different comments by residents about security staff paint a positive picture as well as a general acknowledgement of the work of section security. People repeatedly told me the following story:

> When Burmese soldiers attacked the camps it was the Or Sor who ran away, but the camp security stayed and defended the camp.[11]

Section security is nevertheless criticised for drinking too much alcohol and abusing their position. Security staff members do not all wear uniforms or similar clothes. They are not identifiable to visitors. Although Thai policies forbid camp security to wear military clothes, some of them still wear them. But camp security staff do not wear guns or other items in public that underline their specific membership. Their position is not formalised and recognisable to others, but section members know who the section security staff members are in their respective section. Their membership is performed in public:

Or Sor members are not visible through the way they dress; they are particularly visible through the way they behave at the checkpoint and the localities in which they reside. When *Or Sor* members and camp security play cane ball (*chinlone*)[12] near this checkpoint, it is difficult to see the difference between the border guards. Nevertheless, from the perspective of camp residents, the *Or Sor* represent local Thai authorities and camp security represents the authority of camp residents. While relationships, even families, have been established between *Or Sor* and camp residents, the reciprocal perception of belonging and associating with a specific group remains clear. If an *Or Sor* member is married to a camp resident, he remains an *Or Sor* member married to a camp resident. This is even the case when the married *Or Sor* member lives in the camp for years and participates in the resettlement programme. The localities where members of the two groups usually reside while undertaking their duties as border guards is clearly marked: in the fenced area the *Or Sor*, and on the other side the camp security. What practices are performed by the different groups of border guards when ordinary pedestrians and motorbike drivers pass the checkpoints?

Ordinary Pedestrians and Motorbike Drivers: (Un)passing the Checkpoint

The gate at the checkpoint is open. Border guard 1 stands in front of the checkpoint hut. Border guard 2 walks down the stairs in front of the checkpoint.[13] He looks at the three men passing the checkpoint and passes through the gate himself. The men at the gate do not look up at the border guards, do not slow down and look neither towards the checkpoint nor in the direction of the military zone. Border guard 1 does not look at these men either. Then three students pass through the gate (*recognisable by the way they are dressed*); they are watched by border guard 1. The students do not demonstrate (*make visible to each other*) the fact that they are passing a checkpoint, let alone some obstacle; nor do they look back at the border guard.[14]

Following this movement, a woman with two children passes the gate. She tries to pass through from the right side. Other people standing at the checkpoint making small talk prevent her from coming through on the right side. She needs to slow down. That is why she is not able to walk through the way she had intended. However, she does not wait but seems to change her mind in a matter of seconds, going another way. She walks under and through the open gate, not making eye contact with the checkpoint or the border guard. The border guard then leaves the checkpoint.[15]

These two scenes are exemplary for the entrance situation. Residents do not slow down when passing the checkpoint; there is no ritual, such as an exchange of glances between border guards and pedestrians. Border guards do not prevent people from leaving or entering the camp. Rather, it is made visible in people's practices that here is a mutual expectation on the part of border guards and pedestrians that no practical control will be found at the checkpoint. Only sporadically do border guards, mainly camp security not *Or Sor* members, observe people passing the checkpoint. Even after the 'opening hours', pedestrians continue to pass through the checkpoint in the same way that they would walk along a road.[16] Practices that achieve the passing of a boundary or checkpoint are not observable; residents pass a hindrance as a local accomplishment. When observing motorbike drivers, the incorporation of the checkpoint infrastructure into the drivers' practices was also barely observable.[17] The active ignorance of the *Or Sor* when it comes to people passing the checkpoint becomes even more evident. Their behaviour does not correspond with the ordering and visual representation of the border architecture. The motorbike drivers' practices relate to a system of spatial ordering only in the sense that they must pass some obstacle preventing their movement. The motorbike driver lowers his head and is thus able to pass through the gap under the closed gate.[18] Again, there is no exchange of glances, not even a turn of the head, on the part of the motorbike driver or the border guards.[19] Camp residents pass through a very characteristic infrastructure that differs strongly from other environments in and outside the camp. The objects at the checkpoint make this locality appear exceptional, but they do not have much situational relevance for passing. When passengers pass the checkpoint, they do not perform their practices as being associated with the spatial border-crossing arrangement. Practices of passing a checkpoint are not observable, but practices of passing a hindrance are visible. Border guards do not prevent people from leaving or entering the camp but actively ignore the entering or leaving of ordinary camp residents through the checkpoint. The practices of leaving and entering for pedestrians and motorbike drivers demonstrate an active non-regulation by the border guards. Even after the opening hours, pedestrians or motorbike drivers continue to exit and enter the camp and state related border guards do not seem to mind. This is strengthened by the fact that the *Or Sor* does not usually occupy the checkpoint. With that said, do border objects lose their relevance, function and meaning for pedestrians when they pass these objects simply as hindrances?

People's practices at the checkpoint also make different membership categories visible, in their appearance as well as in their spatial positioning: border guards sit or stand at the checkpoint in an enclosed area; participants pass the checkpoint at a specific point. Through the ways in which they behave they make visible to one another that they are different members of the checkpoint situation. Memberships are performed: border guards are positioned in specific localities and behave in a particular manner. This is the same for people passing the checkpoint: they know where to go and how to pass the checkpoint in a normal manner. Pedestrians hardly notice the checkpoint, while the camp security occasionally see, recognise and observe the passing people. The border guards' presence and behaviour (sometimes observing passing pedestrians) make the idea of a checkpoint/boundary real. The presence of border guards (even though they are not strictly observing people all the time) creates the experience not of passing into a village but of passing into a special zone. Although state-related border guards do not observe the checkpoint systematically, camp-related border guards do. The scenery and the object arrangements support the experience of passing a checkpoint. Seeing or looking at the objects when passing the checkpoint makes people aware that they are entering or leaving a fenced zone, which is special and different from other localities. They see the infrastructure, the objects and how other people deal with the border checkpoint, such as the border guard. Although it does not become relevant in their own practice of passing the checkpoint, they are able to see others' practices regarding the objects. They observe, for example, how the checkpoint situation changes when the military from Bangkok is present. During their visit, the checkpoint is closed and the *Or Sor* practice stricter border control.[20] Pedestrians also observe how vehicles pass through the gate. Jeep drivers must stop at the gate and register themselves in a book that is positioned on a table in the checkpoint hut.

Self-Registration of Jeep Drivers Passing the Checkpoint[21]

In what follows, five scenes are introduced from one video. This specific part of the video lasts around fifteen minutes and shows the different behaviour of Jeep drivers in passing the checkpoint, presented here in chronological order. After describing the single scenes, some detailed observations of the scenes are presented:

Scene 1: Registration and Replacement of Camp Security

The checkpoint is not occupied. An INGO (*Malteser International*) Jeep, recognisable by a sign on the vehicle, arrives at the gate and stops. Driver 1 leaves the car and walks up the stairs into the checkpoint hut. Simultaneously, a camp security member leaves the (*camp security*) building next to the checkpoint, and stands next to the checkpoint, turning his eyes towards the street while the driver finishes his registration, waiting to open the gate. Driver 1, who is just in front of the checkpoint, registers himself in a book on the table in the checkpoint hut. Then an Or Sor member walks down the stairs towards the checkpoint hut. He must have heard the Jeep arriving. The man from the security building returns to the building he came from (*right side*). In the meantime, five pedestrians aim to pass the checkpoint. They slow down, almost to a standstill, and observe the checkpoint scene closely because another Jeep has arrived in front of the gate. Before the Or Sor is able to arrive at the checkpoint hut, driver 1, who has already registered something in the book at the checkpoint, walks down the stairs without looking at the Or Sor. Then the soldier steps in front of the checkpoint hut and looks at his watch. He turns around and positions his body in a way that allows him to pull the line to open the gate. In the meantime, driver 2 leaves his car. Again, two women are passing the gate and take notice of the scene. The Or Sor member is opening the gate and another vehicle arrives at the gate. Driver 2 waits until the Jeep passes through the gate.

Scene 2: Self-Registration and Passing

Another vehicle arrives and driver 3, with a white t-shirt, pushes to the front. The drivers walk up the stairs to the checkpoint together, silently. Driver 3 registers something and the Or Sor examines what he has written from inside the small building. Subsequently, the following people pass through the gate: a woman carrying a baby on her back, a woman carrying a basket on her back with green leaves and holding a small child by the hand, a man with two large bags and another woman with a basket filled with products from the jungle on her back. Driver 3 walks down the stairs and driver 2 begins to register himself in the book. Driver 2 looks at the car, probably in order to write down the license plate number (*which the drivers need to register in the book*). Then, another NGO (*non-governmental organisation*) Jeep (*driver 3*) passes through the open gate. Driver 2 and the soldier talk for a while, and driver 2 returns to his car. He opens the window and laughs in my direction. The Jeep passes through the gate, and the soldier begins to close it behind him.

Scene 3: Gate Closings

While the Or Sor is closing the gate, a motorbike passes through the gate and the soldier slows down his efforts to close it. After the bike has passed through, the Or Sor member finally closes the gate. He remains standing in the checkpoint hut. Another motorbike as well as a pedestrian pass through the gate. One minute after the cars have left, the Or Sor leaves the checkpoint hut, walking up the stairs to the huts where the other Or Sor members reside, even though another Jeep driver is arriving at the gate.

Scene 4: Active Unattendance

Even though another Malteser International NGO vehicle arrives, which is audible to the Or Sor, he does not return to the checkpoint hut but continues to walk up the stairs. The driver leaves his car, registers something in the book. He returns to the car, but no one opens the gate. The driver waits and after a minute a security member goes to the checkpoint hut and opens the gate. The car driver enters the camp and the camp security member closes the gate again. The camp security member then returns to his post in the building, not staying at the checkpoint.

Scene 5: 'Illegal' Practices at the Checkpoint

After a while another Jeep (*from Japanese NGO Jichiro Osaka, visible through signage on the car*) arrives at the gate. Two (*Karen*) women exit the back of the Jeep, carrying large baskets filled with green leaves and other natural products from the jungle used for the roofs in the camp. The two women help each other but also take their time in unloading the heavy baskets. This time, one of the car passengers (*not the driver*) approaches the checkpoint and registers himself in the book. The two women who rode in the back of the Jeep pass the vehicle and look at the driver, who kindly moves his head and looks at each woman (*they are thanking the driver for taking them to the camp*). The two women separately pass the gate and walk into the camp. The men, who registered themselves, now look towards the camp security building. No one seems to open the gate. Then, someone emerges from the (*security*) building, opens the gate and the Jeep passes through, after which he closes the gate again.

All the scenes show how drivers register themselves in a book at the checkpoint and provide relevant information when entering and leaving the camp zone. Border guards do not perform this task. They document date and time of arrival, car registration number, name of the NGO and purpose of stay. There are no instances of aid agency drivers failing to register in the book. There are very routinised mutual expectations: border guards expect drivers to register in the book and drivers expect border guards to open the gate. Drivers register in the book but only occasionally do border guards check what is written in the books. The documentation procedure for aid agencies represents Thai national policy restricting and controlling aid agencies to be present at the camps.

Scenes 1 and 4 highlight the relationship between soldiers and camp security and the differences between these two groups. As noted, the camp security is omnipresent at the checkpoint and authorised to open and close the gate. The *Or Sor* members are not present at the checkpoint itself the whole time. Scene 4 shows that *Or Sor* members are not present at the checkpoint hut and do not control or observe the checkpoint hut all the time. Occasionally they perform their presence. When the *Or Sor* members arrive at the checkpoint hut, camp security gives up their authority over the gate. Camp security members do not stay in the checkpoint hut itself but remain in the camp security building. They only go to the hut in order to open and close the gate. In this way, border guards perform a clear hierarchy and power relationship. Scene three confirms the assumption made earlier: *Or Sor* members show no interest and do not actively control, regulate or prevent passing motorbikes from leaving the camp. They are not checked or controlled; the *Or Sor* in this scene even slows down the activity of closing the gate so that the motorbike driver is able to pass through. Scenes 1 and 3 show how pedestrians observe the practices of drivers who must register at the checkpoint hut. Although pedestrians are not involved in checkpoint practices, such as recording themselves when passing the gate, they observe that Jeep drivers must perform this task. This makes them aware of the fact that this space is different from entering villages or towns and makes them aware that they are living in an exceptional territory.

The last scene introduced here is key, because activities that are officially not allowed are even conducted in front of the checkpoint where border guards are present. Activities and practices that are officially not allowed for aid agency drivers, such as giving camp residents rides to the camp,[22] and camp residents, such as collecting material from the jungle and using this to repair the huts or maybe even selling these natural goods,[23] are openly practiced where state officials are stationed. In this way, local state officials become part of maintaining public camp secrets and local camp orders.

But now there are also Jeep drivers who do not carry out the practices described earlier. Thai vendors who sell food in the camp and pass the checkpoint do not register in the book at all. Instead, people who enter the camp with Jeeps to conduct their business must pay a fee to the *Or Sor*. Villagers who pass through the camps in order to reach their homes do not register. These people are much more strongly bound to the very local and situational system of camp orders. Their practices of entering and leaving are part of local arrangements and negotiations, while the vehicles of aid agencies are not, or only partly, dependent on these local negotiations or arrangements. Vehicles belonging to international aid agencies are covered by international policies and negotiations that lay beyond the local arrangements.

BORDER COMPLEXITIES BETWEEN
ARCHITECTURE AND PRACTICES

The camp is expected to be an area of enclosure and objects are stationed at the camp checkpoint to communicate this. The spatial arrangement of this checkpoint creates an enclosed space and the layout anticipates that border guards will carry out strict controlling practices when people are passing the checkpoint. The ordering of the locality is an arrangement that anticipates practices of passing a boundary point such as slowing down to a walking pace, checking people, queuing and waiting practices, controlling documents, exchange of glances between border guards and pedestrians, and registration. Even though border objects and the architecture of the checkpoint communicate strict control we see a negligent usage and incorporation of the infrastructure. The border negligence corresponds with the control of pedestrians passing the checkpoint. Pedestrians or people who come by motorbike are independent of control measures and observational practices. The passing of retailers, motorbike drivers and pedestrians is characterised by non-control and indifference on the part of the border guards. The hindrances are not border guards but the border markings as objects. Strong routines are observable in passing through the gate, which is treated as a hindrance rather than as a border crossing. Moreover, the security aspect becomes blurred in the process with a low level of control as the result. Soldiers do not rely on or expect interruptions; they do not expect any disturbances. At the same time, the people leaving or entering the camp do not expect to be stopped at the checkpoint. Border guards do not actively control pedestrians, though they seem to observe their movements occasionally. Border-passing practices are only partially implemented; the camp and its closed characteristics are not realised. Diverse aspects of permeability in this intended confinement are possible. This is the case because passing the checkpoint is primarily part of local regulations and underlies active non-regulations.

Still, the architecture of the camp borders and checkpoints are present and visible to pedestrians and motorbike drivers alike. The border negligence and carelessness could be given up any time and control could be reactivated. Potentially, the arrangement could be changed and people could be forced to adapt their gate-passing practices to fit this arrangement. This is put into practice when the Bangkok military visits the camp. As discussed in the previous chapter, during this time a temporary total institution is performed. The presence of the border guards further reinforces that this zone is not representative of a normalcy. Moreover, the entrance continues to demonstrate that the camp is an exceptional space. For example, this space is reproduced and maintained by the presence and the working activities of the border guards. Jeep drivers, specifically drivers from aid agencies, must register at the checkpoint and wait until the border guards open the gate. Control measures and regulations are created and made visible to aid agencies and practiced by aid agency drivers; aid agencies are thus the target group for these control measures, and they cannot withdraw from this system. Members of this group are forced to register. Control is created in and through the interplay of signing into the books and the border guards opening the gate—though these practices are again very much routine, border guards do not check individual Jeep drivers or what they write in the book, and pedestrians are able to observe these 'border passing' practices. In the following section, comparable non-controlling practices are introduced in the context of the camp's public transportation system.

THE PUBLIC CAMP TRANSPORTATION SYSTEM

More than thirty thousand camp residents live in the area where main research has been conducted and no public transportation system is available. This contrasts to Thailand's otherwise very reasonable public transportation system but fits the regulations of Thai authorities—camp residents are not allowed to travel.[24] People who come from Myanmar or Thailand and do not belong to state or aid agencies and want to reach or leave the camps use boats as a means of transportation. Due to the lack of transportation alternatives, camp residents established a camp public transportation system. There is a camp boat leader responsible for controlling and organising the transportation system, resolving conflicts between boat drivers and local Thai authorities. No formal documentation exists to explicate the rules for boat owners and drivers in the camp, but the boat leader explained some rules and the system.

There is a rule, for example, that only boat owners can drive their registered boats. Information about official national or district regulations concerning these boat activities is not available, but the boat leader clarified that a local admission board holds annual meetings at which boat owners are able to register. Although the boat leader had no knowledge about the formal regulations concerning who and when people are awarded these official state boat driving licence, boat owners apply to the board for a licence, and if they are accepted and registered, they are allowed to transport passengers and products along the borderland river.[25] Local boat licences are not restricted to Thai residency and do not require camp registrations. Camp residents can be boat owners and drivers whether they are registered or unregistered camp residents. This system contrasts to regulations for using other vehicles in the camps such as motorbikes and Jeeps. State officials prohibit residents from owning motorbikes and Jeeps; licences are issued only by camp representative organisations which are applicable only in the camp itself and its near surroundings. To the disappointment of state authorities, these boat registration rules are not always followed, which regularly leads to conflicts. According to the boat leader, boat drivers who have not registered with the local board are able to pay additional fees to the *Or Sor*, 'so that they are able to buy some curry'.[26] Apart from being registered with the local admission board, the boat drivers must register with the camp security and the boat leader, who oversees organising the public transportation system in the camp. Boat drivers who are not registered with the admission board are still 'registered' with the boat leader. Otherwise, these boat drivers are not able to leave camp ports.

Another rule the leader explicated is that all boats must carry a Thai flag because the border area was and remains a conflict zone for Burmese and Karen soldiers. These flags prohibit Burmese soldiers from attacking civilian passengers, such as Thai villagers, that also travel by boats in this area, and camp residents. The leader also explained how he organises the public transportation system in order to make it reliable for passengers. There are forty-seven boats registered with the camp boat leader (thirty-two registered small boats and fifteen registered big boats[27]). The drivers and owners of the boats are mostly camp residents. There are only few non-camp registered boats that regularly transport goods and passengers through this camp part of the river. Two boat drivers have Thai registrations, but most are camp residents that hold different administrative statuses.

The boat leader follows a system, which he calls the 'round system', based on two lists—one for small boats and another one for big boats. These lists show whose turn it is to go to Thai villages near the camp.[28] Thus, boat drivers are not allowed to take passengers whenever and wherever they want. This system is like a queuing system, institutionalised through a document that is updated from time to time, from which boat drivers may quit or additional boat drivers may be added. The name of the first list refers to the smaller boats that usually go to villages nearby—every driver who owns a small boat must wait his turn to be allowed to take passengers to this destination. The second document lists the names of the drivers with big boats that are allowed to go to a Thai town located on a Thai main road, which is about a three-hour drive away. Moreover, the boat leader makes sure that boats do not go to far away destinations alone, especially during the rainy season when the river becomes wider and very strong. This is for safety reasons: if a boat capsizes, other boat drivers and passengers are then able to help quickly.[29] The leader explained that he does not make exceptions on these rules and the queuing system, as the previous boat leader did, because this causes major conflicts among boat owners. With this system, everyone can go regularly and at equal opportunity. Apart from this ordered system, boat drivers are free to go to the camp nearby as well as to smaller villages very nearby the camps at any time—though usually owners of big boats do not do so. Additionally, prices for destinations are fixed and defined by the boat leader, meaning that every boat owner/driver gets the same amount and every passenger pays the same fee for a boat ride.

The boat leader observes and controls the boat owners and drivers and makes sure that they behave according to the transportation system's rules and regulations. In case of rule breaking, he gives warnings to drivers, does not allow them to travel by boat for specific timeframes or revokes the licences issued by local state authorities. As the boat leader's house is located near the river, he oversees the ports and the river. Besides that, his house is located near the second checkpoint and opposite the camp leader's house—they keep in touch with one another regularly. The boat leader also has a small shop at his home, selling tea and betel nut, where regular formal and informal meetings among boat drivers take place. He also organises and conducts meetings with local district authorities. The boat leader stated that when boat drivers do not behave properly it is him who gets in trouble with state and camp authorities. In case of major conflicts, he conducts meetings with the camp security and, if there is a serious problem, even with the camp leader and the *Palad*.

The checkpoint at which border guards control the passing of boats is located near the river built on a small hill which allows them to easily oversee the river and observe boats arriving at and leaving from the camp area. The boat drivers are controlled at the checkpoint mainly by the camp security members but *Or Sor* members are present too. How exactly these controlling practices are conducted is explicated in the following.

> Like every morning around 8 a.m. (*not Sundays*), a cluster of boats leaves the camp in order to go to XY—a bigger Thai-Karen village located around a two-hour boat ride from the camp. Camp residents or visitors are picked up by boat drivers at the small ports located in the camp. Before actually leaving the camp area, the cluster of boats has to stop at a small port near the checkpoint. The woman in front of me smiles and says that she is not afraid to travel because I am traveling with her. I wonder about it and think, do we have to be afraid? The boat driver climbs up the mountain to get to the checkpoint occupied by camp security and Or Sor. Border guards look at the papers of some boat drivers but not all. Similar to Jeep drivers, the boat drivers have to register in a book, no individual person is employed to document their identification and observe them, but drivers are responsible for registering their respective vehicles. Passengers do not climb up the mountain and show their documents or identification, and the luggage is not controlled either. The passengers and boats stay on the river and border guards do not come down to the river to see who is traveling and

how much luggage is being transported with the boats. Finally, the individual
boat drivers come back down to their boats. Some boats already start leaving.[30]

These observations confirm considerations made earlier: border guards are
not interested in individual camp residents or visitors. They expect the boat
drivers to come to the checkpoint and to register themselves. Passengers on
the boats do not need to show identification or prove that they have permission to leave the camp; they do not even have to show their faces. Boat drivers climb up the hill to go to the checkpoint. Again, border guards are not
interested in pedestrians but self-registration by drivers is compulsory. The
difference to the other checkpoint we examined is that border guards know,
and further, it is even documented, that camp residents regularly leave and
enter the camp area and are owners of boats. This re-emphasises the argument
made earlier: a locally established system makes mobility opportunities possible that lay beyond national regulation and is even applicable beyond the
camp area, as explicated in the next scene:

> Finally, our boat begins to drive along the river together with another boat.
> Everyone on the boat is freezing and we all get wet. On the way to our main des-
> tination (*the bigger Thai village*) we stop several times—usually we are never
> alone, another boat carrying camp residents or visitors is always nearby. We
> stop at checkpoints where Karen and Thai soldiers are based. Our driver pays
> some people and he also stops to buy beer. We also stop at small ports where
> the boat driver pays Burmese soldiers. The Burmese soldiers do not look at us.
> They do not even recognise me. The money transfer is done in a very calm and
> routine way, silently, with no verbal communication [31]

The 'tax-like contributions' paid to diverse local authorities on both the Thai
and Burmese sides of the river makes clear that the public transportation
system is based on locally established arrangements with different actors
present at the riverside. All boat drivers must pay additional authorities
(Burmese and Thai soldiers) on the way to the bigger Thai towns because the
river is located at the state border of Myanmar and Thailand. Camp residents
establish—in collaboration with the *Or Sor*, district officers and Burmese
soldiers, who profit from this system as well—a reliable public transportation system in the Thai-Burmese borderland area. These arrangements are
normalised practices, routines performed without question. The transfer of
money is done in a very calm and routine manner, almost silently. Boat drivers always pay fees at the same stop. These kinds of fees are fixed—all boat
drivers pay the same amount of money. No paperwork is conducted—only
fees are collected. These 'tax-like contributions' are included in the price of
the boat trip that passengers pay to boat drivers. These observations illuminate the extent to which these fees are useful for camp residents and for sta-

bilising camp orders. If local authorities were to follow national regulations, camp residents would not have this possibility for mobility or to transfer goods and food items by themselves to the camp area. The public transportation system described here would simply not exist. Still, the boat leader did not want to talk about money transfers in detail and ignored questions regarding these issues. This highlights the ambivalent character of camp structure and another public camp secret that is established beyond the camp area. Although officials, such as the boat leader, may not talk about these fees, every boat driver knows about them and boat passengers observe this 'fee practice.' This locally established system gives people the opportunity to be mobile and to transport food items and other goods even if they do not have a Jeep and cannot pass Thai checkpoints on the roads. The paying of fees gives local authorities a reason to accept these practices.

Moreover, occasional interruptions to these mobilities occur. According to the boat leader, he gets information about travel prohibitions from the camp security or the camp leader. The boat leader then gives the information to the boat owners. According to the boat leader, these restrictions can be for safety or political reasons. This was another issue he did not want to discuss. The specific reasons behind the prohibitions are also not known among residents. 'Today it is not the best day to travel, you know?',[32] was a regular comment and an answer to the question of why boats were not travelling. The following scene confirms this assumption:

> I am waiting at the port together with a family and a man. We are waiting at the small port and expect the boats to leave soon. The family is planning to travel to a smaller village nearby. The father of the family asks the boat driver: Are you going now? The boat driver does not answer his question. But the man who is standing just next to the boat driver answers: The Or Sor told him not to go because today is not a good day. He said he will go tomorrow. They said no one will go today.[33]

Pretending not to hear the question might be a method of showing the unwillingness of going into the topic. The response of the man who is standing at the port shows that the father does not expect a response from the boat driver and, further, that the exact reasons for not travelling are not communicated but circumscriptions are used by the man ('not a good day'). Like the interactions in the grocery store discussed in the previous chapter, the exact reasons are not talked about or concealed, but other methods are used to deal with the question and the topic in an appropriate way. This short interaction shows that the problem of other authorities occasionally destroying or interrupting the normal, running order is part of the locally established system and that this is concealed by circumscriptions.

In sum, a locally accomplished system is established because camp residents need to travel and do travel back to Myanmar or to other Thai regions for various reasons. The public transportation system is properly organised: there is a responsible person (boat leader), and boat drivers. There is a fixed system that makes it clear whose turn it is. The organisational character of the system not only refers to the boat drivers but to the passengers too. The prices are transparent, and everyone knows exactly how much the ride costs. There is a quite reliable fixed schedule regarding when and where the boats will leave the camp. The system highlights the informal regulations that we meet in camp constellations time and again. National policies make clear that camp residents are not allowed to travel, but camp residents—in collaboration with authorities in this local context—have established a public camp transportation system.

LOCAL AND SITUATIONAL STATE BORDER REGIMES

Around the camp there is an undeniable buffer zone where there are no checkpoints and where camp residents can move easily without major restrictions or fear of detention. They can move and work within this buffer zone—but what happens beyond this area? Are camp residents able to travel or to be mobile beyond these localities in their host country? Along the Thai–Myanmar border, mobile and fixed checkpoints are positioned on the main roads to communicate that border control is carried out and it is also realised in practise. When public transportation vehicles, which camp residents regularly use, stop at these checkpoints, people who look Burmese are usually asked to show their papers. In case people have no papers or expired documents they have to leave the car, go to the checkpoint huts and pay a fee to the checkpoint guards before the vehicle can travel any further. If they cannot pay a fine to the border guards, they are often, though not always, detained for some days or weeks in a nearby town or are sent back across the border to Myanmar. In case they are detained, they must pay fees to be allowed to leave the premises. For those sent to the border to Myanmar territory, people usually return to Thailand immediately.[34] Some drivers also stop before these checkpoints, and people without documents walk alongside the jungle, while the driver passes the checkpoint. Afterwards, he picks up the passengers again, who pay a fee in exchange for this service.[35] In a border town where a lot of Burmese people live, this situation can be observed regularly as there are many checkpoints at the main roads and many Burmese-looking people without proper documents. In this context, it needs to be emphasised that the checkpoint situation beyond the camp area, in the borderlands in Thailand, in general, is not only problematic for camp residents (Bochmann 2017b). It is problematic for a variety of people without proper documents, such as the millions of Burmese people who live and work in Thailand or people who belong to the ethnic minorities living in the borderland areas. It is estimated that half a million unrecognised people from Myanmar, working in Thailand, would qualify for refugee status (Vungsiriphisal et al. 2011, 12). 'Illegal' human mobility, immigration and working practices are a mass phenomenon in the Thai-Myanmar borderlands that is partly attributable to the very strong historical, economic, political and social linkages that cannot simply be destroyed by national legal acts (Lang 2002, 125ff.). Local employers, governments and police officials make an ambiguous "illegal" mobility system possible (see Brees 2008, 380ff.). The aspect of mobility indicates how ambivalent state regulations can be. The undocumented status of Burmese people working in border towns and villages is a phenomenon that people and local Thai officials deal with daily. The difficulties (Human Rights Watch 2012) and opportunities that go along with working with undocumented status in Thailand encourage camp residents to stay with refugee status or not, but also attract many other people from Myanmar. While Lang argues that Thai policies towards refugees can be characterised by a 'flexibility and overall adherence to the norms of refugee protection' (2002, 101), Brees argues for the necessity of the Thai government changing its policies to legalise and thus regulate refugee labour.

There are opportunities for camp residents to receive white registration cards from district authorities under specific requirements. People with these documents are only allowed to move within specific districts but need to ask for additional permission and documents to move in other districts. There are cases where former camp residents who settled in Thai villages or towns in the borderland areas were able to receive these registration cards two to three times. Then these people were even able to gain Thai citizenship and settled down in Thai villages as Thai-Karen people.[36] But the Thai registration systems are complex and are also partly an area of responsibility of district authorities. Moreover, policies and opportunities regarding the registration procedures change. The inconsistency and opaqueness of these policies becomes more apparent when looking at the opportunities that camp residents have had in becoming regular and legal migrant workers. In one example, camp representatives were even concerned about the prospects of 'their' populations. In a KRC report it is stated that:

> This month, the Thai Government is allowing all illegal migrants to be registered and have legal work permits. This may have some bearing on the refugees. Some camps' people may want to become legal migrant workers instead of being registered refugees. (September 2001, 4)

In contrast to other (forced) migrants, camp residents can also apply for temporary travel documents. According to national regulations, camp residents are not allowed to leave the camp but there are a few, formally regulated, exceptions. In these cases, residents need to apply for travel documents by the district officers. These documents enable residents to legally pass the checkpoints found on the main roads. As camp residents are not allowed to leave the camps, refugee representative organisations who have offices outside the camps are involved in these bureaucratic procedures. The background on this practice is the following: the regulations given by the MOI allow local Thai camp commanders (*Palad*) to provide travel documents, locally called 'camp passes', to displaced persons. These travel documents grant tolerated 'displaced persons' a temporary stay in Thailand with the option to travel more freely. In an Order of the Royal Thai Police, which is one of the few documents accessible to the public regulating the travel of camp residents, it is stated that 'temporary shelter' residents are allowed to leave the camps for educational reasons, missionary reasons, to study Buddhism, occupational training and procedures in the context of resettlement.[37] In practice, KRC staff produce these camp passes, which are signed by the *Palad* or another representative of the district. Applications for these documents are conducted outside the camps, at KRC and district offices. While aid agencies claim that 'new arrivals' or non-registered refugees do not get permission to leave the camps (TBC 2013 Jan-Jun, 65), the camp passes and documents encountered during field research confirm that local authorities do not draw distinctions between unregistered and registered camp residents and issue camp passes to 'new arrivals' or non-registered camp populations. This is a systematic phenomenon and is not only done in exceptional cases.[38] Mostly camp passes are issued only to individuals. But when ceremonies, such as weddings or funerals, are celebrated outside the camp, usually not only individuals but a lot of people and families travel together. That is why it became a common practice to not issue individual camp passes but to issue camp pass lists. The following observations, conducted in the context of a wedding, show characteristics of the application processes of these documents. The wedding couple were ex-camp residents who resettled to the United states years ago and now have US citizenship.[39] They invited many relatives and friends from Myanmar and Thailand, and from different camps. The wedding planners, also ex-camp residents but with Thai citizenship, were taking care of the transportation of guests and the application for the camp passes. The following scene took place after the wedding reception:

> One Jeep driver did not want to leave because the documents for his passengers were not correct. A discussion started about the drivers' camp pass list between the driver, the camp residents and the wedding planners. There were fewer

people on the list than there were in the van because some of them attended the wedding spontaneously and thus, had not applied for camp passes beforehand.[40] Finally, one of the wedding planners decided to go to the local district officer and to the KRC and to register the people who were not on the list. After an hour she came back with a new camp pass list. The wedding organisers called the individual names of guests who should have been on the list, making sure that every person on the paper was in the jeep to go back to the respective camp. But again, a discussion started. Now they were discussing the children that were not recorded on the document but were in the van. The Jeep driver and the wedding planners (*all non-camp residents*) argued that the children should be on the list, but passengers (*camp residents*) argued that this would not be necessary. Finally, the car left with a camp list that did not document the children on board.[41]

The wedding planners felt responsible, and so arranged and paid for the documents for camp residents attending the wedding. The local district officer, together with the locally responsible KRC members, enable and create a bureaucratic system on a local level, thus making it possible for all camp residents to leave the camp, and to move within this respective district on a temporary basis. It was not only registered refugees that received these camp passes, allowing them to legally move within the district. It was documented on the camp pass list that half of the group were not registered as refugees— so called n/a (new arrivals) as documented in the paper. New arrivals are not recoded by UNHRC or Thai authorities but are registered with the local camp system and are partly included in the feeding figures of the TBC. According to aid agency staff,[42] these people are not allowed to apply for a camp pass but they do nevertheless—and they get camp passes, giving them legal permission by local state officials to move within the district territory. The local bureaucratic system established between KRC members and local district authorities is also a practical reaction to the camp circumstances of plural registration or even non-registration. Even without proper documents (UN or host-state registrations) camp residents are able to apply for camp passes, which allows them to legally move within the district. Local arrangements between district officers and KRC officers make it possible for non-registered camp residents to apply for camp passes and to be safe at the checkpoints.

The previous considerations show that it is possible for camp residents to travel within Thailand, albeit on a temporary basis. On the other hand, they show that movement of camp residents without papers could potentially become problematic, regulations are untransparent and children have a status that can be locally negotiated with border guards. The wedding planners, for example, are worried about their guests. They do not want their guest to get in trouble, they want to make sure that they travel safely, but in the end, they accept the claims of camp residents that children are safe even without documents. It has been shown that the regulations about these camp passes are not transparent; should children be on the list or not? The observed scenes, as well as the documents, show that only people over nineteen years of age are on the lists. Children or young people under nineteen were not categorised as people who need to be checked or that need documents. But the scenes point to other phenomena as well. Namely that resettled ex-camp residents maintain and even strengthen this local system.

These observations, as well as the camp's public transportation system and the mobility restrictions and opportunities at the borderland area, demonstrate that camp mobility strongly determines camp orders. A refugee camp is not a microcosm for intensive modes of governing and restrictions on the part of state bodies or aid agencies. The camp is under the competence of local arrangements and systems. Locally established mobility rules may change occasionally but are quite stable and reliable for camp residents. The practice of passing a camp checkpoint paints a picture of the camp as an open space with some situational closings. Still, camp residents notice border architectures and observe Jeep drivers and border guards' practices, which maintains the idea that people are living in, and entering or leaving, an enclosed space. At the same time, border guards practice active non-regulations and support ordinary pedestrians in passing the gate as a simple hindrance. The practices at the port confirm that local systems of mobility are created that make genuine mobility in this apparent confinement possible. Even though boat drivers as well as their passengers are occasionally restricted in this system, these restrictions are normalised in peoples' practices. Usually, a reliable public transportation system exists that creates and stabilises camp mobility orders and makes opportunities such as opening a grocery store in the camp possible. The 'tax-like contributions' paid by boat drivers to local authorities at the state borders is reliable as well—it is done in a very routine and normalised fashion. Thus, camp borders and state borders are situational and locally accomplished.

The weak presence of the central state does not show off chaotic circumstances or an unordered state border situation. Rather, it makes a situational and locally accomplished border regime at checkpoints possible, which stabilises and maintains the order of the camp. Checkpoints and regulations beyond the camp environment show that there are restrictions but also that there are alternative ways and local systems for dealing with borders. Locally established bureaucratic systems make it possible for camp residents with unclear statuses to pass checkpoints without being imprisoned or sent to the other side of the border. Ceremonies, such as weddings celebrated by former camp residents who resettled and hold Western citizenship, also point to the transnational linkages of camp orders and this local system. These people have the money to pay for camp passes for a lot of people and in this way stabilise and strengthen this system. But it is important to notice that there are three important circumstances under which these characteristic practices take place. First, there are strong historical and political linkages that exist in the Thai-Burmese borderland area. Local state authorities from Myanmar and Thailand know each other and cooperate. These serve as a basis for building up such a local mobility system. Second, the scenes described take place in peripheral localities and in border situations where the camp and its outside are interlinked. Third, 'illegal' human mobilities is a mass phenomenon in Thailand that people deal with on a daily basis, particularly in border towns and areas. Still, these findings confirm arguments made in contemporary state border studies where scholars continuously refer to and emphasise the permeability of state borders (Newmann 2003, 15; Bochmann 2020).

NOTES

1. Though, host state guidelines allow exceptions. These are explicated subsequently.
2. (Field notes, talk with camp residents 3).
3. (Field notes, talk with ex-camp resident who will resettle in 2014 to the US, as well as her family members).
4. (Email response from an NGO worker when asked in an e-mail whether it is more difficult for camp residents to travel because of the political change in Thailand in 2014).
5. (Interview protocol, aid agency 3).
6. (Interview protocol, CBO 1).
7. (Poster, IMG 9700).
8. (Poster, DSCF 3887).
9. In the past, Thai police staff members were also present at the camp checkpoint, but not much has changed since these staff members left the checkpoint locality.
10. (Poster, DSCF 2447).
11. (Field notes, section).
12. Chinlone is a popular, non-competitive sport in Myanmar.
13. At a later stage it is described how these two men show that they are border guards.
14. (Video, DSCF 3887, mobility).
15. (Video, DSCF 3887, mobility).
16. (Video, DSCF 3890, mobility).
17. (Video, DSCF 3892, mobility).
18. (Video, DSCF 3892, mobility).
19. (Video, DSCF 3892, mobility).

20. I was not able to observe the situation at the checkpoint when military from Bangkok were visiting the camp but was told by camp residents that the checkpoint would be difficult to pass on these specific days.

21. (Video, DSCF 4093, mobility).

22. Usually, international aid agencies are asked not to take camp residents or other people to the camp. The UNHCR, TBC and bigger aid agencies are especially strict on this policy. Smaller NGOs do not follow these rules.

23. This is also observable in scene 2. This rule is mentioned in section meetings regularly and discussed in chapter 4.

24. There are camps in Thailand that are easily accessible through the public transportation system such as Mae La Camp. There are even motorbike taxi drivers, bringing people from one section to the other at the main road along the Thai-Burmese border.

25. During the section meeting introduced in chapter 3, section staff members point out the rule that boat drivers have to register with state officials.

26. (Interview protocol, boat leader).

27. A big boat costs around fifty thousand to one hundred thousand baht, and a small boat costs around thirty thousand to forty thousand baht.

28. (DSCF 5688, 5689).

29. (Interview protocol, boat leader).

30. (Field notes, mobility).

31. (Field notes, mobility).

32. (Field notes, mobility).

33. (Video, DSCF 4472, mobility).

34. (Interview 3, field notes borderland mobility). Other studies confirm this practice (see Jackson and Associates 2012, 16).

35. (Field notes, borderland mobility).

36. I was invited to weddings of former camp residents, now US citizens, organised by former camp residents who are now Thai citizens. In addition, I talked to several people in Mae Sot, Sangklaburi, Chiang Mai and in smaller Thai villages located around the camps who originate from the borderlands in Myanmar and who gained Thai citizenship. All these people fled Burma in the 1980s and the 1990s.

37. (Order of the Royal Thai Police, No. 777/2551).

38. (Photo, camp pass list).

39. It is not an unusual practice that resettled ex-camp residents marry in Thailand.

40. (Field notes, mobility).

41. (Video, DSCF 3432, mobility).

42. (Interview protocol, aid agency 2).

Chapter Eight

The Power of Microstructures in Camp Systems

This study frames refugee camps as 'multiply inflected, contradictory spaces' (Peteet 2005, 31), where institutional and structural constraints, human creativity and micro-processes intersect. While some camp studies tend to highlight structural constraints by an external camp regime, this work puts emphasis on the human creativity and micro-processes, in which structural constraints are made visible. This book answers the research questions of how people deal with living in long-term, but supposedly temporary and precarious, spaces with plural governance and legal structures by taking public camp life, situations and interactions as well as the concept of microstructures at centre stage. It highlights that public camp life is organised and established according to powerful microstructures that are part of camp governance structures. These microstructures can be easily overlooked because they are rooted in very local events and interactions and are characterised by the necessity of being maintained in situational dynamics and by its non-documentation. But these microstructures provide stability, durability and reliability and entail forms of resistance, autonomy and sovereignty towards other camp structures. Thus, social orders and stability are achieved within exceptional spaces with the help of microstructures that local actors present in public camp life. This study, moreover, confirms the richness and usefulness of a micro-analytical approach, taking an ethnomethodological approach when studying camp orders. From this perspective, the constitution of social order is identifiable in the observable processes of joint actions, in which a camp regime becomes visible. The disponibility of camp structures is not taken for granted but is only observable in people's methods and performances. In this way, the observability and relevance of a camp regime for the social orders accomplished in specific situations and interactions is guaranteed. This means that camp structures are neither assumed to be omni-relevant nor are they ignored, but the focus is shifted to everyday accomplishments in which people make camp structures relevant. From this perspective, we can challenge the politically and theoretically overloaded camp conceptions. Although ethnomethodology is widely understood as a microsociology, its fundamental concern with local orders or ordering is a concern with social practices, which the methods people use to produce both microstructures and macrostructures and the links between the two (Hilbert 1990; Rawls 2002). This study shows how we can examine the social practices where structures are made visible by the participants and accomplished by and for the participants. As stated, the presence of structures is not denied but neither is the existence of these structures affirmed. The question of structures is left behind in favour of examining people's social practices—or members' methods, ethnomethods. Social camp orders are understood as a product of the members' shared methods, partly situating camp rules, norms and structures within situations and events. In this way, theoretically-applied camp dimensions such as containment, temporariness, exclusion, marginalisation and exception are not treated as objective camp realities but as a local achievement produced by camp members.

This book is biased by mainly focussing on camp residents' practices and local state authorities in public camp life. Microstructures are certainly observable in other contexts, such as the working practices of staff members of the humanitarian regime or state authority staff at a national level as well as at meetings between the camp leader and aid agency staff members. These occasions are, however, less relevant for public camp life, unless camp members refer to them in public camp life as explicated in this ethnography. Still, the research findings are limited because they are solely based on studying public camp life and the respective observable orders and structures introduced in these situations. It is limited to people's practices carried out in public and does not represent people's narratives, thoughts and dreams. Another limitation refers to the picture of public harmony this study might draw. More situations of struggles and conflicts need to be focussed on. Powerful microstructures do not only support stability and agency but obviously also create spaces of conflict, violence and disorder.

CONTRIBUTION TO REFUGEE CAMP STUDIES

Refugee camps cannot simply be defined by a logic of power, governmentality, state sovereignty, social exclusion, containment or as representing the *nómos of the modern* because it incarnates a permanent state of exception (Agamben 1998). This study has demonstrated that camp orders are not reducible to a biopolitical regime creating a needy refugee, controlled and

regulated by the external environment. Refugee camps are also not suffi-
ciently and exclusively described by disciplinary technology, or places of
'standardised, generalisable technologies of power in the management of
displacement' (Malkki 1995b, 498). Even though biopolitics—regulations
that are oriented towards a collective—are indeed part of camp orders such
as humanitarian aid structures, camp residents and people present in public
camp life are not only subjected through these. This ethnography complements findings that highlight the multiplicity, heterogeneity and complexity
of power relations in refugee camps (Maestri 2017; Hanafi and Long 2010;
Inhetveen 2010) and where camp sovereignty is described as layered (Turner
2001), plural (McConnachie 2012), hybrid (Ramadan and Fregonese 2017)
and contentious (Maestri 2017). Based on these results, I emphasise that camp
residents and other actors present in public camp life are not simply victims
of imposed camp structures enacted by these (plural) actors. First of all, the
different actors of the political order of the camp such as the humanitarian aid
organisations, their donors, refugee representative bodies, pre-camp actors
and host states are interested in the enforcement of different regulations and
norms. Additionally, these different actors do not present homogeneous entities in themselves, following consistent strategies and interests, allowing a
simple top-down approach to apply to camp institutions. This plural situation
leads to structural contradictions and paradoxes that people present in public
camp life have to deal with. One example of a structural contradiction is the
characteristic of containment, which is often described in the context of refugee camps but is not applicable to possible ("illegal" but often systematically
tolerated) mobility opportunities. Other studies confirm that refugee camps
cannot be simply understood as human forms of containment, but rather the
mobility and economic opportunities camp residents have is relevant in camp
life (Jansen 2018; Werker 2007; Horst 2006; Jacobsen 2005;). Established
"illegal" mobilities as identified in Burmese refugee camps, meanwhile Bhutanese refugee camps in Thailand (Bochmann 2010) are not necessarily established by regulations or governmentality of a camp regime but are strongly
bound to (historical) structures of the region as well as social and cultural
structures of the camp's environments. The regional and historical context
in which camps are established also need to be considered and integrated
when trying to understand public camp orders. Moreover, camp governance
structures are not only plural but partly characterised by an under-regulation
or non-regulation of important domains. This is where the necessity for residents to establish microstructures in the camps comes into play.

This research shows how camp residents, staff members of refugee representative organisations but also locally present state authorities have to
find local, consistent and practical solutions to the situation of plurality and

non-regulation. Thus, they play an underestimated part of the creation, maintenance and reinforcement of camp orders and governance. In this way, this
study complements research findings that emphasise the powerful role of
camp residents and refugee representative organisations (Fiddian-Qasmiyeh
2011; Frechette 2002). As particular actors such as aid agency staff, donors
or pre-camp authorities are not present daily (at least in Burmese refugee
camps), their relevance in creating microstructures in public camp life is
limited to the way camp residents and local state authorities make them
relevant in daily actions. For example, McConnachie summarises the role of
the state in the context of Burmese refugee camps the following way: 'the
host state plays an essential role in defining conditions and circumstances of
encampment at a political level but on a daily basis is largely invisible, even
irrelevant, to the refugee population' (2014b, 11). Yet, the findings of this
book make clear that not only the state but also other actors are indeed part
of the daily basis considering the above given points and the results outlined
in this study. Though, forms of containment, exceptionality and temporality
that state actors or international actors intend to create are fractured through
powerful microstructures. Thus, microstructures can also become a response
to state policies or even the national state order of things. The aforementioned
plural camp structures, the gap between regulations and local realisations
as well as under- or non-regulations need to be incorporated and dealt with
in public camp life. Public camp life becomes part of the political order or
regime of the camp. This is what we need to acknowledge when studying
camp plurality.

This research agrees with other scholars who call for empirically-grounded
studies of camps, challenging camp conceptions and grand camp theories
(Holzer 2013; Peteet 2005). Instead of identifying refugee camp characteristics such as extraterritoriality, exception and exclusion (Agier 2011, 20),
containment (McConnachie 2016) or along temporal and spatial dimensions
in order to answer the question, What are camps? (Turner 2015), this study
raises questions such as, How are camps made to be contained, excluded
or interim? When and by whom? These questions shed more light on our
understanding of refugee camps and appreciate much more the complexity
of refugee camp orders. By raising these questions, this study makes very
clear that regulations, rules and policies that are produced by the various
actors who are part of establishing camp orders also need to be incorporated
in public camp life. Plural governance structures are visible in the described
microstructures because local actors who are present in public camp life
must deal with these in one way or another. Somewhat ambivalent and plural
regulations that are introduced into the social situations of public camp life
must be incorporated in local orders. Studying these microstructures, we also

get insights on the reasons of the gap between these (plural) regulations and their local realisations. This depends on who is present and who is interested in enforcing them.

What characterises many refugee camps that exist long-term is the established and institutionalised provisory and interim state. The temporary nature of camps is first and foremost given by external structures such as state regulations and international discourses but also its architecture. If long-term states of exception and temporariness were a relevant component of public camp life, we could assume people would make attempts to actively achieve and preserve them. The characteristics of liminality described by Turner (1964) are certainly observable in the beginning when camps are newly established. Liminality, however, does not determine life in camps in the long-term. An exceptional situation cannot simply be applied to public camp life as it is barely observable in people's practices. People's everyday life worlds are incompatible with temporariness and stand-by modus, they are not permanently waiting. While observing people's daily practices, the temporary perspective was difficult to identify because people make the camp their home. Residents establish camp normality without constantly thinking about what to do next. As these spaces become permanent and entire generations grow up in these environments; people simply have to live their lives and engage with the situation. People build up long-term relationships in refugee camps. Durability and sustainability are observable and identifiable in people's situated practices. A sense of the interim may leave its marks on camp life, but this feature is not a determining factor. The interim and temporary character of the camp becomes blurred in public camp life. Camp residents tend to produce normality even in situations where they are restricted in their normal state of affairs and are reminded of the exceptional space they live in; for instance, when residents have to close down their shops and hide their motorbikes and cars, or when people have to wait for products because boats are not allowed to travel to the camps. Camp normality is a product of diverse, loosely coupled activities and practices that nevertheless give hints about the structural problems faced by the institutional arrangements of refugee camps. The exceptionality of the camp and its extraterritorial status become routine. The closer one looks at the situationally achieved local orders and ethnomethods, the more one can perceive public camp life producing a normal social order rather than an abnormal life people in camps are forced to live. Not only in camp life, but even in civil war situations, people tend to normalise their experiences (Koloma Beck 2012).

Still, the political structure of plurality and the established interim state has consequences for the social orders of camps. Particularly, the pluralities and the long-term provisory character of refugee camp institutions strengthen and reinforce the possibility to establish local microstructures in public camp life—partly as an answer to the camp regime, partly not. The strength of microstructures and their power in establishing some degree of stability is traced back to the fact that refugee camps are states of plural governance and exceptionality. Thus, established interim spaces such as refugee camps in the Global South enable the establishment of powerful microstructures. Social orders of refugee camps incorporate not only (plural) governance and jurisdiction structures but also microstructures and situationally achieved local orders.

Social Orders of Camp Institutions

Governance and Jurisdiction Structures (Policies, Regulations, Rules)	Microstructures Established by Participants of the Situation	Situationally Achieved Local Orders – Ethno Methods

I introduce the power of locally established microstructures in the dimensions of camp governance, mobility and economic practices. Microstructures such as the establishment of public secrets, public bureaucracy, miniature examinations, the achievement of local and situational discipline, the organised temporariness and the established "illegal" mobilities are strongly related to the situational context. To remind the reader of some examples explicated throughout this research: the performances of the public address system by camp residents demonstrates how announcements create a public discipline and maintain a stable, durable and reliable temporary state of public life. The system is used to warn the camp public about state restrictions and enables them to change their 'normal' behaviour on a temporary basis. This shows how the camp public resists other structures they are aware of and refer to while allowing them to accomplish autonomous structures in their normal way. Loudspeaker announcements function not only as a central form of governing but at the same time as temporal and community-making.

By studying section meetings among camp residents, evidence is given that on such occasions common camp knowledge is produced and public camp secrets are established that have the function of maintaining the stability of the section and the camp alike. But here, again, regulations by powerful actors such as host state authorities and humanitarian agencies come into play and are incorporated. Based on the analysis of section meetings, the power of section residents becomes visible as well as their good organisational reasons to falsify documents. This is a great example of how powerful microstructures become and show a great degree of autonomy and sovereignty that are heavily traced back to the local and situational dynamics. While aid agency rules might change occasionally, the establishment and maintenance of public secrets provide stability to camp residents.

The ration distribution system, which initially seems to be in control of aid agencies, shows that all residents take part in creating public camp structures such as bureaucracy and miniature examination where the equal treatment of camp residents is made visible and is performed, not for the good of aid agency, but for the camp public themselves. During the section meetings and the ration distributions, I show how formal positions such as being part of the local self-governance structures break up ordinary gender orders. Not only through the usage of loudspeakers but also in section meetings and the distribution system, (self-)governance and camp autonomy is performed, maintained and made visible to the camp public.

People's working practices or economic activities that are strongly bound to their mobility show how people achieve normality in the camp and how they tend to normalise situations where established "illegal" practices are also situationally prevented by powerful state actors. Kibreab argues in his article about the myth of dependency among camp refugees that material well-being is the key to non-material advancement (1993, 330). Based on the results of my study, I argue that the practices of achieving material well-being is the key to producing a normal life (see Oka 2014).

The motorbike driver passing through the closed camp checkpoint exemplifies the relations between normality and temporariness. The border checkpoint is visible and needs to be passed but is passed in such a routine way that the very idea of passing a checkpoint, which represents an exceptional space, is gone. Local state officials do not regulate or control passers-by. The camp border situation demonstrates that residents, in collaboration with local authorities, can withdraw from national regulations and control such as that governance becomes part of these locally accomplished microstructures. The camp border, and its openings and closings, is the result of diverse activities within local orderings, which are situationally accomplished—turning into stable microstructures people can rely on. The enclosed character of the camp border is not an objective condition of camp life.

It can be assumed that refugee camps located in rural and difficult-to-access areas, which have existed for decades, can only be circumstantially enclosed and controlled in relation to particular ends. The peripheral location of the camp and the area around it enables participants (including camp residents and local authorities) to act free from national state observation or regulation. Local systems and even situational arrangements are in place. The refugee camp constellation and its boundaries are characterised by local openness and flexibility that enables mobility for people and products beyond state and even local regulations. When state officials visit the camp and people close their shops and paint a picture of an enclosed and economically poor camp, it is part of the social order, which again integrates the ambivalent governance and jurisdiction structures into ordinary life. People incorporate the ambivalences into everyday life and find ways of dealing with them. These diverse examples show that microstructures make a significant contribution to the stability of the camp and its stable relation to its surroundings.

Public camp life may in part be describable as life in a city or a village, but camp life is nevertheless part of a dominant discourse (maintaining the temporary, liminal and marginal character) and is maintained by its surroundings, which camp residents also perceive (Jansen 2011, 123; Herz 2013; Dorai 2010). The refugee camp is a very particular, extraterritorial political unit between and within nation states. Its characteristics—such as immobility, inactivity and frozen time—exist in the dominant discourse but also, situationally speaking, occasionally become relevant and are incorporated into people's practices. Indeed, camps are being, simultaneously, a symptom of and a cure for the national order of things (Malkki 1992; Diken and Laustsen 2005). And this is what distinguishes them from ordinary villages and cities, even though participants of public camp life work on resisting it.

NEW PERSPECTIVES ON CAMP THEORY

The research findings from this case study provide a basis for the further development of camp theory because current theories and conceptions on camps neglect to incorporate the complex local realities of camp life found in empirical data. Hitherto, camp theory does not acknowledge the multiple layers of camp orders at a very local and situational level. People's lived experiences, and the local microstructures established within and beyond these spaces, are not integrated into common perceptions of camps. Studying phenomena that occur in streams of here-and-now situations and the practice of everyday life (de Certeau 1984) contributes to our understanding of camps because they are indeed part of social camp orders. Particularly, a microanalytical, ethnomethodological perspective helps to remove these blind spots that the theory has been producing and enriches theoretical approaches that try to come to terms with the camp. The outcomes of this research, for example, in the domains of camp governance, open economy and human mobility, make clear that the local practices of camp residents and local state authorities—people present in public camp life—challenge camp conceptions such as containment, exclusion and quarantine. Particularly, *the power of microstructures* has the potential to be integrated in camp theory because they highlight aspects of camp orders that camp theory seems to have neglected and underestimated until now. Or, to put it more succinctly: the microstructures are a necessary theoretical complement to understanding different forms of encampment. Hence, I argue that these locally and situationally achieved microstructures must be accomplished in any camp context because residents or inmates or local actors have to respond in one way or another to non-regulations and regulations alike in a camp regime. This is also linked to what Garfinkel describes as the 'impossible task of "repairing" the essential incompleteness of any set of instructions no matter how carefully or elaborately written they might be' (1967, 30). In this sense, camp inmates have agency not only in terms of representing their own self-interests but particularly in terms of being actively involved in managing and dealing with the rules and regulations of the external environment in case they become part of social situations. As outlined in chapter 1, we also learned from Arendt and Giddens that, even in total institutions, powerless situations are difficult to imagine, not least because the powerful depend on the cooperation of the controlled or ruled (Arendt 1970, 51; 1986, 312; Giddens 1988, 64ff.). Also, Popitz refers to the role of the suppressed to maintain power relations (1992, 185).

But again, I want to make clear that camp theory provides satisfactory tools to grasp camp complexity, highlighting specifically the role of the external environment. Theoretical approaches tend to underscore powerful camp structures, emphasising the segregation, containment, exclusion and exceptional character of camps, where people are controlled and have limited agency. Camp institutions enable bureaucratic acts and regulations to easily supervene and allow 'the penetration of regulation into even the smallest details of everyday life through the mediation of the complete hierarchy that assure[s] the capillary functioning of power' (Foucault 1979, 198). Mechanisms, characteristics and procedures that are oriented towards collectives are identifiable in camp institutions of different kinds. Camp conceptions are describable as total and disciplinary institutions but are better described with the help of governmentality and biopolitics. This is because the regulation and mechanisms are oriented towards a collective and not towards individuals. Additionally, in the camp environments the accessibility towards a smaller collective in a restricted space is easier. That is why control, discipline and regulation mechanisms are much easier to enforce. The requirement for the exercise of power involves restricting the mobility of the oppressed; the ongoing pursuit of power depends on the accessibility of the group being controlled as well as on their inability to escape from the respective territory. This seems to be the case for camp institutions. It is true, from the perspective of the environment, based on the spatial regime and the concentration of people, a collective of liminality, marginality and inferiority is produced. A central aspect for these perspectives on camps and its orders is the environment, which cannot be ignored because it makes a decisive contribution to maintaining the camp as well as the camp collective, particularly regarding liminality, inferiority and marginality—which also has its function for wider society (Soguk 1999; Foucault 1984; Turner 1969). But it seems that conceptions regarding people's practices and their agency outside of these regulating power mechanisms are not considered. People's practices, inmates or camp residents, or people in public camp life remain in the totalitarian structures and types of power-subjected collectives. Camp residents are perceived as creatures of an external context, as enactors of rules and scripts provided by the wider institutional environment. Then, camp life seems to be fundamentally shaped or even constituted by the external environment, where people find themselves 'neither here nor there; they are "betwixt and between" the positions assigned and arrayed by law, custom, convention and ceremonial' (Turner 1969, 95). The egalitarianism found among residents, the collective treatment experienced, the equalising processes (Goffman 1981; Turner 1969) as well as the concepts of liminality, marginalisation and inferiority do not represent camp complexities adequately. When understanding camp life, we need to consider the microstructures that deal with all these possible and potential enforcements. My approach emphasises the power of microstructures, taking them as the centre state of the research. At the same time, this study acknowledges the great power of the camp's surroundings. The structures and the discourses surrounding the camp establish the camp as a camp, the life in a camp as life in a camp, and a camp collective as a camp collective. Also, the characteristics such as containment, exclusion, exceptionality and marginalisation are primarily established through the perspectives and discourses on camps and in this way may become part of public camp life. Society produces camps and camp characteristics that can become part of public camp life but do not necessarily do so. Public camp life tries to work on fracturing these characteristics imposed by its surroundings.

Considering these arguments, it is also worthwhile to recap Foucault's premise of the heterotopia (1984) and stress its relevance for setting up camp characteristics. Time structures in camps do not necessarily come to a standstill and time structures in everyday life do not present temporariness. Indeed, there are temporal camp orders that are presented by discourses and camp structures that differ from time structures in camp environments. Moreover, camps demarcate spaces where the systems of openings and closings that isolate camps from their environments exist. But the degree of the openings and closings varies strongly and is changeable. They characterise the way in which camps function for their surroundings and simultaneously question them. Camps demonstrate the illusion of a perfectly ordered and normed society such as the nation-state system that every person belongs to a territory and a people. The environment plays a significant role in producing a homogeneous camp collective and from this we learn a lot about our society and our global governance system. Malkki (1992) refers to this phenomenon as the role refugees play in polluting and, simultaneously, maintaining the 'national order of things'. This is transferable to environments other than refugee camps. But *the power of microstructures* needs to be acknowledged and better integrated into these common perceptions as well as the fact that camps remain a provisory and actors want to leave it as a provisory, such as states, the national order of things or the humanitarian regime. Particularly, this characteristic allows for the establishment of local microstructures, breaking with the underlife Goffman had in mind (1961, 169).

According to theoretical conceptions, camps are describable as spaces where, in one way or the other, the following features come into play:

Temporariness
Legal Exclusion
Compulsive Character
'Self-Governance' Structures
Power Relations and Bureaucracy
Shared Accommodation in a Limited Space
Containment, Isolation from the Environment
Pronounced and Highly Regulated Hierarchies

In order to understand camp complexities, we need to reframe the question of what camps are, into questions of how camps are constructed, by whom and when, and to apply these kinds of questions to the above outlined dimensions. How is temporariness constructed, by whom and when? How is legal exclusion constructed, when and by whom? How is the isolation from the environment achieved, by whom and when? This enables researchers to study and perceive legal and political camp orders or regimes as well as these characteristics not as objective realities, as social facts, but as the ongoing accomplishments of socially organised practices. Moreover, this allows a shift towards perspectives focussing on the detailed study of small-scale phenomena occurring in social situations, because such studies give a better understanding of the way humans do things and the kinds of 'objects' they use to construct and order their affairs.

These considerations as well as *the power of microstructures* are generally applicable to other research contexts as well, for example, to discussions about border regimes and (im)mobilities. In fact, the concept of powerful microstructures contributes to debates on border studies and the autonomy of migration (Papadopoulos and Tsianos 2013, 178ff.), where the links between state border regimes, migrants' practices, and their ways of dealing with restrictions are emphasised and illuminated (Walter 2011). The theoretical-methodological grounding introduced here shifts the focus from the question of what a migration, refugee or border regime does to people, to that of how people respond to these structures and how these structures become relevant and perpetuate social orders in everyday life. This perspective is a response to critique of the term 'autonomy' (of migration), which is not romanticised or equated with freedom or independence from state regulations (Scheel 2013); rather, structures and regimes are included in people's lived experiences when they are made relevant. The conceptual framework introduced above speaks in favour of a situational analysis of state and border regimes and studying people's ongoing and non-controllable creative responses, talk and actions regarding state and border regimes (see also Hess and Tsianos 2010, 243ff. on this debate).

FROM TOTALISED CAMP SYSTEMS TO SITUATIONAL CAMP SETTLEMENTS

In academic debates about refugee accommodation, a distinction between organised encampment and 'disorganised' self-settlements has been suggested (Bakewell 2014, 127). However, forms of encampment may include 'anything from a small, militarised fenced centre housing refugees in dormitories guarded by soldiers, to a huge agriculture settlement (. . .) consisting of villages deeply embedded into the local economy (. . .)' (130). Thus, a distinction between the organised and the disorganised does not seem to be appropriate when it comes to understanding social orders in refugee camp contexts because there is a huge variation of situations. Some people are constantly guarded and controlled by soldiers; for others, life is ordered by making a living through agricultural work or running a grocery store. Life in 'disorganised' self-settlements may be far more controlled and regulated than life in a camp. Hitchcox compares different types of Vietnamese refugee camps in Southeast Asia in the late 1980s. She distinguishes between different forms of encampment along the categories of open (1990, 100) and closed prison-like camps (102–3). These categories are linked to the working opportunities that are permitted, other than with agencies or the administration (112). Additionally, Hitchcox categorises camps according to their levels of refugee participation in camp management (155ff.) and their levels of safety

(160ff.). While she discusses correlations between these categories, she does not further elaborate on them, although this would help to systematically distinguish different types of refugee camps. Agier differentiates between four types of refugee camps: (1) self-organised settlements, which are installed under the gaze of national authorities and aid agencies but where international aid is almost absent; (2) retention or transit centres, particularly those located at borders such as the European border with Africa; (3) UNHRC/UNRWA organised refugee camps in the Global South, including camps where refugees receive rations or have access to land and are self-reliant; and (4) internally displaced persons camps, so-called IDPs, where displaced people are accommodated and cared for without the need to cross a national border (2010, 36). This distinction is based on the geographies/localities of centralised refugee accommodations rather than their structural characteristics, but it remains unclear why Agier does not include accommodation centres for asylum seekers in Europe, America or Australia, where people are accommodated until their legal status is decided upon. Based on these debates and the more historical and general camp cartographies introduced in chapter 1, in the following section, an alternative way of perceiving camps is suggested, one that is not another typology of camps (see Möller 2014; Kotek and Rigoulot 2001; Arendt 1962).

To capture multiple forms of camps, a graded list is suggested, ranking from totalised camp systems to more situational camp settlements. The graded list aims to provide tools to empirically capture camp environments and to give empirically-grounded studies of camps an analytical framework from which to study camps. The terms 'camp' and 'settlement' are used here in an analytical way, which differs from the way the UNHCR uses these terms as administrative categories (Schmidt 2003). Three dimensions have been identified in this study and are relevant when it comes to differentiating types of camps: governance/jurisdiction, mobility and economy. The last two dimensions correspond with claims made by Diken, who argues for the following characteristics of camp life:

> living on a small amount of support payments or even food vouchers with no cash allowance, which pushes the asylum seeker out of the normal functioning of the economic system; to be prevented from finding paid work, living according to the governments choice of residency, and minimum geographical mobility. (Diken 2004, 92)

Diken defines the camp along the dimensions of mobility and economic behaviour because he is mainly concerned with centralised refugee accommodation located in the Global North (Diken and Laustsen 2005) where self-governance practices are limited mainly because people do not stay for long. For Diken and Laustsen, the domination of external governance over the accommodation centres is evident and confirmed by diverse studies (2005). However, the relevance of governance and jurisdictional structures needs to be explicated for an adequate understanding of the social orderings in camps. These three dimensions help to differentiate when we should speak of a camp-like institutions and when we should speak of situational camp-like settlements. The following illustration visualises the two extremes as a gradient of existing camp systems:

Totalized Camp Systems --- **Situational Camp Settlement**

Governance, (Im)Mobility, Economy

A high degree of realised external governance and jurisdiction, regulation and control, and a low degree of realised outside mobility and economic activities define camp-like institutions. Whereas, a low degree of realised external governance and jurisdictions, and a high degree of realised outside mobility and economic activities define a settlement where camp structures become relevant only occasionally. The aspect of realisation is important and only identifiable by empirically-grounded studies of camps. The aspect of realisation is connected to the camps intended to be provisory institutions. Here, the necessity of the micro-analytical approaches to camps becomes evident. The strength of micro-analytical approaches is to identify the constitution of social order in people's practices, in which structures and discourses become visible but need to be situated. From this perspective, the constitution of social order is identifiable in the observable processes of joint actions in which camp structures become visible. The disponibility of camp structures cannot be taken for granted but is observable in people's methods and presentations (Garfinkel and Sacks 1970). In this way, the observability and relevance of camp structures for the social orders accomplished in specific situations is guaranteed. This means that camp structures are not assumed to be relevant, nor are these structures ignored as such, but the focus shifts to everyday accomplishments in which people make camp structures relevant and visible. On the one hand, this approach acknowledges the provisory and complexity of camp institutions. On the other hand, this approach suggests people's agency in these institutions. Based on these assumptions, refugee centres in Europe, America and Australia, transit centres at the African-European border, or Mexican-US border come closer, at least from a theoretical perspective, to what has been understood as camps with a characteristic structure (see Diken and Laustsen 2005, 57). This might be opposed to camp systems and settlements as we find them in African and Asian contexts.

Bibliography

Abdi, A. M. 2005. 'In Limbo: Dependency, Insecurity and Identity Amongst Somali Refugees in Dadaab Camps'. *Bilhaan: An International Journal of Somali Studies* 5(7): 17–34.

Adelman, H. 1998. 'Why Refugee Warriors are Threats'. *The Journal of Conflict Studies* 18(1): 1–16.

Agamben, G. 1998. *Homo Sacer. Sovereign Power and Bare Life*. Stanford: Stanford University Press.

———. 2000. *Means Without End. Notes on Politics. Vol. 20: Theory Out of Bounds*. Minneapolis: University of Minnesota Press.

———. 2002. *Homo Sacer. Die Souveränität der Macht und das Nackte Leben*. Frankfurt am Main: Suhrkamp.

Agier, M. 2002a. 'Between War and City: Towards an Urban Anthropology of Refugee Camps'. *Ethnography* 3(3): 317–41.

———. 2002b. 'Still Stuck Between War and City: A Response to Bauman and Malkki'. *Ethnography* 3(3): 361–66.

———. 2010. 'Humanity as an Identity and its Political Effects: A Note on Camps and Humanitarian Government'. *Humanity: An International Journal of Human Rights, Humanitarianism, and Development* 1(1): 29–45.

———. 2011. *Managing the Undesirables, Refugee Camps, and Humanitarian Government*. Cambridge, Malden: Polity Press.

Alexander, J. C. 1987. *Twenty Lectures: Sociological Theory Since World War II*. New York: Columbia University Press.

Andersen, K. E. 1979. 'Deference for the Elders and Control Over the Younger Among the Karen in Thailand'. *Folk* 21 and 22: 313–25.

Applebaum, A. 2003. *Der Gulag*. Berlin: Siedler Verlag.

Arendt, H. 1943/1986. 'Wir Flüchtlinge'. In M. Knott, ed., *Zur Zeit. Politische Essays*. Berlin: Rotbuch.

———. 1962. 'The Origins of Totalitarianism'. Cleveland, New York: Meridian Books. The World Publishing Company.

———. 1970. *Macht und Gewalt. Bd. 1.* München: Piper.

Armanski, G. 1993. *Maschinen des Terrors. Das Lager (KZ and Gulag) in der Moderne.* Münster: Westfälisches Dampfboot.

Atkinson, P., and M. Hammersley. 1994. 'Ethnography and Participant Observations'. In N. Denzin, and Y. Lincoln, eds., *Handbook of Qualitative Methods* (248–61). Thousand Oaks, CA: Sage.

Augé, M. 1995. *Non-Places. Introduction to an Anthropology of Supermodernity.* London, New York: Verso.

Aung, L. R. 2016. 'Laiza: Kachin Borderlands—Life after the Ceasefire'. In W. Tantikanangkul, and A. Pritchard, eds., *Politics of Autonomy and Sustainability in Myanmar. Change for New Hope. New Life?* (37–56). Singapore: Springer.

Bakewell, O. 2007. 'Editorial Introduction: Researching Refugees: Lessons from the Past, Current Challenges and Future Directions'. *Refugee Survey Quarterly* 26(3): 6–14.

———. 2008. 'Research Beyond Categories: The Importance of Policy Irrelevant Research into Forced Migration'. *Journal of Refugee Studies* 21(4): 432–53.

———. 2014. 'Encampment and Self-Settlement'. In E. Fiddian-Qasmiyeh, G. Loescher, K. Long, and N. Sigona, eds., (127–38). Oxford: Oxford University Press.

Banki, S., and H. J. Lang. 2008. 'Protracted Displacement on the Thai-Burmese Border: The Interrelated Search for Durable Solutions'. In H. Adelmann, ed., *Protracted Displacement in Asia: No Place to Call Home* (59–81). Aldershot: Ashgate.

Barth, F. 1969. *Ethnic Groups and Boundaries: The Social Organisation of Culture Difference.* Oslo: Unversitetsforlaget.

Baumann, Z. 2002. 'In the Lowly No Where Villes of Liquid Modernity: Comments on and around Agier'. *Ethnography* 3(3): 343–49.

BBC. 1991–2004. 'Burmese Border Consortium: Programme Reports'. Bangkok: accessible @ www.theborderconsortium.org, last access 14 February 2017. Retrieved February 2017

Bergmann, J. 1985. 'Flüchtigkeit und Methodische Fixierung Sozialer Wirklichkeit: Aufzeichnung als Daten der Interpretativen Soziologie'. In W. Bonß, and H. Hartmann, eds., *Entzauberte Wissenschaft. Zur Relativität und Geltung Soziologischer Forschung: Sonderband 3 der Zeitschrift für Soziologie* (299–20). Göttingen: Schwarz.

———. 1988. *Ethnomethodologie und Konversationsanalyse: Kurseinheit 1–3.* Hagen: Fernuniversität Hagen.

———. 1990. 'On the Local Sensitivity of Interactions'. In I. Markoà, and K. Foppa, eds., *The Dynamics of Dialogue* (201–26). Hemel, Hemstead: Harvester Wheatsheaf.

———. 2011. 'Von der Wechselwirkung zur Interaktion—Georg Simmel und die Mikrosoziologie Heute'. In *Georg Simmels Große "Soziologie": Eine Kritische Sichtung nach Hundert Jahren* (125–48). Bielefeld: Transcript.

Bettina, G., and A. Kramer. 2014. *Welt der Lager: Zur 'Erfolgsgeschichte' einer Institution.* Hamburg: Hamburger Edition.

Betts, A., L. Bloom., J. Kaplan and N. Omata. 2014. *Refugee Economies: Rethinking Popular Assumptions.* Oxford: University of Oxford.

Bevir, M. 2012. *Governance: A Very Short Introduction*. Oxford: Oxford University Press.

Birkholz, S., A. Bochmannand J. Schank. n.d. 'Ethnographie und Teilnehmende Beobachtung'. In A. Wagemann, and M. Siewert, eds., *Handbuch Methoden der Politikwissenschaften*. Wiesbaden: Springer.

Bochmann, A. 2010. 'Citizenship Ethnography: Perspectives on Membership in the Context of Bhutanese Refugee Camps in Nepal. Bielefeld': Unpublished Diploma Thesis.

———. 2017a. 'Institution Lager: Theoretische Grundlagen und die Macht Lokaler Mikrostrukturen'. In S. Lessenich, *Geschlossene Geselllschaften. Verhandlungen des 36. Kongress der Deutschen Gesellschaft für Soziologie*. Wiesbaden: Springer.

———. 2017b. 'Soziale Ordnungen, Mobilitäten und Situatives Grenzregime im Kontext Burmesischer Flüchtlingslager in Thailand'. *Peripherie* 145(37): 29–51.

———. 2019. 'The Power of Local Microstructures in Refugee Camps'. *Journal of Refugee Studies* 32(1): 63–85.

———. 2020. 'Researching State Borders: Situations, Materiality and Global Discourses. UniGR-CBS Borders in Perspective thematic issue'. Identities and Methodologies of Border Studies: Recent Empirical and Conceptual Approaches, forthcoming.

———., and Daroussis, D. 2011. 'Returned Graduates and Their Ties: Mechanisms of Social Support'. In T. Faist, and N. Sieveking, *Unravelling Migrants as Transnational Agents of Development: Social Spaces Between Ghana and Germany*. Münster: Lit Verlag.

Bochmann, A., and K. Inhetveen. 2017. *Orte der Dauerhaften Vorläugfigkeit: Bundeszentrale für politische Bildung*, Kurzdossiers: Zuwanderung, Flucht und Asyl.

Bochmann, A., D. Negnal and T. Scheffer. 2019. 'Die Aufladung der Gegenstände: Das ethnographische Forschungsprogramm einer politischen Soziologie'. *Soziologie* 48: 438–42.

Boden, D. 1994. *The Business of Talk*. Cambridge: Polity Press.

Boli, J., and G. M. Thomas. 1997. 'World Culture in the World Polity: A Century of International Non-Governmental Organisations'. *American Sociological Review* 62(2): 172–90.

Bousquet, G. 1987. 'Living in a State of Limbo: A Case Study of Vietnamese Refugees in Hong Kong Camps'. In S. Morgan, and E. Colson, eds., *People in Upheaval* (34–53). New York: Center for Migration Studies.

Bowles, E. 1998. 'From Village to Camp: Refugee Camp Life in Transition on the Thai-Burma Border'. *Forced Migration Review* 2: 11–14.

Brees, I. 2008. 'Refugee Business: Strategies of Work on the Thai-Burma Border'. *Journal of Refugee Studies* 21(3): 380–97.

———. 2009. *Livelihoods, Integration and Transnationalism in a Protracted Refugee Situation*. Ghent: Ghent University.

Burma Lawyers' Council. 2007. 'Analysis of the Situation of the Refugee Camps: From the Rule of Law Aspect'. *Thailand Journal of Law and Policy* 1(11): 1–6.

Butenschön, N. A., Ö. Stiansen and K. Vollan. 2015. *Power-Sharing in Conflict-Ridden Societies: Challenges for Building Peace and Democratic Stability*. Surrey, Burlington: Ashgate.

Callahan, M. P. 2007. *Political Authority in Burma's Ethnic Minority States: Devolution, Occupation and Coexistence*. Washington: East-West Centre Washington.

———. 2013. *Making Enemies, War and State Building in Burma*. Ithaca, NY: Cornell University Press.

Cannon, J. P., and W. D. Perreault. 1999. 'Buyer-Seller Relationships in Business Markets'. *Journal of Marketing Research* 26(4).

Cha, D. C., and C. A. Small. 1994. 'Policy Lessons from Lao and Hmong Women in Thai Refugee Camps'. *World Development* 22: 1045–59.

Cicourel, A. V. 1981. 'Notes on the Integration of Micro- and Macro Levels of Analysis'. In K. Knorr-Cetina, C. A. V., K. Knorr-Cetina, and A. Cicourel. eds., *Advances in Social Theory and Methodology*. New York: Routledge.

Clark, C., and T. Pinch. 1988. 'Micro-Sociology and Micro Economics: Selling by Control'. In N. G. Fielding, and N. Fielding, eds., *Actions and Structures: Research Methods and Social Theory* (117–41). London: Sage.

Crisp, J. 1999. 'Who has Counted the Refugees? UNHCR and the Politics of Numbers'. *New Issues in Refugee Research*. UNHCR, 12.

da Costa, R. 2006. 'The Administration of Justice in Refugee Camps: A Study of Practice', UNHCR. Geneva: accessible@ unhcr.org, last access 17 February 2017.

Davies, C. A. 2008. *Reflexive Ethnography: A Guide to Researching Selves and Others*. London, New York: Routledge.

Davies, S. E. 2007. *Legitimising Rejection: International Refugee Law in Southeast Asia*. Leiden, Boston: Martinus Nijhoff.

de Certeau, M. 1984. The Practices of Everyday Life. Berkeley: University of California Press.

Diken, B. 2004. 'From Refugee Camps to Gated Communities: Biopolitics and the End of the City'. *Citizenship Studies* 8(1): 83–106.

Diken, B., and C. B. Laustsen. 2005. *The Culture of Exception: Sociology Facing the Camp*. London, New York: Routledge.

Dorai, M. K. 2010. 'From Camp Dwellers to Urban Refugees? Urbanization and Marginalization of Refugee Camps in Lebanon'. In M. Khalidi, ed., *Manifestations of Identity: The Lived Reality of Palestinian Refugees in Lebanon* (1–21). Lebanon: Institute for Palestine Studies.

Douglas, B. 2003. 'The Art of Surviving the Gulag. Baltimore: The Baltimore Sun.

Dudley, S. H. 2010. *Materialising Exile: Material Culture and Embodied Experience Among Karenni Refugees in Thailand*. New York, Oxford: Berghahn Books.

Dzeamesi, M. 2008. 'Refugees, the UNHCR and Host Governments as Stakeholders in the Transformation of Refugee Communities: A Study into the Buduburam Refugee Camp in Ghana'. *International Journal of Migration, Health and Social Care* 4(1): 28–41.

Elford, L. 2008. 'Human Rights and Refugees: Building a Social Geography of Bare Life in Africa'. *African Geographical Review* 27(1): 65–79.

Elias, N., and J. L. Scotson. 1965. *The Established and the Outsiders: A Sociological Inquiry into Community Problems*. Boston: Cass and Company.

Essed, P., G. Frerks and J. Schrijvers. 2005. *Refugees and the Transformation of Societies: Agency, Policies, Ethics and Politics*. New York, Oxford: Berghahn Books.

Fellesson, M. 2003. *Prolonged Exile in Relative Isolation: Long Term Consequences of Contrasting Refugee Policies in Tanzania*. Uppsala: Uppsala Universitet.

Fiddian-Qasmiyeh, E. 2011. *Protracted Sahrawi Displacement: Challenges and Opportunities Beyond Encampment*. Oxford: University of Oxford Press.

Foucault, M. 1977/2014. *Der Wille zum Wissen, Sexualität und Wahrheit*. Frankfurt am Main: Suhrkamp.

———. 1979. *Discipline and Punish: The Birth of the Prison*. New York: Vintage Books.

———. 1980. *Power/Knowledge: Selected Interviews and Other Writings 1972–1977 by Michel Foucault*. New York: Harvester Wheatsheaf.

———. 1984. 'Of Other Spaces: Utopias and Heterotopias'. *Architecture, Mouvement, Continuitè* 10: 1–9.

———. 1994. *Überwachen und Strafen. Die Geburt des Gefängnisses*. Frankfurt: Suhrkamp.

———. 1998. *The History of Sexuality: The Will to Knowledge*. London: Penguin.

Frechette, A. 2002. *Tibetans in Nepal: The Dynamics of International Assistance Among a Community in Exile*. New York, Oxford: Berghahn Books.

Fresia, M., and A. von Känel. 2016. 'Beyond Space of Exception? Reflections on the Camp Through the Prism of Refugee Schools'. *Journal of Refugee Studies* 29(2): 250–72.

Garfinkel, H. 1967. *Studies in Ethnomethodology*. Englewood Cliffs: John Wiley & Sons.

———. 1996. 'Ethnomethodology's Program'. *Social Psychology Quarterly* 59(1): 5–21.

Garfinkel, H., and A. W. Rawls. 2002. *Ethnomethodology's Program. Working Out Durkheim's Aphorism*. Lanham, MD: Rowman & Littlefield.

Garfinkel, H., and H. Sacks. 1970. 'On Formal Structures of Practical Actions'. In J. McKinney, and E. Tiryakian, eds., *Theoretical Sociology. Perspectives and Developments* (337–66). New York: Appleton-Century Crofts.

Garfinkel, H., and L. D. Wieder. 1992. 'Two Incommensurable Asymmetrically Alternate Technologies of Social Analysis'. In G. Watson, and R. Seiler, eds., *Text in Context: Contributions to Ethnomethodology* (175–206). London: Sage.

Garfinkel, H., M. Lynch and E. Livingston. 1981. 'The Work of a Discovering Science Constructed with the Materials from the Optically Discovered Pulsar'. *Philosophy of Social Science* 11: 131–58.

Giddens, A. 1988. *Die Konstitution der Gesellschaft: Grundzüge einer Theorie der Strukturierung*. Frankfurt am Main: Campus.

Gilbert, S. 2005. *Music in the Holocaust: Confronting Life in the Nazi Ghettos and Camps*. Oxford: Oxford University Press.

Glaser, B., and Anselm L. Strauss. 1967. *The Discovery of Grounded Theory: Strategies for Qualitative Research*. New Brunswick, London: Aldine Transaction.

Gluckmann, M. 1968. *Analysis of a Social Situation in Modern Zululand.* Manchester: Manchester University Press.

Goffman, E. 1961. *Asyle. Essays on the Social Situation of Mental Patient and Other Inmates.* New York: Anchor Books.

———. 1963. *Behaviour in Public Places: Notes on the Social Organization of Gatherings.* New York: Free Press.

———. 1971. *Relations in Public: Microstudies of the Public Order.* New York: Harper & Row.

———. 1974. *Rahmen-Analyse: Ein Versuch* über *die Organisation von Alltagserfahrungen.* Frankfurt am Main: Suhrkamp.

———. 1977. 'The Arrangement Between the Sexes'. *Theory and Society* 4(3): 301–31.

———. 1981. *Forms of Talk.* Philadelphia: University of Pennsylvania Press.

———. 1983. 'The Interaction Order: American Sociological Association, 1982 Presidential Address'. *American Sociology Review* 48(1): 1–17.

———. 2002. 'On Fieldwork'. In D. Weinberg, ed., *Qualitative Research Methods* (148–53). Malden: Blackwell Publishers.

Goodwin, Charles 1981. Conversational Organisation: Interaction between Speakers and Hearers. New York: Academic Press.

Goodwin, C. 2007. 'Interactive Footing'. In E. Holt, and R. Clift, eds., *Reporting Talk: Reporting Speech Interaction* (16–46). Cambridge: Cambridge University Press.

Gravers, M. 2007. 'Conversion and Identity: Religion and the Formation of Karen Ethnic Identity in Burma'. In M. Gravers, ed., *Exploring Ethnic Diversity in Burma* (227–59). Copenhagen: NIAS Press.

Greiner, B. and Kramer, A.: Die Welt der Lager. Zur 'Erfolgsgeschichte' einer Institution. Hamburg: Hamburger Edition HIS Verlag.

Greve, J., and B. Heintz. 2005. 'Die "Entdeckung" der Weltgesellschaft'. In *Weltgesellschaft. Theoretische Zugänge und Empirische Problemlagen: Sonderband der Zeitschrift für Soziologie* (89–119). Stuttgart: Lucius und Lucius.

Griek, I. 2006. 'Traditional Systems of Justice in Refugee Camps: The Need for Alternatives'. *Refugee Reports* 27(2): 1–5.

Haddad, E. 2008. *The Refugee in International Society: Between Sovereigns.* Cambridge: Cambridge University Press.

Hafner-Burton, E., and K. Tsutsui. 2005. 'Human Rights in a Globalizing World: The Paradox of Empty Promises'. *American Journal of Sociology* 110(5): 1373–411.

Hammersley, M., and Atkinson, P. 2007. *Ethnography. Principles in Practice.* London, New York: Routledge.

Hanafi, S., and T. Long. 2010. 'Governance, Governmentalities, and the State of Exception in the Palestinian Refugee Camps of Lebanon'. *Journal of Refugee Studies* 23: 134–59.

Harrell-Bond, B. 1986. *Imposing Aid—Emergency Assistance to Refugees.* Oxford, New York, Nairobi: Oxford University Press.

————. 1999. 'The Experience of Refugees as Recipients of Aid'. In A. Ager, ed., *Refugees: Perspectives on the Experience of Forced Migration* (136–68). London: Pinter.

Harrell-Bond, B., and E. Voutira. 1992. 'Anthropology and the Study of Refugees'. *Anthropology Today* 8(4): 6–10.

Harvey, G. E. 1967. 'History of Burma'. In S. Cocks, ed., *Burma Under British Rule*. Bombay: K. and J. Cooper.

Have ten, Paul. 1999. *Doing Conversation Analysis: A Practical Guide*. Los Angeles, London, New Delhi, Singapore: Sage.

Heintz, B., D. Müller and H. Schiener. 2006. 'Menschenrechte im Kontext der Weltgesellschaft: Die Weltgesellschaftliche Institutionalisierung von Frauenrechten und ihre Umsetzung in Deutschland, der Schweiz und Marokko'. *Zeitschrift für Soziologie* 35(6): 424–48.

Herz, M. 2013. *From Camp to City: Refugee Camps of the Western Sahara*. Basel: Lars Müller Publishers.

Hess, S., and V. Tsianos. 2010. 'Ethnographische Grenzregimeanalyse: Eine Methodologie der Autonomie der Migration'. In A. Hess, and B. Kasparek , eds., *Grenzregime: Diskurse, Praktiken, Institutionen in Europa* (243–64). Berlin: Assoziation.

Hester, S., and P. Eglin. 1997. *Culture in Action: Studies on Membership Categorization Analysis*. Washington, DC: University Press of America.

Hester, S., and D. Francis. 2004. *An Invitation to Ethnomethodology: Language, Society and Social Interaction*. London, Thousand Oaks, New Delhi: Sage.

Hilbert, R. A. 1990. 'Ethnomethodology and the Micro-Macro Order'. *American Sociological Review* 55(6): 794–808.

Hilhorst, D., and B. Jansen. 2013. 'Humanitarian Space as Arena: A Perspective on Everday Politics of Aid'. In D. Hilhorst , ed., *Disaster, Conflict and Society in Crisis: Everday Politics of Crises Response* (187–204). Abingdon, New York: Routledge.

Hirschauer, S. 2014. Intersituativität: Teleinteraktionen und Koaktivitäten Jenseits von Mikro und Makro. *Sonderheft: Zeitschrift für Soziologie*: 109–33.

Hitchcox, L. 1990. *Vietnamese Refugees in Southeast Asian Camps*. Hampshire, London: Macmillan.

Holzer, E. 2012. 'A Case Study of Political Failure in a Refugee Camp'. *Journal of Refugee Studies* 25(2): 257–81.

————. 2013. 'What Happens to Law in a Refugee Camp'. *Law and Society Review*, 47(4): 837–72.

————. 2015. *The Concerned Woman of Buduburam: Refugee Activists and Humanitarian Dilemmas*. Ithaca, NY: Cornell University Press.

Horst, C. 2006. *Transnational Nomads: How Somalis Cope with Refugee Life in the Dadaab Camps of Kenya*. New York, Oxford: Berghahn Books.

Human Rights Watch. 2012. 'Ad Hoc and Inadequate: Thailand's Treatment of Refugees and Asylum Seekers'. accessible @ www.hrw.org, last access 1 March 2017.

Hyndman, J. 1997. 'Refugee Self-Management and the Question of Governance'. *Refuge* 16(2): 16–22.

―――. 2000. *Managing Displacement: Refugees and the Politics of Humanitarianism*. Minneapolis, London: University of Minnesota Press.

Inhetveen, K. 2006. 'Situative Fluchten. Mobilität und Macht in einem Sambischen Flüchtlingslager'. In K. Inhetveen, ed., *Flucht als Politik. Berichte von fünf Kontinenten* (81–102). Köln: Rüdiger Köppe Verlag.

―――. 2010. 'Die Politische Ordnung des Flüchtlingslagers. Akteure―Macht―Organisation'. Bielefeld: Transcript.

―――. 2013. 'Another Kind of Empowerment? Refugees, Imported Power Structures, and the International Refugee Regime in a Zambian Refugee Camp'. *Trialog* 112/113: 54–59.

IOM/NRC/UNHCR. 2015. *Camp Management Toolkit*. accessible @ www.global cccmcluster.org, last access 14 February 2017.

Jackson, E., and Associates, Ltd. 2012. 'Adaption, Resilience and Transition: Report of the Formative Evaluation of Camp Management in the Burmese Refugee Camps in Thailand'. accessible @ www.etjackson.com, last access 17 February 2017.

Jacobsen, K. 2005. *Refugee Camp Economy*. Bloomfield: Kumarian Press.

―――. 2014. 'Livelihoods and Forced Migration'. In E. Fiddian-Quasmiyeh, G. Loescher, K. Long, and N. Sigona, eds., *The Oxford Handbook of Refugee and Forced Migration Studies* (99–111). Oxford: Oxoford University Press.

Janmyr, M. 2013. *Protecting Civilians in Refugee Camps: Unable and Unwilling States, UNHCR and International Responsibility*. Leiden: Martinus Nijhoff.

Jansen, B. J. 2009. *The Accidental City: Urbanisation in an East-African Refugee Camp*. Urban Agriculture Magazin 21: 11–12.

―――. 2011. *The Accidental City: Violence, Economy and Humanitarianism in Kakuma Camp, Kenya*. Wageningen: Wageningen University.

―――. 2018. *Kakuma Refugee Camp: Humanitarian Urbanism in Kenya's Accidental City*. London: Zed Books.

Kapferer, B. 2010. 'Introduction: In the Event―Toward an Anthropology of Generic Moments'. *Social Analysis* 54(3): 1–27.

Keenan, P. 2013. *By Force of Arms: Armed Ethnic Groups in Burma*. New Delhi: VijBooks India Pvt.

Kibreab, G. 1987. *Refugees and Development in Africa: The Case of Eritreans Fleeing to Sudan*. Trenton: Red Sea Press.

―――. 1993. The Myth of Dependency Among Camp Refugees in Somalia 1979–1989. *Journal of Refugee Studies* 6(4): 321–49.

―――. 1996. *People on the Edge in the Horn: Displacement, Land Use and the Environment*. Oxford: James Currey Publishers.

Kipgen, N. 2014. *Democratisation of Myanmar*. New Delhi, London, New York: Routledge.

Knorr-Cetina, K. 1981. 'Introduction: The Micro-Sociological Challenge of Macro-Sociology: Towards a Reconstruction of Social Theory and Methodology'. In K. Knorr-Cetina, and A. Cicourel, eds., *Advances in Social Theory and Methodology: Towards an Integration of Miro and Macro-Sociologies* (1–48). Boston, London, Henley: Routledge and Kegan Paul.

Knudsen, A. 2009. 'Widening the Protection Gap: The "Politics of Citizenship" for Palestinian Refugees in Lebanon, 1948–2008'. *Journal of Refugee Studies* 22(1): 51–73.

Kogon, E. 1980. *The Theory and Practice of Hell: The German Concentration Camps and the System Behind Them*. New York: Berkley Books.

Koloma Beck, T. 2012. *The Normality of Civil War*. Frankfurt am Main: Campus.

König, M. 2005a. *Menschenrechte*. Frankfurt am Main: Campus.

———. 2005b. 'Weltgesellschaft, Menschenrechte und der Formenwandel des Nationalstaates'. In W. T. Soziologie, B. Heintz, R. Münch, and H. Tyrell, eds., *Soziologie, Weltgesellschaft: Theoretische Zugänge und Empirische Grundlagen. Sonderband der Zeitschrift für Soziologie* (374–93). Stuttgart: Lucius and Lucius.

Kotek, Joel and Rigoulot, Pierre. 2001. *Das Jahrhundert der Lager. Gefangenschaft, Zwangsarbeit, Vernichtung*. Berlin: Propyläen.

KRC. 1984–2017. Karen Refugee Committee. 'Monthly Reports'. Mae Sot: accessible @ www.burmalibrary.org, last access 14 February 2017. Retrieved January 2017, from http://www.burmalibrary.org/docs15/KRCMR-2013-06-red.pdf.

———. 2008. Karen Refugee Committee. 'Code of Conduct'. Mae Hong Son: accessible @ www.pseataskforce.org/uploads/tools/1351628020.pdf, last access 14 February 2017. Retrieved October 2016, from www.pseataskforce.org: http://www.pseataskforce.org/uploads/tools/1351628020.pdf.

Kyu, M. M. 2016. 'Kokang: The Rise of the Chinese Minority—The New Neo-Libera State'. In W. P. Tantikanangkul, ed., *Politics of Autonomy and Sustainability in Myanmar. Change for New Hope. New Life?* (13–36). Singapore: Springer.

La, T. D. 2017. 'Fighting Continues with No Sign of Letup in Kachin and Shan State'. Kachin State: accessible @ www.burmalink.org, last access 14 February 2017. Retrieved January 2017.

Lall, M. 2016. *Understanding Reform in Myanmar: People and Society in the Wake of Military Rule*. London: Hurst Publishers.

Lang, H. J. 2002. *Fear and Sanctuary: Burmese Refugees in Thailand*. Ithaca, NY: Cornell Southeast Asia Program.

Latour, B. 2006. 'Über Technische Vermittlung: Philosophie, Soziologie und Genealogie'. In A. Belliger, and D. Krieger, eds., *ANThologie: Ein Einführendes Handbuch zur Akteur-Netzwerk Theorie* (483–528). Bielefeld: Transcript.

Leigh, M. D. 2011. *Conflict, Politics and Proselytism: Methodist Missionaries in Colonial and Postcolonial Upper Burma, 1887–1966*. Manchester, New York: Manchester University Press.

Lepper, G. 2000. *Catgeories in Text and Talk: A Practical Introduction to Categorization*. London: Sage.

Levitt, P., and Nyberg-Sörensen, N. 2004. 'The Transnational Turn in Migration Studies. Global Commission on International Migration, Geneva'. *Global Migration Perspectives*, No. 6.

Lindley, A. 2010. *The Early Morning Phone Call: Somali Refugees' Remittances. Studies in Forced Migration*. New York, Oxford: Berghahn.

Lischer, S. K. 2005. *Dangerous Sanctuaries: Refugee Camps, Civil War and the Dilemma of Humanitarian Aid*. London, Ithaca: Cornell University Press.

Loescher, G., and J. Milner. 2005. *Protracted Refugee Situations: Domestic and International Security Implications*. New York, London: Routledge.

Long, L. D. 1993. *Ban Vinai: The Refugee Camp*. New York: Columbia University Press.

Ludewig-Kedmi, R. 2002. *Opfer und Täter Zugleich? Moraldilemmata Jüdischer Funktionshäftlinge in der Shoah*. Gießen: Psychosozialverlag.

Lynch, M. 1993. *Scientific Practice and Ordinary Action: Ethnomethodology and Social Studies of Science*. New York: Cambridge University Press.

———. 2007. 'The Origins of Ethnomethodology'. In S. Turner, and M. Risjord, eds., *Handbook of the Philosophy of Science. Philosophy of Anthropology and Sociology* (485–515). Amsterdam: Elsevier.

MacDonald, A. P. 2013. 'The Tatmadaw's New Position in Myanmar Politics'. accessible @ www.eastasiaforum.org, last access 17 February 2017.

Maestri, G. 2017. 'The Contentious Sovereignties of the Camp: Political Contention Among State and Non-State Actors in Italian Roma Camps'. *Political Geography* 60: 213–22.

Malkki, L. H. 1989. *Purity and Exile: Transformations in Historical-National Consciousness Among Hutu Refugees in Tanzania*. Harvard: Dissertation. Harvard University.

———. 1992. 'National Geographic: The Rooting of Peoples and the Territorialization of National Identity Among Scholars and Refugees'. *Cultural Anthropology* 7(1): 24–44.

———. 1995a. *Purity and Exile: Violence, Memory and National Cosmology Among Hutu Refugees in Tanzania*. Chicago, London: University of Chicago Press.

———. 1995b. 'Refugees and Exile: From "Refugee Studies" to the National Order of Things'. *Annual Review of Anthropology* 24: 495–523.

———. 2002. 'News from Nowhere: Mass Displacement and Globalized 'Problems of Organization'. *Ethnography* 3(3): 351–60.

Marshall, H. I. 1922/1997. *The Karen People of Burma: A Study in Anthropology and Ethnology*. Bangkok: White Lotus Press.

Mbembe, A. 2000. 'At the Edge of the World: Boundaries, Territoriality, and Sovereignty in Africa'. Public Culture 12(1): 259–84.

McConnachie, K. 2012. 'Rethinking the "Refugee Warrior": The Karen National Union and Refugee Protection on the Thai-Burma Border'. *Journal of Human Rights Practice* 4(1): 30–56.

———. 2014a. 'Forced Migration in Southeast-Asia and East Asia'. In E. Fiddian-Qasmiyeh, G. L. Loescher, and N. Signa, eds., *The Oxford Handbook of Refugee and Forced Migration Studies* (626–38). Oxford: Oxford University Press.

———. 2014b. *Governing Refugees: Justice, Order and Legal Pluralism*. Routledge: New York.

———. 2016. 'Camps of Containment: A Genealogy of the Refugee Camp.' *Humanity: An International Journal of Human Rights, Humanitarianism, and Development* 7(3): 397–412.

McGuiness, M. E. 2003. 'Legal and Normative Dimensions of the Manipulation of Refugees'. In S. Stedman, and F. Tanner, eds., *Refugee Manipulation: War, Politics, and the Abuse of Human Suffering*. Washington: Brooking Institution Press.

Meyer, J. W., et al. (1987. 'The World Polity and Authority of the National-State'. In *Institutional Structure: Constituting State, Society and the Individual* (41–70). Newbury Park: Sage.

———. 2005. *Weltkultur: Wie die Westlichen Prinzipien die Welt Durchdringen*. Frankfurt am Main: Suhrkamp.

———. 2010. *World Society: The Writings of John M. Meyer*. Oxford, New York: Oxford University Press.

Meyer, J., J. Boli, G. Thomas and F. Ramirez. 1997. 'World Society and the Nation State'. *American Journal of Sociology* 103(1): 144–81.

Milner, J., and G. Loescher. 2011. 'Responding to Protracted Refugee Situations: Lessons from a Decade of Discussion'. *Forced Migration Policy Briefing*, No.8.

Mitchell, C. J. 2006. 'Case and Situation Analyis'. In T. Evens, and D. Handelman, eds., *The Manchester School: Practice and Ethnographic Praxis in Anthropology* (23–48). Oxford, New York: Berghahn Books.

Moerman, M. 1965. 'Ethnic Identification in a Complex Civilisation: Who are the Lue?' *American Anthropologist* 67(5): 1215–230.

———. 1974. 'Accomplishing Ethnicity'. In R. Turner, ed., *Ethnomethodology. Selected Readings* (54–68). Harmondsworth, Middlesex, England: Penguin Education.

———. 1993. 'Adriane's Threat and Indra's Net: Reflection on Ethnography, Ethnicity, Identity, Culture, and Interaction'. *Research on Language and Social Interaction* 26(1): 85–98.

Möller, B. 2014. *Refugees, Prisoners and Camps: A Functional Analysis of the Phenomena of Encampment*. Hampshire: Palgrave Macmillan.

Montclos de, M.-A., and P. M. Kagwanja. 2000. 'Refugee Camps or Cities? The Socio-Economic Dynamics of the Dadaab and Kakuma Camps in Northern Kenya'. *Journal of Refugee Studies* 13(2): 205–22.

MyanmarPeaceMonitor. 2017. Website. Yangoon: accessible www.mmpeacemonitor .org, last access 14 February 2017.

Newmann, D. 2003. 'On Border and Power: A Theoretical Framework'. *Journal of Border Studies* 18(1): 13–25.

O'Connor, B. 2016. 'Violence in Northern Myanmar Overshadows Peace Process: Fighting Continues in Northern Myanmar as Union Peace Conference Negotiations Commence'. Shan State: accessible @ www.aljazeera.com, last access 14 February 2017. Retrieved January 2017, from http://www.aljazeera.com/indepth /inpictures/2016/09/violence-northern-myanmar-overshadows-peace-process -160901090748423.html.

Odgen, M. 2008. *Refugee Utopias: (Re)Theorizing Refugeeism Through Cultural Production of the Hmong Diaspora*. Minneapolis: University of Minnesota.

Oka, R. C. 2014. 'Coping with the Refugee Wait: The Role of Consumption, Normalcy, and Dignity in Refugee Lives at Kakuma Refugee Camp'. *American Anthropologist* 116(1): 23–37.

Orth, K. 2007. 'Gab es eine Lagergesellschaft? "Kriminelle" und Politiische Häftlinge im Konzentrationslager'. In N. Frei, S. Steinbacher, and B. Wagner, eds., *Ausbeutung, Vernichtung,* Öffentlichkeit: *Neue Studien zur Nationalsozialistischen Lagerpolitik* (109–33). München: de Gruyter.

Owens, P. 2009. 'Reclaiming "Bare Life". Against Agamben on Refugees'. *International Relations* 23(4): 567–82.

Papadopoulos, D., and V. Tsianos. 2013. 'After Citizenship: Autonomy of Migration, Organisational Ontology and Mobile Commons'. *Citizenship Studies* 17(2): 178–96.

Park, R. E. 1928. 'Human Migration and the Marginal Man'. *American Journal of Sociology* 33(6): 881–93.

Pearce, K. J. 2009. 'Media and Mass Communication Theories'. In S. Littlejohn, and K. Foss, eds., *Encyclopaedia of Communication Theory* (624–28). London, Thousand Oaks: Sage.

Peteet, J. 2005. *Landscape of Hope and Despair: Palestinian Refugee Camps.* Philadelphia: University of Pennsylvania Press.

Pollner, M., and R Emerson. 2001. 'Ethnomethodology and Ethnography'. In P. Atkinson, A. Coffey, S. Delamont, J. Lofland, and L. Loflan, eds., *Handbook of Ethnography.* London, Thousand Oaks, New Delhi: Sage.

Popitz, Heinrich. 1992. Phänomene der Macht. Tübingen: J.C.B. Mohr, Paul Siebeck

Pottier, J. 1996. 'Why Aid Agencies Needs Better Understanding of the Communities they Assist. The Experience of Food Aid in Rwandan Refugee Camps'. *International Journal of Disaster Studies and Practices* 20(4): 324–37.

Pritchard, A. 2016. 'Introduction'. In W. Tantikanangkul, and A. Pritchard, eds., *Politics of Autonomy and Sustainability in Myanmar.* Singapore: Springer.

Ramadan, Z. 2013. 'Spatialising the Refugee Camp'. *Transactions of the Institute of British Geographers* 38: 65–77.

Ramadan, A., and S. Fregonese. 2017. 'Hybrid Sovereignty and the State of Exception in the Palestinian Refugee Camps in Lebanon'. *Annals of the American Association of Geographers,* 107(4): 949–63.

Rawls, A. 2002. 'Editors Introduction'. In H. R. Garfinkel, ed., *Ethnomethodology's Program: Working Out Durkheim's Aphorism* (1–76). Lanham, MD: Rowman & Littlefield.

———. 2008. 'Harold Garfinkel, Ethnomethodology and Workplace Studies'. *Organization Studies* 29(5): 701–32.

Riak Akuei, S. 2005. 'Remittances and Unforseen Burdens: The Livelihoods and Social Obligations of Sudanese Refugees'. *Global Migration Perspectives* 18: 774–86.

Roberts, B. 2006. *Micro Social Theory.* New York: Palgrave Macmillan.

Robinson, C. N. 2000. 'Refugee Warriors at the Thai Cambodian Border'. *Refugee Survey Quarterly* 19(1): 23–37.

Royal Thai Police. 2004. 'Order of the Royal Thai Police. No. 777/2551'. Bangkok: accessible @ www.immigration.go.th, last access 14 February 2017. Retrieved January 2016, from www.immigration.go.th:http://www.immigration .go.th/nov2004/doc/temporarystay/policy777-2551en.pdf.

Sacks, H.; Schegloff, E.A.; Jefferson, G. 1974. A Simplest Systematics for the Organization of Turn-Taking for Conversation. Language: 40/40,1, pp. 696–735.

Sacks, H. 1984. 'On Doing "Being Ordinary"'. In J. Atkinson, and J. Heritage, eds., *Structures of Social Action: Studies in Conversation Analysis* (413–29). Cambridge, London, New York: Cambridge University Press.

———. 1995. *Lectures on Conversation*. Oxford/Cambridge: Blackwell.

Sagy, T. 2009. *Outside the Pale of the Law: The Processing of Disputes in Budduburam Refugee Camp in Ghana*. Ann Arbor, MI: UMI Dissertation Service.

Sakhong, L. 2013. 'Introduction'. In P. Keenan, and P. Keena, ed., *By Force of Arms: Armed Ethnic Groups in Burma*. Delhi: VjJ Books India Pvt Ltd.

Salehyan, I., and K. S. Gleditsch. 2006. 'Refugees and the Spread of Civil War'. *International Organization* 60: 335–66.

Scheel, S. 2013. 'Studying Embodied Encounters: Autonomy of Migration Beyond its Romanticization'. *Postcolonial Studies* 16(3): 279–88.

Schegloff, E. A. 1997. 'Whose Text? Whose Context?' *Discourse and Society* 8: 165–87.

Schiocchet, L. 2014. 'Palestinian Refugees in Lebanon: Is the Camp a Space of Exception'. Mashriq and Mahjar. *Journal of Middle East Migration* 2(1): 130–60.

Schmidt, A. 2003, Jan. 'FMO Thematic Guide: Camps versus Settlements'. accessible @ www.forcedmigration.org, last access 17 February 2017. http://www.forcedmigration.org/research-resources/expert-guides/camps-versus-settlements/fmo021.pdf.

Schmidt, R. 2012. *Soziologie der Praktiken: Konzeptuelle Studien und Empirische Analysen*. Frankfurt am Main: Suhrkamp.

Schmitt, C. 1985. *Political Theology: Four Chapters on the Concept of Sovereignty*. Chicago: University of Chicago Press.

Schnell, F. 2013. 'Der Gulag als Systemstelle Sowjetischer Herrschaft'. In B. Greiner, and A. Kramer, eds., *Die Welt der Lager. Zur 'Erfolgsgeschichte' einer Institution* (134–65). Hamburg: Hamburger Edition HIS Verlag.

Schütz, A. 1964. 'The Stranger: An Essay in Social Psychology'. In A. Brodersen, ed., *Collected Papers II: Studies in Social Theory* (91–105). The Hague: Martinus Nijhoff.

Schwartzman, H. B. 1989. *The Meeting. Gatherings in Organizations and Communities*. New York, London: Plenum Press.

Scott, J. C. 2009. *The Art of Not Being Governed: An Anarchist History of Upland South-East Asia*. New Haven, CT: Yale University Press.

Selth, A. 2015. 'Myanmar's Coercive Apparatus: The Long Road to Reform'. In D. Steinberg, ed., *Myanmar: The Dynamics of an Evolving Polity* (13–36). London: Lynne Rienner Publisher.

Sgovio, T. 1979. *Dear America*. New York: New York Partners.

Shacknove, A. E. 1985. 'Who is a Refugee?' *Ethics* 95(2): 274–84.

Shami, S. 1996. 'Transnationalism and Refugee Studies: Rethinking Forced Migration and Identity in the Middle East'. *Journal of Refugee Studies* 9(1): 3–26.

Sheth, J. N. 1976. 'Buyer-Seller Interaction: A Conceptual Framework'. *Advances in Consumer Research* 3: 382–86.

Simmel, Georg. 1908/1992. Der Raum und die Räumlichen Ordnungen der Gesell-schaft. Edited by G. Simmel. *Soziologie. Untersuchungen über die Formen der Vergesellschaftung.* Berlin: Duncker & Humbolt, pp. 460–526.

———. 1916/2003. 'Das Problem der Historischen Zeit'. In U. Kösser, H.-M. Kruckis, and O. Rammstedt, eds., *Goethe, Deutschlands Innere Wandlung, das Problem der Historischen Zeit, Rembrandt* (287–304). Frankfurt am Main: Suhrkamp.

———. 1917/1970. *Grundfragen der Soziologie* (Individuum und Gesellschaft). Berlin: Walter de Gruyter.

Smith, M. J. 1994. *Ethnic Groups in Burma: Development, Democracy and Human Rights.* London: Anti-Slavery International.

———. 1999. *Burma Insurgency and the Politics of Ethnicity.* London: Zed Books.

Sofsky, W. 1993. *Die Ordnung des Terrors: Das Konzentrationslager.* Frankfurt am Main: Fischer.

Soguk, N. 1999. *States and Strangers: Refugees and Displacements of Statecraft.* Minneapolis, London: University of Minnesota Press.

South, A. 2004. 'Political Transition in Myanmar: A New Model for Democratiza-tion'. *Contemporary Southeast Asia: A Journal of International and Strategic Affairs* 26(2): 233–55.

———. 2007. 'Conflict and Displacement in Burma/Myanmar'. In M. Skidmore, and T. Wilson, eds., *Myanmar: The State, Community, and Environment* (54–81). Canberra: ANU Press.

———. 2008. *Ethnic Politics in Burma. States of Conflicts.* London: Routledge.

———. 2011. *Burma's Longest War: Anatomy of the Karen Conflict.* Netherlands: Transnational Institute and Burma Center.

———. 2015. 'Governance and Political Legitimacy in the Peace Process'. In *Myanmar: The Dynamics of an Evolving Polity* (159–90). London: Lynne Rienner Publisher.

Speer, S. 2002. 'Debate. "Natural" and "Contrived" Data: A Sustainable Distinction?' *Discourse Studies* 4: 511–25.

Spoorenberg, T. 2015. 'Myanmar's First Census in More than 30 Years: A Radical Revision of the Official Population Count'. *Population and Societies* 527(11): 1–4. Retrieved from http://ined.

Spradley, J. P. 1979. *The Ethnographic Interview.* Chicago, San Francisco: Holt, Rinehart, Winston.

Steinberg, D. I. 2013. *Burma/Myanmar: What Everyone Needs to Know.* Oxford, New York: Oxford University Press.

———. 2015. *Myanmar: The Dynamics of an Evolving Polity.* London: Lynne Ri-enner Publisher. Steinberg, D., and Hongwei, F. 2012. *Modern China-Myanmar Relations: Dilemmas of Mutual Dependence.* Copenhagen: NIAS Press.

Stucki, A. 2013. 'Streitpunkt Lager: Zwangsumsiedlung an der Imperialen Periph-erie'. In B. Greiner, and A. Kramer, eds., *Die Welt der Lager: Zur 'Erfolgsge-schichte' einer Institution* (62–86). Hamburg: Hamburger Edition HIS.

Taylor, R. H. 2007. 'British Policy Towards Myanmar and the Creation of the "Burma Problem"'. In N. Hanesan, and K. Hliang, eds., *Myanmar, State, Society and Ethnicity* (70–95). Singapore: ISEAS Publishing.

———. 2015. *Trends in Southeast Asia. The Armed Forces in Myanmar Politics: A Terminating Role?* Singapore: ISEAS Publishing.

TBBC. 2004–2012. 'Thai Burmese Border Consortium'. *Programme Reports.* Bangkok: accessible @ www.theborderconsortium.org, last access 14 February 2017.

TBC. 2012–2016. 'The Border Consortium. Programme Reports'. Bangkok: accessible @ www.theborderconsortium.org, last access 14 February 2017.

———. 2013. 'Poverty, Displacement, and Local Governance in Southeast Burma/ Myanmar'. Yangon: accessible @ www.theborderconsortium.org, last access 14 February 2017.

Thawnghmung, A. M. 2008. *The Karen Revolution in Burma: Diverse Voices, Uncertain Ends*. Singapore: East-West Center.

———. 2012. *The 'Other' Karen in Myanmar: Ethnic Minorities and the Struggle Without Arms*. Lanham, MD: Lexington.

Thompson, S. 2008. 'Community-Based Camp Management'. *Forced Migration Review* 20: 26–28.

Topich, W., and Leitich, K. 2013. *The History of Myanmar*. Santa Barbara, California: Greenwood.

Turnell, S. 2012. 'Myanmar in 2011: Confounding Expectations'. *Asian Survey* 52(1): 157–64.

Turnell, S., A. Vicary and W. Bradford. 2008. *Migrant Worker Remittances and Burma: An Economic Analysis of Survey Results*. Sydney: Burma Economic Watch. Macquire University.

Turner, S. 2001. *The Barriers of Innocence: Humanitarian Intervention and Political Imagination in a Refugee Camp for Burundians in Tanzania*. Roskilde: Roskilde University.

———. 2004. 'Under the Gaze of the "Big Nations": Refugees and Rumours and the International Community in Tanzania'. *African Affairs* 103: 227–47.

———. 2006. Biopolitics and Bare Life in a Refugee Camp: Some Conceptual Reflections. In K. Inhetveen, ed., *Flucht als Politik. Berichte von fünf Kontinenten* (39–62). Köln: Rüdiger Köppe Verlag.

———. 2010. *Politics of Innocence: Hutu Identity, Conflict and Camp Life*. New York, Oxford: Berghahn Books.

———. 2015. 'What is a Refugee Camp? Explorations of the Limits and Effects of the Camp'. *Journal of Refugee Studies* 29(2): 139–48.

Turner, V. 1964. 'Betwixt and Between: The Liminal Period in Rites de Passage'. In J. Helm, ed., *Religion, Symposium on New Approaches to the Study of Religion* (4–20). Seattle, WA: University of Washington Press.

———. 1969. *The Ritual Process: Structure and Anti-Structure*. Ithaca, NY: University Press.

UN. 2016. 'United Nation Committee for Development Policy: List of Least Developed Countries'. Accessible @ www.un.org, last access 14 February 2017.

UNHCR. 2014. 'UNHCR Statistical Yearbook 2014'. Geneva: accessible @ www
.unhcr.org, last access 14 February 2017. Retrieved from http://www.unhcr.org
/statistics/country/566584fc9/unhcr-statistical-yearbook-2014-14th-edition.html.
————. 2015. 'Global Trends: Forced Displacement in 2015'. Geneva: accessible @
www.unhrc.org, last access 14 February 2017.

van Gennep, A. 1909. *The Rites of Passage*. London: Routledge and Kegan Paul.

van Hear, N. 2003. 'From Durable Solution to Transnational Relations: Home and
Exile Among Refugee Diasporas'. *New Issues in Refugee Research*. UNHCR, 83.
————. 2006. 'Refugees in Diaspora: From Durable Solution to Transnational Relations'. *Refuge* 23(1): 9–14.

van Hoyweghen, S. 2001. 'Mobility, Territoriality, and Sovereignty in Postcolonial
Tanzania'. *New Issues in Refugee Research*. UNHCR, 49.

Veroff, J. 2010. *Justice Administration in Meheba Refugee Settlement: Refugee Perceptions, Preferences, and Strategic Decisions*. Oxford: Oxford University.

Vogler, P. 2007. 'Into the Jungle of Bureaucracy: Negotiating Access to Camps at the
Thai-Burmese Border'. *Refugee Survey Quarterly* 26(3): 51–60.

Voutira, E., and B. Harrell-Bond. 1996. 'In Search for the Locus of Trust: The Social
World of the Refugee Camp'. In V. Daniel, and J. Knudson, eds., *(Mis)trusting
Refugees*.

Vungsiriphisal, Premjai. 2011. *Sustainable Solution to the Discplaced Person Situation on the Thai-Myanmar Borders*. Chulalongkron University: Asian Research
Center for Migration, Institut of Asian Studies. Bangkok.

Wacquant, L. 2001. 'Deadly Symbiosis: When Ghetto and Prison Meet and Mesh'.
Punishment and Society 3(1): 95–134.

Walter, W. 2011. 'Foucault and Frontiers: Notes on the Birth of the Humanitarian
Border'. In U. Bröckling, S. Krasmann, and T. Lemke, eds., *Governmentality: Current Issues and Future Challenges* (138–64). London: Routledge.

Weber, M. 1972. *Wirtschaft und Gesellschaft*. Tübingen: Mohr.

Werker, E. 2007. 'Refugee Camp Economies'. *Journal of Refugee Studies*, 20(3):
461–80.

Wilson, K. 1992. 'Enhancing Refugees: Own Food Acquistition Strategies'. *Journal
on Refugee Studies* 5(4): 226–46.

Wright, T. 2014. 'Media and Representations of Refugees and Other Forced Mi-
grants'. In E. Fiddian-Qasmiyeh, G. Loescher, K. Long, and N. Sigona, eds.,
The Oxford Handbook of Refugee and Forced Migration Studies. Oxford: Oxford
University Press.

Zimmerman, D. H. 1969. 'Tasks and Troubles: The Practical Bases of Work Activities in a Public Assistance Agency'. In D. Hanse, ed., *Explorations in Sociology
and Counselling*. Boston: Houghton Mifflin.
————. 1974. 'Fact as a Practical Accomplishment'. In R. Turner, ed., *Ethnomethodology: Selected Readings* (128–43). Middlesex, Baltimore, Victoria: Penguin
Education.

Index

About the Author

Annett Bochmann is a postdoctoral researcher in Germany at Siegen University, in the Department of General Sociology. Since 2008 she has been researching in refugee-camp contexts and in border regions in Asia. As a political sociologist, she seeks to combine her interests in social theory with empirical insights gained through qualitative methods—especially long-term ethnographic fieldwork, interaction and discourse analysis.

www.ingramcontent.com/pod-product-compliance
Lightning Source LLC
Chambersburg PA
CBHW022309280326
41932CB00010B/1040